MW01532888

ONTARIO

QUEBEC

NEWFOUNDLAND

NEW BRUNSWICK

PRINCE EDWARD ISLAND

NOVA SCOTIA

MAINE · Fredericton

Quebec ·

Montreal ·

Ottawa ·

Bangor ·

VT. · Montpelier

N.H. · Concord

MASS. · Boston

CONN. · Providence
R.I.

Albany ·

Hartford ·

N.J. · New York

Sault Ste. Marie ·

MICHIGAN

WISCONSIN

· Eau Claire

·aul

· Cadillac

Toronto ·

· Buffalo

NEW YORK

PENNSYLVANIA

· Milwaukee

· Grand Rapids

Detroit ·

ILLINOIS

Chicago ·

· South Bend

· Toledo · Cleveland Williamsport ·

· Atlantic City

INDIANA OHIO

· Peoria

· Pittsburgh

Philadelphia ·

·ds

· Baltimore · Dover
MD. DEL.

W. VA. Washington DC ·

·City

Springfield ·

Indianapolis ·

· Cincinnati

St. Louis ·

· Louisville Charleston ·

· Roanoke · Norfolk
VIRGINIA

KENTUCKY

· Paducah

N. CAROLINA

· Winston-Salem

·NSAS

TENNESSEE · Nashville

· Charlotte

· Memphis

ALABAMA GEORGIA

S. CAROLINA

· Columbia

Birmingham ·

· Atlanta

· Charleston

·JISIANA
·reveport

· Jackson

Savannah ·

MISSISSIPPI

Mobile · FLORIDA

Jacksonville ·

New Orleans ·

· Tampa

Miami ·

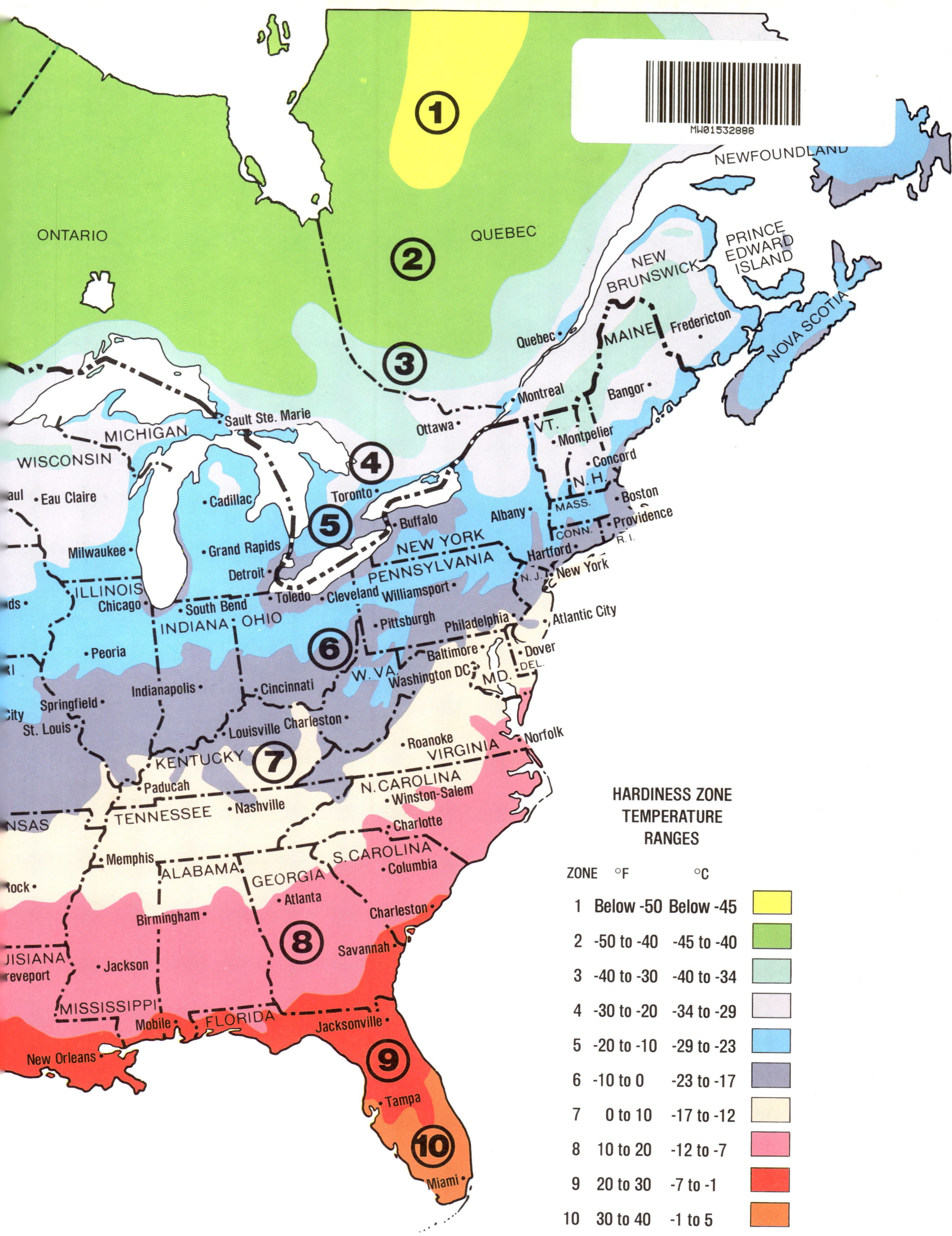

HARDINESS ZONE
TEMPERATURE
RANGES

ZONE	°F	°C
1	Below -50	Below -45
2	-50 to -40	-45 to -40
3	-40 to -30	-40 to -34
4	-30 to -20	-34 to -29
5	-20 to -10	-29 to -23
6	-10 to 0	-23 to -17
7	0 to 10	-17 to -12
8	10 to 20	-12 to -7
9	20 to 30	-7 to -1
10	30 to 40	-1 to 5

Pictorial Library

Pictorial Library

OF LANDSCAPE PLANTS

Volume Two
Southern Hardiness Zones 6-10

by

Ruth Fortune Woods, Ph.D.

merchants publishing company
kalamazoo, michigan

ISBN 0-89484-095-9 (Volume 2)

ISBN 0-89484-026-6 (Set)

Library of Congress Catalog Card No. 81-82113

ᴹ

merchants publishing company • 20 mills street • kalamazoo, michigan 49001

First Edition 1989

Printed in the United States of America

Contents

Introduction

HOW TO USE THIS BOOK

Volume Two of the *Pictorial Library* contains a selection of landscape plant materials for Hardiness Zones 6-10. These zone numbers correspond to those on the hardiness zone maps of North America featured in full color on the endpapers of this book.

Each volume of the *Pictorial Library* is designed to illustrate ornamental and fruiting plants in typical landscape settings, showing the characteristics of each plant for identification as well as for visual appreciation. A special *Tropical* section is included in this volume which covers Zones 9 and 10 specifically.

Within each of the plant categories that make up the ten sections of this volume, the plants are alphabetically arranged by their botanical names. If you are interested in a particular plant category (e.g. Deciduous Shrubs), simply turn to the appropriate section and locate it alphabetically by its botanical name. To locate a plant by common or botanical name, refer to the index where both are listed.

Broadleaf Evergreens. These shrubs retain their leaves in all but the coldest areas of the Zones for which they are recommended. Those that are cold sensitive are referred to as semi-deciduous or semi-evergreen. Many have outstanding foliage which brightens winter months, and some have magnificent blooms. They are valued as accents, foundation or background plantings, borders, screens or hedges. Page 1.

Coniferous Evergreens. This section includes shrubs and trees of the conifer (cone-producing) or needle-leaf types. They are "evergreen" in habit and beautify the landscape all year long. Page 75.

Deciduous Shrubs. These shrubs include some of the most brilliantly colored, flowering shrubs available. They make outstanding accents. Many are often used as foundation plants, but they do not offer the wintertime protection afforded by the evergreens. Page 107.

Flowering Trees. These are small to medium sized trees that give outstanding color and maximum ornamental effect. They provide excellent bird shelters. Most can be used on small lots and in confined areas such as patios and dooryard gardens. Page 157.

Ground Covers. Landscape plants shown in this section are used both to beautify and to reduce maintenance labor. By covering the ground totally, these plants reduce weeds and erosion problems. Broadleaf evergreens and coniferous evergreen types are pictured here. Page 185.

Hedges & Screens. A wide variety of plant materials is featured here and includes evergreens, semi-evergreens, deciduous and monocot (grasslike) plants. Hedges and screens are integral elements of landscape design, and several ways to use them are shown here. Page 201.

Roses. The most popular types of these beautiful plants are shown in this section. The most formal roses plus border, miniature and tree roses are illustrated. Page 227.

Shade & Ornamental Trees. These are the larger deciduous and evergreen trees, all valued for cooling summer shade. Some have unique branch form, bark color and/or seed pods/capsules. Trees of unusual growth habit and ornamentals not necessarily grown for showy bloom are included as well. Page 235.

Tropicals. This section features plants particularly suited to Zones 9 and 10. Tropical and subtropical palms are shown as well as palmlike cycads. Succulents and grasslike specimens add to a wide variety of distinctive, showy plants. Page 283.

Vines. Some of the most colorful and effective landscape effects can be achieved with vines. This section includes dedicuous, evergreen and tropical appearing specimens. With most, the floral show is outstanding. Page 311.

Acknowledgments

The author acknowledges with thanks those who have contributed to this work:

—Dr. Robert J. Black, Urban Hort. Spec., Fla. Coop. Ext. Serv., Univ. of Fla.; Dr. Donald I. Dickmann, Prof., Dept. of Forestry, Mich. St. Univ. and Mr. James A. Faiszt, Ext. Spec., Virg. Coop. Ext. Serv., Virg. Poly. Tech. & St. Univ.; Dr. Louis F. Wilson, North Central Forest Experiment Station, U.S.D.A. Forest Service: *consultants.*

E.S. 'Bud' Reasoner, Pres., Reasoner's Nurseries, Oneco, Fla.; George L. Tabor III, Glen St. Mary's Nursery Co., Glen St. Mary, Fla. and Audrey Teasdale, Botanist, Monrovia Nursery Co., Azusa, Calif.: *resource material source persons.*

—Muriel & Arthur Orans, Hort. Photo.; Mrs. Clarence E. Lewis (from the Clarence E. Lewis collection); Pam Cox, Moore Miniature Roses—Sequoia Nursery; Maggie Oster, All Am. Rose Selections; Maxine Gilliam, Weeks Wholesale Rose Grower, Inc. and Merchants Pub. Co. Film Library: *photography.*

—Dean Clark, Art Director; Bob Snover and Richard Whittington, Color Separators; Max Hale, Typographer; Kimberly Marshell, and Nina Feirer, Editors: *production.*

Broadleaf Evergreens

GLOSSY ABELIA *Abelia x grandiflora*

Abelia x grandiflora is a dense, semi-evergreen shrub that reaches a height and spread of 3-5′ (.9-1.5m) in 4-5 years. Severe winters will cause leaf fall and all top growth may be killed back by very low temperatures (0°F or -17°C).

Rose-white, tubular 1″ (2.5cm) flowers bloom in profuse clusters on current season's growth from June through fall.

Young leaves are reddish in the spring, maturing to a glossy dark green. Fall color is a shiny bronze-purple. Leaves are often held through milder winters.

Soil: Plant in a medium-coarse to medium textured, well-drained soil that has been enriched with leaf mold or compost.

Light: It needs full sun or light shade and shelter from strong winds.

Pruning: Prune in early spring. Hedges may be sheared, though clipping out of individual stems is preferred.

Uses: Use for a foundation planting, formal/informal hedge or shrub border.

PINK ABELIA *Abelia x grandiflora 'Edward Goucher'*

This evergreen (Zones 8 & 9) or semi-deciduous (Zones 6 & 7) shrub is a low grower that matures at 3-5′ (.9-1.5m).

Orchid-pink bell-shaped flowers with orange throats present a beautiful display from June through October.

The small, glossy green leaves take on a red tinge in colder areas.

Soil: Plant in a well-drained, fertile soil. Feed and water regularly during the season of bloom.

Light: Abelia does best in full sun but will tolerate light shade.

Pruning: Prune according to desired shape.

Uses: This dwarf abelia is excellent as an informal hedge, or as a border or edge planting.

JAPANESE AUCUBA *Aucuba japonica*

Zones: 7-9

This dense evergreen shrub will reach a height and spread of up to 6-15′ (1.8-4.5m) in 10-20 years. The species is dioecious (male and female on separate plants).

Small, inconspicuous white flowers bloom in early spring, followed by brilliant red berries which ripen in fall and persist through winter. Plant both male and female for good production.

Leaves up to 6″ (15cm) long are glossy dark green with a thick leathery texture.

Soil: *Aucuba* does best in a moist, well-drained soil but tolerates drought once established.

Light: The plant does best in light to moderate shade, as sun burns the leaves.

Pruning: Pruning is rarely needed. If desired, clip individual branches in early spring.

Uses: The shrub makes an ideal container plant for patio-indoor use, is attractive as a border planting or is showy in a woodland garden.

4

GOLDEN JAPANESE AUCUBA

Aucuba japonica 'Crotonifolia'

This very showy evergreen shrub grows to 6-10′ (1.8-3m) and has outstanding foliage which contrasts beautifully with other dark green shrubs.

The deep green 6″ (15cm) leaves are boldly splashed with white and gold.

Soil: *Aucuba* does best in a moist, well-drained soil but will tolerate drought once it is established.

Light: The plant does best in light to moderate shade, as the sun burns the leaves.

Pruning: Pruning is rarely needed. If desired, clip individual branches in early spring.

Uses: The shrub makes an ideal container plant for patio/indoor use, is attractive as a border planting and is showy in a woodland garden.

WINTERGREEN BARBERRY *Berberis julianae*

Zones: 6-8

This upright, semi-evergreen shrub retains its leaves in milder climates. If unpruned, it will reach 6′ (1.8m) with a spread of about 5′ (1.5m). The stems are armed with three-pronged spines.

Tiny ¼″ (6mm), yellow blossoms line the stems in the spring, and are followed by blue to black berries which persist into winter.

The long, glossy green leaves have spiny edges.

Soil: *Berberis* does best in any well-drained garden soil. It will grow in moist soil extremes as well, including those with high lime content.

Light: It prefers full sun to light shade and will tolerate heat and drought, but not wind.

Pruning: To create desired shape, shear several times each season to maintain dense, formal appearance. Specimen plants rarely need pruning except to contain irregular growth.

Uses: Excellent as a hedge. It also makes an attractive shrub border, specimen or accent.

WINTERGREEN BARBERRY *Berberis julianae*

JAPANESE BOXWOOD *Buxus microphylla var. japonica*

Zones: 7-9

Buxus microphylla is a slow-growing, compact evergreen shrub which matures to 4-6' (1.2-1.8m) if not pruned. The plants may be shaped into stunning globes, pyramids or screens.

Inconspicuous creamy white flowers bloom at ends of branches in the spring.

The small ½-1" (1.3-2.5cm) light green, oval leaves often turn brown to bronze in cooler climates.

Soil: Plant in moist, well-drained soil and mulch with a 1" (2.5cm) layer of coarse peat moss, woodchips or peanut shells to retain moisture in the summer. Water regularly during dry spells until established (1-2 years).

Light: Plant in full sun or partial shade but protect from winter winds with burlap or other screening.

Pruning: Shear or prune according to the landscaping objective.

Uses: This is an excellent choice for formal/ informal hedges. Plant 15-30" (38-75cm) apart and remove upper one third of all growing shoots to encourage bushy growth.

KOREAN BOXWOOD *Buxus microphylla var. koreana 'Wintergreen'*

Zones: 7-9

This low evergreen shrub grows to 2' (60cm) and spreads to 4' (1.2m) in 8-10 years.

Inconspicuous creamy white flowers bloom at the ends of branches in the spring.

The small ¼-½" (.6-1.3cm) glossy dark green, oval leaves are retained throughout the winter.

Soil: Plant in moist, well-drained soil and mulch with a 1" (2.5cm) layer of coarse peat moss, woodchips or peanut shells to retain moisture in the summer. Water regularly during dry spells until established (1-2 years).

Light: Plant in full sun or shade but protect from winter winds with burlap or other screening.

Pruning: Shear or prune according to the landscaping objective.

Uses: 'Wintergreen' is an excellent choice for formal-informal hedges. Plant 15-30" (38-75cm) apart and remove upper one third of all growing shoots to encourage bushy growth.

'Welleri' is a wide-spreading evergreen shrub that grows 2-5' (.6-1.5m) high and 5-10' (1.5-3m) wide in about 15-20 years.

Inconspicuous, small white flowers bloom at branch ends in the spring.

The 1-1½" (2.5-3.8cm), oval leaves have a delicate fragrance, particularly in warmer climates. Fall color is bronze in colder areas.

An additional variety *B.s.* 'Suffruticosa' is very low and slow growing with a dense, compact branching habit which is ideal for edging. It is also available in silver-edged forms.

Soil: Plant in moist, well-drained soil and mulch with a 1"(2.5cm) layer of coarse peat moss, woodchips or peanut shells to retain moisture in the summer. Water regularly during dry spells until established (1-2 years).

Light: It is not particular and does well in full sun or shade. Protect from winter winds with burlap or other screening.

Pruning: Shear or prune according to the landscaping objective.

Uses: 'Welleri' is an excellent choice for formal/ informal hedges. Plant 15-30' (38-75cm) apart and remove upper one third of all growing shoots to encourage bushy growth.

COMMON CAMELLIA *Camellia japonica cultivars*

Camellia japonica is a large evergreen shrub or small tree; variable in size, rate of growth, habit, form of- and season of bloom and color.

A wide variety of showy flower forms range from single to semi- and formal double, peony, anemone, rose, 'rabbit ears' and fimbriata. Colors range from white to red, violet, rose, pink and may be variegated, bordered and/or streaked. Size of bloom varies from 2½ to 7″ (6-18cm). For full season bloom, varieties are available in early, midseason and late flowering.

Large, glossy dark green leaves may grow up to 4″ (10cm) long.

Soil: Camellias must have a good well-drained soil that is rich in organic matter. Add peat moss, leaf mold or compost if necessary. Fertilize with commercial acid plant food during and following bloom. Keep roots cool with a 2″ (5cm) mulch.

Light: Plant *C. japonicas* in partial shade and protect them from strong winds.

Pruning: Prune lightly to shape and remove faded blooms.

Uses: Camellias are very formal and make beautiful specimens in large gardens, or as a background planting. They may also be espaliered.

BETTY SHEFFIELD SUPREME CAMELLIA

Camellia japonica 'Betty Sheffield Supreme'

Zones: 7-9

This camellia is a slow to moderate growing evergreen shrub with upright form to 6-8′ (1.8-2.4m).

The beautiful variegated flowers are a medium large peony form, white in color with a deep pink to red border on each slightly wavy petal. It is a midseason bloomer. Large, glossy dark green leaves may grow up to 4″ (10cm) long.

Soil: Camellias must have a good well-drained soil that is rich in organic matter. Add peat moss, leaf mold or compost if necessary. Fertilize with commercial acid plant food during and following bloom. Keep roots cool with a 2″ (5cm) mulch.

Light: Plant *C. japonica* in partial shade and protect from strong winds.

Pruning: Prune lightly to shape and remove faded blooms.

Uses: Camellias are very formal and make beautiful specimens in large gardens, or as a background planting. They may also be espaliered.

FINLANDIA CAMELLIA   *Camellia japonica 'Finlandia'*

'Finlandia' is a compact evergreen shrub that grows to about 6' (1.8m).

The medium large flowers are semi-double in form with pale pink, swirled, fluted petals. It is an early to midseason bloomer.

Large, glossy dark green leaves may grow up to 4" (10cm) long.

Soil: Camellias must have a good well-drained soil that is rich in organic matter. Add peat moss, leaf mold or compost if necessary. Fertilize with commercial acid plant food during and following bloom. Keep roots cool with a 2" (5cm) mulch.

Light: Plant *C. Japonicas* in partial shade and protect them from strong winds.

Pruning: Prune lightly to shape and remove faded blooms.

Uses: Camellias are very formal and make beautiful specimens in large gardens, or as background plantings. They may also be espaliered.

MATHOTIANA RUBRA CAMELLIA   *Camellia japonica 'Mathotiana Rubra'*   Zones: 7-10

'Mathotiana Rubra' is a vigorous upright evergreen shrub that grows to 6-10' (1.8-3m). This variety is more cold hardy than some others.

The very large rose form flowers are a deep crimson red, blooming midseason.

Large, glossy dark green leaves may grow up to 4" (10cm) long.

Soil: Camellias must have a good well-drained soil that is rich in organic matter. Add peat moss, leaf mold or compost if necessary. Fertilize with commercial acid plant food during and following bloom. Keep roots cool with a 2" (5cm) mulch.

Light: Plant *C. japonica* in partial shade and protect it from strong winds.

Pruning: Prune lightly to shape and remove faded blooms.

Uses: Camellias are very formal and make beautiful specimens in large gardens, or as background plantings. They may also be espaliered.

MRS. TINGLEY CAMELLIA *Camellia japonica 'Mrs. Tingley'*

'Mrs. Tingley' is an upright, compact evergreen shrub that grows to 8′ (2.4m).

The superb, medium-size salmon-pink flowers are formal double and bloom mid- to late season.

Large glossy dark green leaves may grow up to 4″ (10cm) long.

Soil: Camellias must have a good well-drained soil that is rich in organic matter. Add peat moss, leaf mold or compost if necessary. Fertilize with commercial acid plant food during and following bloom. Keep roots cool with a 2″ (5cm) mulch.

Light: Plant *C. japonicas* in partial shade and protect them from strong winds.

Pruning: Prune lightly to shape and remove faded blooms.

Uses: Camellias are very formal and make beautiful specimens in large gardens, or as a background planting. They may also be espaliered.

SASANQUA CAMELLIA *Camellia sasanqua cultivars*

Camellia sasanqua is a graceful, broadleaf evergreen which varies in form from upright and dense to compact, spreading and/or climbing. It is more versatile for landscape use because it thrives in full sun or partial shade, and is somewhat more cold hardy than *C. japonica.*

The flowers may be single, semi- or large double or peony in form. Colors range from white through pink, rose, orchid-pink, orange and red. Petals may be fluted, cupped, frilled or edged with a contrasting color.

Leaves are a shiny dark green, 1½-3½" (3.8-9cm) long and one-third as wide.

Soil: Camellias must have a good, well-drained soil that is rich in organic matter. Add peat moss, leaf mold or compost if necessary. Fertilize with commercial acid plant food during and following bloom. Keep roots cool with a 2" (5cm) mulch.

Light: *Camellia sasanqua* thrives in full sun or partial shade if water is plentiful and the plant is protected from strong, drying winds.

Pruning: Prune lightly to shape and keep compact. Remove faded blooms.

Uses: Sasanqua camellias make excellent hedges and screens, or may be used for accents. foundations or espaliers.

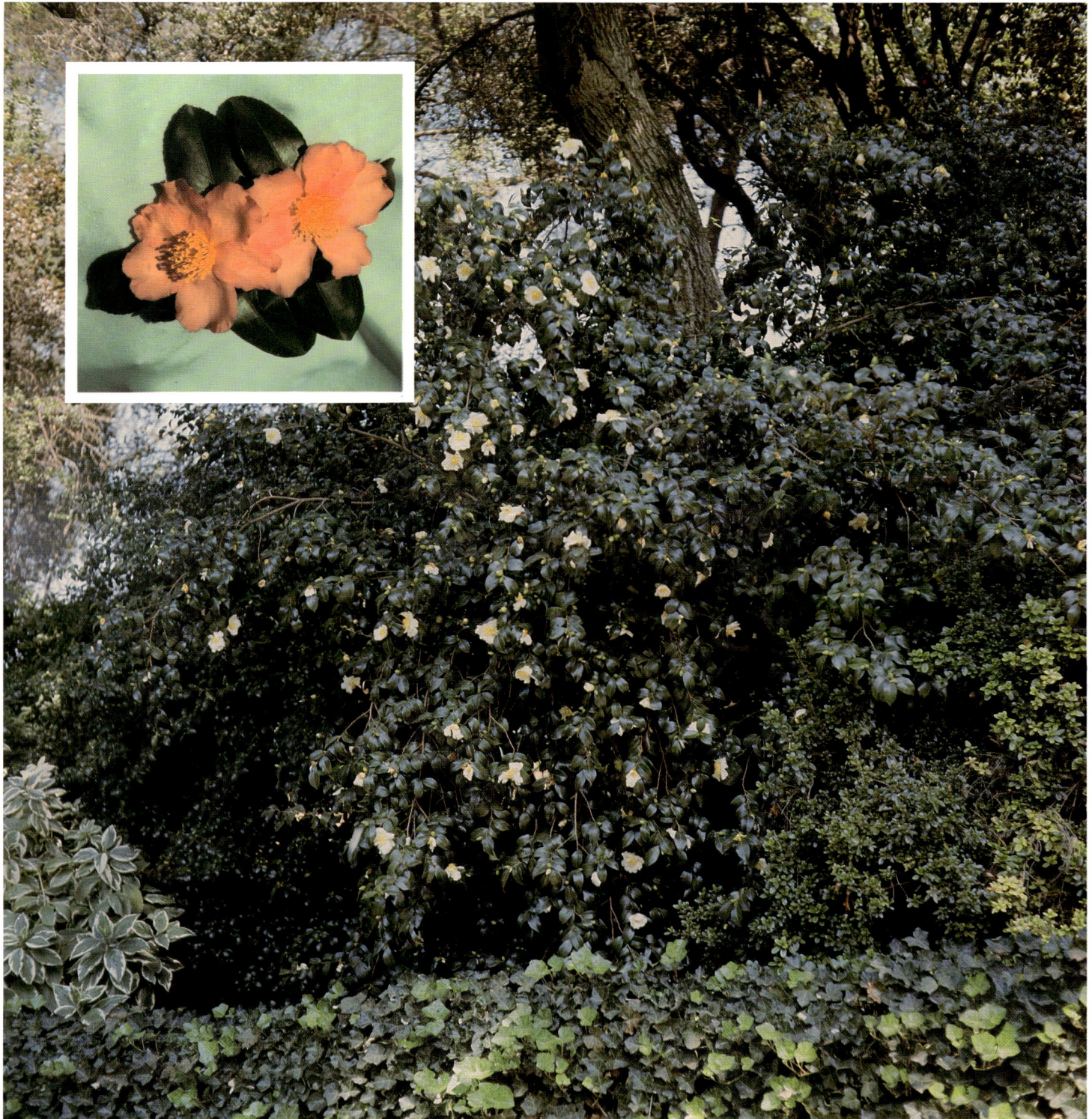

BOXWOOD BEAUTY NATAL PLUM   *Carissa grandiflora 'Boxwood Beauty'*   Zones: 9 & 10

This fast-growing, exceptionally low, compact woody shrub grows to 2′ x 2′ (60cm x 60cm) and is a thornless variety. It is well suited to coastal areas where wind and salt spray could be a problem.

The 2″ (5cm) star-shaped, white flowers have a delicate fragrance and bloom throughout the year. One to 2″ (2.5-5cm) plum-shaped fruit follow the blooms.

Abundant 3″ (8cm) dark, shiny, deep green oval leaves create a dense, rounded appearance.

Soil: Plant in a medium-coarse to medium textured soil with good drainage.

Light: Plant in full sun and a warm, south or west-facing position.

Pruning: Prune lightly for a screen or heavily for a formal hedge.

Uses: 'Boxwood Beauty' is suitable as an accent, foundation, specimen or hedge; it makes a good seashore plant as well.

FANCY NATAL PLUM   *Carissa grandiflora 'Fancy'*

Zones: 9 & 10

'Fancy' is a fast-growing, upright, woody shrub that reaches 6′ (1.8m), making it an excellent screen.

The 2″ (5cm) star-shaped, white flowers have a delicate fragrance and bloom throughout the year. Unusually large, red, plum-shaped fruit follow the blooms.

Abundant 3″ (8cm) dark, shiny, deep green oval leaves create a dense, rounded appearance.

Soil: Plant in a medium-coarse to medium textured soil with good drainage.

Light: Plant in full sun and a warm, south or west-facing position.

Pruning: Prune lightly for a screen or heavily for a formal hedge.

Uses: 'Fancy' is excellent as a screen or hedge.

PATTERLEAF *Cocculus laurifolius*

Cocculus laurifolius is a slow to moderate-growing evergreen shrub or small tree. Usually multistemmed, it spreads as wide as it is high, with gracefully arching branches. If staked and trained as a single trunk tree, it becomes umbrella shaped.

Stiff, leathery, deep green, oblong 6″ (15cm) leaves have raised, yellowish parallel veins.

Soil: It does well in medium-coarse to medium textured soils and will tolerate other types if sufficient moisture is available.

Light: This adaptable plant will grow in sun or dense shade.

Pruning: Prune or shape as desired.

Uses: Plant as a foundation, background or border, or shape for an attractive screen. It may also be pruned and trained as an espalier.

BRIGHT BEAD COTONEASTER

Cotoneaster glaucophyllus

Cotoneaster glaucophyllus is a low, rounded, dense evergreen shrub that grows to 2-3' (60-90cm). Foliage initiates from the base of the plant, outward, in graceful, arching branches.

Tiny white flowers which resemble wild roses are followed by dense clusters of bright red ¼" (.6cm) berries.

The leaves are small, rounded and shiny dark green with whitish underneath.

Soil: These plants do best in poor garden soil and require very little care. They may be used effectively for erosion control on dry slopes and banks.

Light: Plant this shrub in full sun.

Uses: This is an ideal plant for ground cover or rock gardens due to its "ground hugging" ability. It is also suitable for borders, edgings, foregrounds and for container plantings.

ROCK SPRAY COTONEASTER *Cotoneaster microphyllus*

This evergreen spreading shrub has main branches that trail and secondary (rooting) branches that grow upright. The height is 2-3' (.6-.9m) with a spread of 6' (1.8m) or more.

The tiny leaves $\frac{5}{16}$" (.8cm) are dark green above, and silvery underneath. Rose-red ¼" (.6cm) berries provide a striking contrast against the beautiful leaves.

Soil: These plants do best in poor, well drained garden soil, and require very little care. They may be used effectively for erosion control on dry slopes and banks.

Light: Plant in full sun for best flower and berry production.

Pruning: Prune out undesirable upright branches if a low, sprawling effect is desired.

Uses: Use in large rock gardens or place in a position where it can spill over a wall.

ROCK SPRAY COTONEASTER

THREADLEAF FALSE ARALIA
Dizygotheca elegantissima, Aralia elegantissima   Zone: 10

This graceful evergreen shrub, usually considered a house plant, grows into a tropical looking, multitrunked tree or bush to about 12′ (3.6m) when planted out.

Juvenile thread-leaf foliage has narrow bronzy leaflets extending from slender cream-mottled stems. Mature leaves have coarser leaflets to 12″ (30.5cm).

Soil: Plant in a well-drained soil with high moisture-holding capacity. Add leaf mold, peat moss or compost if needed. Water and feed regularly.

Light: Plant in partial shade.

Pruning: Stake and train it if the tree form is desired.

Uses: The lacy foliage of this plant is very showy against a solid wall. It is equally effective as an accent, foundation, patio or container planting.

TRAILING HOP BUSH *Dodonaea viscosa*

Zones: 8-10

This fast-growing evergreen shrub has an excellent spreading habit, with heavy-leaved stems that trail, twine and hug the ground.

Flowers are insignificant, followed by pinkish, winged fruit that add late summer interest.

Willowlike, 4″ (10cm), deep green leaves cover the stems profusely. *Dodonaea viscosa* 'Purpurea' (shown in the inset) has bronze-green leaves that turn to a deep wine color in the winter.

Soil: This highly tolerant plant grows well in any kind of soil and withstands drought and strong wind.

Light: Plant this *Dodonaea* in full sun.

Uses: Use as a formal or informal hedge, or as a border or accent planting. It is particularly effective for erosion control on difficult sites.

EBBING'S SILVERBERRY

Elaeagnus macrophylla 'Ebbingii'

'Ebbingii' is a vigorous upright evergreen shrub that matures at about 10′ (3m). Early growth is rapid and produces dense, hardy shrubs which require little or no care.

Small fragrant flowers are followed by ¼″ (.6cm) red berries with silver flocking.

The foliage is unique, as the 2-4″ (5-10cm) leaves have iridescent silver spots, and the stems have brown scales.

Soil: Plant in any good garden soil that is well drained.

Provide moderate moisture until it is well established.

Light: Plant in full sun or partial shade. It is extremely hardy and tolerates heat, wind and seaside conditions.

Pruning: Shape as desired for landscape objective.

Uses: To use as a hedge or screen, plant 10-12″ (25-30cm) apart. 'Ebbingii' would also be good as an accent, foreground planting or espalier.

THORNY ELAEAGNUS *Elaeagnus pungens*

Elaeagnus pungens is a large, spreading evergreen shrub that grows to a height of 8-15′ (2.4-4.5m) in 8-10 years. The branches are spiny and covered with rust-brown dots.

The small, fragrant, waxy white flowers bloom in late fall. Oval ½″ (1.3cm), berrylike fruits are red with a silvery covering.

Grayish green 1-2″ (2.5-5cm) leaves have wavy edges and rust-brown dots.

Soil: Plant in any good garden soil that is well drained.

Provide moderate moisture until well established.

Light: Plant in full sun or partial shade. It is extremely hardy and tolerates heat, wind and seaside conditions.

Pruning: Prune at any time. Shear as a hedge or shape by clipping out individual stems.

Uses: To use as a hedge or screen, plant 10-12″ (25-30cm) apart. *Elaeagnus pungens* also makes an excellent accent, foreground planting or espalier. Good wildlife shrub.

BRONZE LOQUAT *Eriobotrya deflexa*

Eriobotrya deflexa is a large, fast-growing, evergreen shrub which is easily trained into a small, single-stem tree.

Dense clusters of creamy-white flowers appear in the spring. This plant does not produce edible fruit.

Oval, pointed, large, 5-10 ″ (13-25cm) shiny-green leaves are a bright copper color when young.

Soil: Plant in any good garden soil that is well drained. It will tolerate some drought, but produces a better show of foliage and flowers with plenty of water.

Light: Give it full sun or partial shade.

Pruning: When pruning to shape, take great care to sterilize the tools *Eriobotrya* is subject to Fireblight *(Erwinia emylovora),* which is easily spread from one plant to another.

Uses: This shrub would make a fine espalier, or a lawn tree if it were trained to a single stem.

RED GUM *Eucalyptus camaldulensis*

This rapidly-growing, wide-spreading evergreen tree grows to 80-130′ (25-40m) high. It has smooth bark that is red when young and mottled tan with age. Branches are long, slender and gracefully arching.

White flowers with a pinkish cast hang in drooping clusters during the summer, and are followed by pea-size seed capsules.

The long, slender, lance-shaped leaves are medium green.

Soil: Plant in a well-drained soil and water and feed during establishment. Eucalyptus will tolerate some drought after 2-3 years.

Light: Plant in full sun or partial shade.

Uses: This would make an excellent specimen or shade tree for highways, broad streets or parks.

BIGLEAF WINTERCREEPER OR EVERGREEN BITTERSWEET

Euonymus fortunei var. vegeta

Zones: 6-9

This evergreen shrubby spreader has erect stems to a height of 4′ (1.5m) and spreads to about 5′ (1.5m) in 8-10 years.

The rounded, oval, 1½″ (4cm) leaves are a glossy dark green all year long.

Eye-catching orange-red fruit that resembles bittersweet makes a colorful accent.

This genus is very hardy, and tolerant of poor soil conditions, high temperature, wind and salt spray.

Soil: Plant *Euonymus* in almost any soil and give it moderate watering until it is well established.

Light: Full sun and good air circulation are required in areas of high humidity, as it is highly susceptible to mildew. Light shade is suitable in a hot, dry climate.

Pruning: Prune at any time to shape. It also responds well to shearing.

Uses: Use as a low hedge, ground cover, foundation planting or train as an espalier.

GOLD SPOT EUONYMUS   *Euonymus japonica 'Aureo-marginata'*

This densely-branched, upright. medium-sized shrub grows 4-5' (1.2-1.5m). Its compact, fast growth responds well to pruning and shaping.

The shiny, deep green leaves have brilliant gold margins.

The genus is very hardy, and tolerant of poor soil conditions, high temperature, wind and salt spray.

Soil: Plant Euonymus in almost any soil and give it moderate watering until it is well established.

Light: Full sun and good air circulation are required in areas of high humidity, as it is highly susceptible to mildew. Light shade is suitable in a hot, dry climate.

Pruning: Prune at any time to shape. It also responds well to shearing.

Uses: Use as a low hedge, ground cover, foundation planting or train as an espalier.

SPREADING EUONYMUS *Euonymus kiauschovicus*

This *Euonymus* is somewhat hardier than *E. japonica,* and tolerates reasonably colder temperatures. The spreading, semi-evergreen (evergreen in milder climates) shrub has a height and spread of 4-5' (1.2-1.5m) in 5-6 years.

Insignificant flowers appear in September, and are followed by clusters of red and white berries.

Glossy dark green leaves hold their color all year in mild climates.

The genus is very hardy, and tolerant of poor soil conditions, high temperature, wind and salt spray.

Soil: Plant *Euonymus* in almost any soil and give it moderate watering until it is well established.

Light: Full sun and good air circulation are required in areas of high humidity. as it is highly susceptible to mildew. Light shade is suitable in a hot, dry climate.

Pruning: Prune at any time to shape. It also responds well to shearing.

Uses: Plant as a specimen accent or group planting.

JAPANESE ARALIA *Fatsia japonica (Aralia sieboldii)*

Zones: 8-10

This fast-growing evergreen shrub reaches both a height and spread of 6-10′ (1.8-3m) at maturity. It has a distinctively tropical appearance with large, glossy, fan-shaped leaves.

Clusters of small white flowers appear in the fall and winter, followed by small, shiny, blue-black fruit.

The dark green, deeply lobed 16″ (40cm) leaves unfold from long, dominant stalks.

Soil: Plant in any moderate to good garden soil that is well-drained. It will grow in a low fertility/moisture situation, but it does best with regular feeding and watering.

Light: Plant in full shade and protect from strong wind.

Pruning: Clip the old growth to maintain desired size.

Uses: Use *Fatsia* as an attractive foundation, specimen or border planting. If small size is desired, a container planting would be suitable.

30

WEEPING FIG *Ficus benjamina*

Ficus benjamina is a large, tropical evergreen tree which can grow to 30′ (9m) or more and spreads at least half its height.

Shiny-green, oval, pointed, 5″ (13cm)-long leaves hang on graceful, drooping branches.

Soil: Ficus thrives in a rich, moist, but well-drained soil.

Beautiful foliage results with frequent, light feeding. Do not overwater, however.

Light: Adjusts well to full sun or deep shade.

Uses: Use as an accent, specimen, or foundation plant, but protect from frost or wind. Weeping Figs can also be pruned into a hedge.

FIDDLELEAF FIG *Ficus lyrata*

Ficus lyrata is a large, tropical evergreen tree or shrub which can grow up to 20' (6m) or more, with a trunk up to 6″ (15cm) wide.

The huge, dark green, fiddle-shaped leaves may grow up to 16″ (40cm) long, and more than 8″ (20cm) wide.

Soil: *Ficus* thrives in a rich, moist, but well-drained soil.

Beautiful foliage results with frequent, light feeding. Allow the soil to become moderately dry, then water thoroughly.

Light: Plant in either sun or shade, but position in an area that is protected from prevailing winds and potential frost.

Uses: Use as an accent, specimen or foundation. A swimming pool location would be excellent.

FIDDLELEAF FIG *Ficus lyrata*

GARDENIA *Gardenia jasminoides*

Zones: 8-10

Gardenia jasminoides is a beautiful evergreen shrub with rich foliage and highly fragrant white flowers. Several forms are available, including dense-bushy (*G.j.* 'Mystery'), compact (*G.j.* 'Veitchii') and a petite miniature (*G.j.* 'Radicans').

Gardenia produces abundant, velvety, creamy white double blooms from May through November.

The leaves are a narrow, glossy bright green.

Soil: Plant in a rich, well-drained soil with excellent moisture-holding capacity. Condition the soil with peat moss or ground bark. Mulch around the plants with peat moss or ground bark. Feed every 3-4 weeks during the growing season with an acid plant food.

Light: Plant in full sun in coastal areas and filtered shade in warmer, inland areas.

Pruning: Prune to remove unattractive branches.

Uses: Gardenias are beautiful as hedges, screens, accents, in raised beds or as espaliers.

SILK OAK *Grevillea robusta*

This fast-growing evergreen tree matures at about 50-60' (15-18m). It is symmetrical in youth, and develops a wide, broad crown when older. *Grevillea* is particularly well suited to hot, dry climates.

Large clusters of striking, bright, golden orange flowers appear in the spring. This floral show makes an outstanding display when situated with a dark green background.

Large fernlike leaves are golden green to deep green above, and silvery beneath.

Soil: Plant in ordinary, well-drained garden soil. It will adapt to poor, rocky, dry soil once it is established.

Light: Plant *Grevillea* in full sun.

Pruning: It has brittle stems which are easily damaged in high winds, so cut the leader at planting time to promote sturdier branches.

Uses: This is an excellent choice for a specimen, tall screen or street tree.

SHRUBBY VERONICA

Hebe x 'Patty's Purple'

This densely-branched, evergreen shrub grows to about 3′ (.9m) in height.

Purplish blue flowers on narrow spikes bloom throughout the summer.

½″ (1.3cm) green leaves are particularly attractive on wine red stems.

Soil: Hebe needs a good rich garden soil that is well drained, yet holds plenty of moisture.

Light: Plant in full sun. It does best in cooler coastal areas and is salt and wind tolerant.

Pruning: Prune after flowering to keep the plants compact and bushy.

Uses: Use for group plantings, as a specimen or as an informal hedge.

SHRUBBY VERONICA

Hebe x *'Veronica Lake'*

Zones: 9 & 10

'Veronica Lake' is a densely-branched, evergreen shrub which grows to 3′ (.9m). Foliage is larger than 'Patty's Purple' and bloom period is longer.

Abundant short spikes of lilac flowers appear in late spring and during the summer.

The dark green, oblong leaves are 1½″ (4cm) long.

Soil: Hebe needs a good rich garden soil that is well drained, yet holds plenty of moisture.

Light: Plant in full sun. It does best in cooler coastal areas and is salt and wind tolerant.

Pruning: Prune after flowering to keep the plants compact and bushy.

Uses: Use for group plantings, as a specimen or as an informal hedge.

CHINESE HIBISCUS

Hibiscus rosa-sinensis, Compact Bush Form

Hibiscus rosa-sinensis, compact bush form, is one of several forms of this tropical evergreen shrub. It matures at 5-7' (1.5-2.1m). All *H. rosa-sinensis* hybrids have beautiful, dense, glossy foliage.

Flowers in this species vary from 4-8" (10-20cm) wide and may be single or double. The variety *H. rosa-sinensis* 'Crown of Bohemia', featured here, has double, gold flowers with a deep orange-red throat.

The leaves of 'Crown of Bohemia' are oval, shiny, deep green, and have finely-toothed edges.

Soil: Plant this species in a rich, well-drained soil that has a good moisture-holding capacity. If internal soil drainage is reduced, plant in raised beds or choose another location. If organic matter is low, mix half the top soil from the hole with equal amounts of peat moss, compost or muck.

Light: Hibiscus needs full sun and protection from winds and potential frost.

Pruning: Prune poorly-shaped young plants when planting, to encourage good form. Pinch branch ends during bloom season for more flowers.

Uses: Use for an outstanding accent, specimen, border, screen, hedge or mass planting.

Hibiscus rosa-sinensis, open upright form, is a vigorous, evergreen shrub that will reach up to 15′ (4.5m) at maturity.

The variety *H. rosa-sinensis* 'White Wings', featured here, has beautiful, single, 4-6″ (10-15cm) white flowers with a red throat.

The leaves of 'White Wings' are oval, shiny, deep green with finely-toothed edges.

Soil: Plant this species in a rich, well-drained soil that has a good moisture-holding capacity. If internal soil drainage is reduced, plant in raised beds or choose another location. If organic matter is low, mix half the top soil from the hole with an equal amount of peat moss, compost or muck.

Light: Hibiscus needs full sun and protection from winds and potential frost.

Pruning: Prune poorly-shaped young plants when planting, to encourage good form. Pinch branch ends during bloom season for more flowers.

Uses: Use for an outstanding accent, specimen, border, screen, hedge or mass planting.

CHINESE HIBISCUS
Hibiscus rosa-sinensis, Tall Compact Form

Zone: 10

Hibiscus rosa-sinensis, tall compact form, is a hardy, vigorous evergreen shrub that will grow up to 15′ (4.5m) with very dense branching.

The variety *H. rosa-sinensis* 'Brilliant', featured here, has single, bright red flowers that bloom abundantly for most of the year.

The leaves of 'Brilliant' are oval, shiny, deep green with finely-toothed edges.

Soil: Plant this species in a rich, well-drained soil that has a good moisture-holding capacity. If internal soil drainage is reduced, plant in raised beds or choose another loca-tion. If organic matter is low, mix one half the top soil from the hole with equal amounts of peat moss, compost or muck.

Light: Hibiscus needs full sun and protection from winds and potential frost.

Pruning: Prune poorly-shaped young plants when planting, to encourage good form. Pinch branch ends during bloom season for more flowers.

Uses: Use for an outstanding accent, specimen, border, screen, hedge or mass planting.

CHINESE HIBISCUS
Hibiscus rosa-sinensis, Upright Bush Form

Zone: 10

Hibiscus rosa-sinensis, upright bush form, is a vigorous, tall, densely-branched evergreen shrub that grows to 15′ (4.5m).

The variety *H. rosa-sinensis* 'Kona', featured here, has lavish, double, ruffled, 4″ (10cm) or more, rose-pink flowers.

The leaves of 'Kona' are oval, shiny, deep green with finely-toothed edges.

Soil: Plant this species in a rich, well-drained soil that has a good moisture-holding capacity. If internal soil drainage is reduced, plant in raised beds or choose another location. If organic matter is low, mix half the top soil from the hole with an equal amount of peat moss, compost or muck.

Light: Hibiscus needs full sun and protection from winds and potential frost.

Pruning: Prune poorly-shaped young plants when planting, to encourage good form. Pinch branch ends during bloom season for more flowers.

Uses: Use for an outstanding accent, specimen, border, screen, hedge or mass planting.

ALTHAEA or ROSE OF SHARON *Hibiscus syriacus*

Hibiscus syriacus is a fast-growing, upright evergreen shrub that spreads broadly as it matures. The branches are pliable and easily trained into a tree form if desired. Freestanding height reaches 6-12′ (1.8-3.6m).

Flowers may be single or double with bloom in late summer and fall. Colors range from white to pink, red and purple.

The medium-sized, three-lobed green leaves are coarsely toothed.

Soil: Plant this species in a rich, well-drained soil that has a good moisture-holding capacity. If internal soil drainage is reduced, plant in raised beds or choose another location. If organic matter is low, mix half the top soil from the hole with an equal amount of peat moss, compost or muck.

Light: Hibiscus needs full sun and protection from winds and potential frost.

Pruning: Prune in the spring to remove winterkilled shoot tips. Shorten extra-long shoots after flowering.

Uses: Use this Hibiscus in borders, against a wall, or on a trellis. It is also beautiful as an accent or screen.

41

ENGLISH or CHRISTMAS HOLLY *Ilex aquifolium*

Ilex aquifolium is an evergreen shrub or tree with slow growth up to 40′ (12m). Both male and female plants are needed for good berry production, although some newly developed varieties are self-pollinating and self-fruitful. Large clusters of bright red berries follow inconspicious white flowers.

The glossy, thick, medium green leaves have sharp points with or without long spines. *Ilex aquifolium* 'Ferox Aurea' or GOLD HEDGEHOG (shown in the inset) is a striking variety with spiny, gold-blotched leaves.

Soil: *Ilex* does well in a rich, slightly acid garden soil. Good drainage is essential yet the moisture-holding capacity must be ample. Mulch around the plants with leaf mold or compost.

Light: Plant *Ilex* in sun or shade, but berry production is favored in a sunny location.

Pruning: Prune when needed for desired shape.

Uses: Use for a hedge, foundation planting, accent, specimen or screen.

CHINESE HOLLY *Ilex cornuta cultivars*

Ilex cornuta cultivars are evergreen shrubs or small trees, the largest having open growth to about 10′ (3m). All fertile varieties have very large, longlasting bright red berries.

Ilex cornuta 'Burfordii', BURFORD HOLLY (main illustration), is a vigorous, upright, densely-branched, nearly spineless medium size shrub.

Ilex cornuta 'Burfordii Nana', DWARF BURFORD HOLLY (lower right), grows to only 1½-2′ (45-60cm) in 5 years, and has nearly spineless leaves.

Ilex cornuta 'Compacta', DWARF CHINESE HOLLY (lower left), is a compact, mounding, non-fruiting low grower with spines at the leaf corners and tips.

Soil: Plant in rich, slightly acid garden soil with good drainage and good moisture-holding capacity.

Light: Plant 'Burfordii' and 'Burfordii Nana' in full sun for berry production. 'Compacta' does well in sun or shade.

Pruning: Prune when needed for desired shape.

Uses: These cultivars may be used as a hedge, accent, specimen, screen, border or espalier.

Ilex crenata cultivars are dense, erect evergreen shrubs with small, narrow, finely-toothed leaves. All produce attractive black berries.

Ilex crenata 'Convexa', JAPANESE HOLLY (main illustration), is a compact, densely-branched shrub that reaches 4-6'x 6' (1.2-1.8m x 1.8m). The long, glossy green leaves have cupped edges.

Ilex crenata 'Globosa', DWARF JAPANESE HOLLY (upper right), matures at about 2-3' (60-90cm).

Ilex crenata 'Helleri', HELLER'S JAPANESE HOLLY (lower left), is a dwarf form, 1' x 2' (30cm x 60cm), with small, oval, dark green leaves.

Soil: Plant in rich, slightly acid garden soil with good drainage and good moisture-holding capacity.

Light: Plant in full sun for good berry production.

Uses: These cultivars may be used as an accent, foundation, specimen, hedge or screen. 'Helleri' and 'Globosa' are best suited to low hedges, edgings, patio plantings or as ground covers.

SOUTHERN MAGNOLIA, BULL BAY *Magnolia grandiflora*

Magnolia grandiflora is a medium size evergreen tree with a pyramidal branching form.

Cup-shaped, fragrant white flowers to 8-12″ (20-30cm) across bloom in early summer. The age of bloom is unpredictable, but plants from grafts may bloom in 2-3 years after planting.

The leaves are large, glossy deep green with wavy edges.

Soil: This magnolia does well in a soil with only moderate internal soil drainage and moderate fertility.

Light: Plant in full sun and against a warm wall in cooler areas. The tree is very heat tolerant.

Uses: *Magnolia grandiflora* makes an excellent street or lawn tree, showy accent or beautiful specimen.

OREGON GRAPE *Mahonia aquifolium*

Mahonia aquifolium is an evergreen shrub that grows to a height and spread of 3-6' (.9-1.8m) in 5-6 years.

Short clusters of bright yellow flowers appear at the ends of the stems in the spring.

Blue-black, grapelike fruit follow the flowers and persist through early summer. The fruit may be used to make jelly.

Hollyleaf-shaped leaflets make up the spiny, leathery, dark green leaves. The new growth is typically bronze. Mature growth may be bronze in cold temperatures.

Soil: Plant in a rich, well-drained soil that has a good moisture-holding capacity. *Mahonia* thrives in a slightly acid (pH 5.0-5.5) environment, but does well in neutral or alkaline soils as well. Add peat moss, leaf mold or compost to the soil in the planting hole.

Light: Plant in light or full shade.

Pruning: Prune tall canes (stems) back to the ground in early spring for a succession of vigorous young shoots.

Uses: Use for foundation plantings, as shrub borders or as specimens, or accents.

OLEANDER *Nerium oleander*

This upright, rounded evergreen shrub reaches 8-10′ (2.4-3m) with a spread as wide. If trained, it may resemble a single or multi-stem, olive-type tree. *Nerium* is available in a variety of colors, flower forms and leaf color variations.

Clusters of flowers bloom all through the summer, in white, pink, yellow, salmon and/or red.

The 4-12″ (10-30cm) long narrow, leathery dark green leaves provide a beautiful display all year long.

Soil: This shrub thrives in most any soil and is tolerant of drought, poor drainage and high salt conditions.

Light: Plant in full sun. It thrives in heat and tolerates intense, reflected light.

Pruning: Prune early in the spring to desired shape. Cut old growth close to the ground. All plant parts are poisonous to humans and animals, as well as the smoke if cuttings are burned.

Uses: Use as a specimen tree or in shrub form use as a hedge, screen or windbreak.

SWEET OLIVE *Osmanthus fragrans*

Osmanthus fragrans is a broad, compact, rounded evergreen shrub with a moderate growth rate to 10′ (3m) or more. It can be trained as a small tree.

Tiny, white, inconspicuous flowers produce a strong, apricotlike fragrance, spring through summer in cooler areas, and scattered throughout the year in warm zones.

The 4″ (10cm), oval, medium green leaves have finely-toothed edges. *Osmanthus heterophyllus* 'Aureus' (featured on the right) is a showy, variegated form.

Soil: Plant in any moderately well to well-drained soil. This adaptable species is well suited to heavy clays.

Light: Osmanthus does best in full sun but tolerates light to medium shade.

Pruning: Prune to desired shape. It is easily shaped to an upright form for a narrow location.

Uses: Use as a small tree, hedge, screen backgound or espalier.

Photinia x fraseri is a wide-spreading evergreen shrub that matures at about 10' (3m).

Small clusters of fragrant white flowers appear in the early spring.

The 2-5" (5-13cm) long leaves are a brilliant bronze-red when young, maturing to a glossy dark green with light green undersides.

Soil: Photinia thrives in a good, well-drained garden soil, high in organic matter with moderate moisture-holding capacity. Add peat moss or leaf mold to improve the soil.

Light: Plant in full sun.

Prune: Prune to desired shape.

Uses: Use as an accent, foundation, hedge or border. Photinia will make an attractive espalier or may be trained to a single-stemmed, small tree.

JAPANESE PHOTINIA *Photinia glabra*

Photinia glabra is a broad, dense evergreen shrub that grows to 10′ (3m) or more. The showy foliage gives landscape interest throughout the year.

Fragrant white flowers in 4″ (10cm) clusters are followed by red berries that eventually turn black.

The striking, oval, 3″ (8cm) leaves are bronze when young and glossy green with bright red undersides when mature. Bronze-red individual leaves are also scattered throughout the mature leaves adding unique interest during the fall and winter.

Soil: *Photinia* thrives in a good, well-drained garden soil, high in organic matter with moderate moisture-holding capacity. Add peat moss or leaf mold to improve the soil.

Light: Plant in full sun.

Pruning: Prune to desired shape.

Uses: Use as an accent, foundation, hedge or border. *Photinia* will make an attractive espalier or may be trained to a single-stemmed, small tree.

MOCK ORANGE   *Pittosporum tobira*

This large, dense evergreen shrub will grow to 15' (4.5m) or taller, but can be kept to about 6' (1.8m) with cutting back and thinning.

Clusters of creamy white flowers appear in the spring, and emit an orange blossom fragrance. Green fruit that turn brown and split to show orange seeds, follow the blossoms.

The 4-5" (10-13cm) long, thick, glossy, leathery, dark green leaves have rounded ends.

Soil: Plant in a rich well-drained garden soil with high moisture-holding capacity. Add peat moss or leaf mold to enrich the soil. Water regularly and feed in the spring with a complete fertilizer.

Light: *Pittosporum* does best in full sun.

Pruning: Prune to desired shape.

Uses: Use as a screen or hedge, mass planting, foundation or border.

BLUE CAPE PLUMBAGO   *Plumbago auriculata (P. capensis)*   Zones:9 & 10

This semi-evergreen shrub reaches 12' (3.6m) or more with support, or forms a sprawling bush which grows to 6-10' (1.8-3m) if left untrained.

Showy, phloxlike, blue-white flowers bloom in clusters throughout the summer.

The 1-2" (2.5-5cm) long leaves are light to medium green.

Soil: Plumbago tolerates coarse textured soils, low moisture and low fertility, once it is established. However, good soil drainage is essential.

Light: Plant in full sun.

Pruning: Prune out old or damaged growth.

Uses: Use as an accent, foundation, screen, ground cover, mass planting or bank cover.

ELEPHANT BUSH or PURSLANE TREE *Portulacaria afra*

This thick-stemmed succulent shrub or small tree grows to 12′ (3.6m) and resembles a huge jade plant. It is fast growing, with flexible, tapering branches.

Small, thick, ½″ (1.3cm) leaves are round and fleshy. The cultivar *P. afra* 'Variegata' has smaller greenish yellow leaves marked with white.

Soil: Plant in a coarse to medium textured soil with good drainage. Water when surface soil has dried to a depth of 2-3″ (5-8cm).

Light: Plant in full sun. It will withstand intense heat and considerable drought.

Uses: Use as an informal screen, foundation, tall ground cover, unclipped hedge or container/patio planting.

CAROLINA LAUREL CHERRY

Prunus caroliniana

Prunus caroliniana is an evergreen tree or shrub. As a shrub, it is densely-branched and useful as a formal hedge or screen. If trained as a tree, it forms a broad, round crown, and matures at about 40' (12m). *Prunus caroliniana* 'Compacta' (shown upper left) is more dense and is easily sheared to a hedge, or clipped into formal shapes.

Small, creamy white flowers bloom in 1" (2.5cm) clusters from February through April. Small, black cherrylike fruit follow the blossoms.

The 2-4" (5-10cm) long leaves are a smooth-edged, shiny green.

Soil: *Prunus* does well in average garden soil with good drainage. It will withstand moderate drought once it is established.

Light: Plant in full sun. Avoid areas where salt spray is a possibility.

Pruning: Prune or train to desired shape.

Uses: This *Prunus* is excellent in natural form as a windbreak, screen or specimen. Train as a small tree for an accent planting.

ORANGE PYRACANTHA or SCARLET FIRE THORN

Pyracantha coccinea 'Lalandei'

Zones: 6-9

Pyracantha coccinea 'Lalandei' is a rounded evergreen shrub that grows 8′ x 10′ (2.4m x 3m). It will reach 20′ (6m) if trained against a wall.

Clusters of tiny ¼″ (.6cm), fragrant flowers appear in the spring. Orange, long-lasting berries develop after the flowers.

The narrow, oval dark green leaves are 1-1½″ (2.5-3.7cm) long.

Soil: *Pyracantha* thrives in a well-drained soil of moderate texture. Keep it away from irrigation sprinklers as it should not be continually wet.

Light: Plant in full sun for good berry production.

Pruning: To control size, pinch young growth and prune long branches before growth initiation.

Uses: This shrub is well suited to barrier plantings, screens, hedges, backgrounds or situated against a wall.

GRABERI FIRE THORN   *Pyracantha fortuneana 'Graberi'*   Zones 7-9

This upright, evergreen shrub grows to a height and spread of about 10′ (3 m). It is prized for its bright fruit, beautiful foliage, variety of landscape uses and easy culture.

Numerous clusters of white flowers appear in the spring on spurs projecting from the previous year's wood.

Huge clusters of bright red fruit adorn the woody stems from midfall through winter.

The oval leaves are a glossy green with rounded ends.

Soil: *Pyracantha* thrives in a well-drained soil of moderate texture. Keep it away from irrigation sprinklers as it should not be continually wet.

Light: Plant in full sun for good berry production.

Pruning: To control size, pinch young growth and prune long branches before growth initiation.

Uses: This shrub is well suited to barrier plantings, screens, hedges, backgrounds or situated against a wall.

FORMOSA FIRE THORN *Pyracantha koidzumii*

Zones: 8-10

Pyracantha koidzumii is a large, upright shrub with a height and spread of 8-10′ (2.4-3m).

Clusters of tiny ¼″ (.6cm), fragrant flowers appear in the spring.

Large, bright red berries follow the flowers.

Attractive gray-green leaves have a notch at the tip.

Soil: *Pyracantha* thrives in a well-drained soil of moderate texture. Keep it away from irrigation sprinklers as it should not be kept continually wet.

Light: Plant in full sun for good berry production.

Pruning: To control size, pinch young growth and prune long branches before growth initiation.

Uses: Use as a specimen, screen or border. It would also be attractive as an espalier or positioned on a trellis.

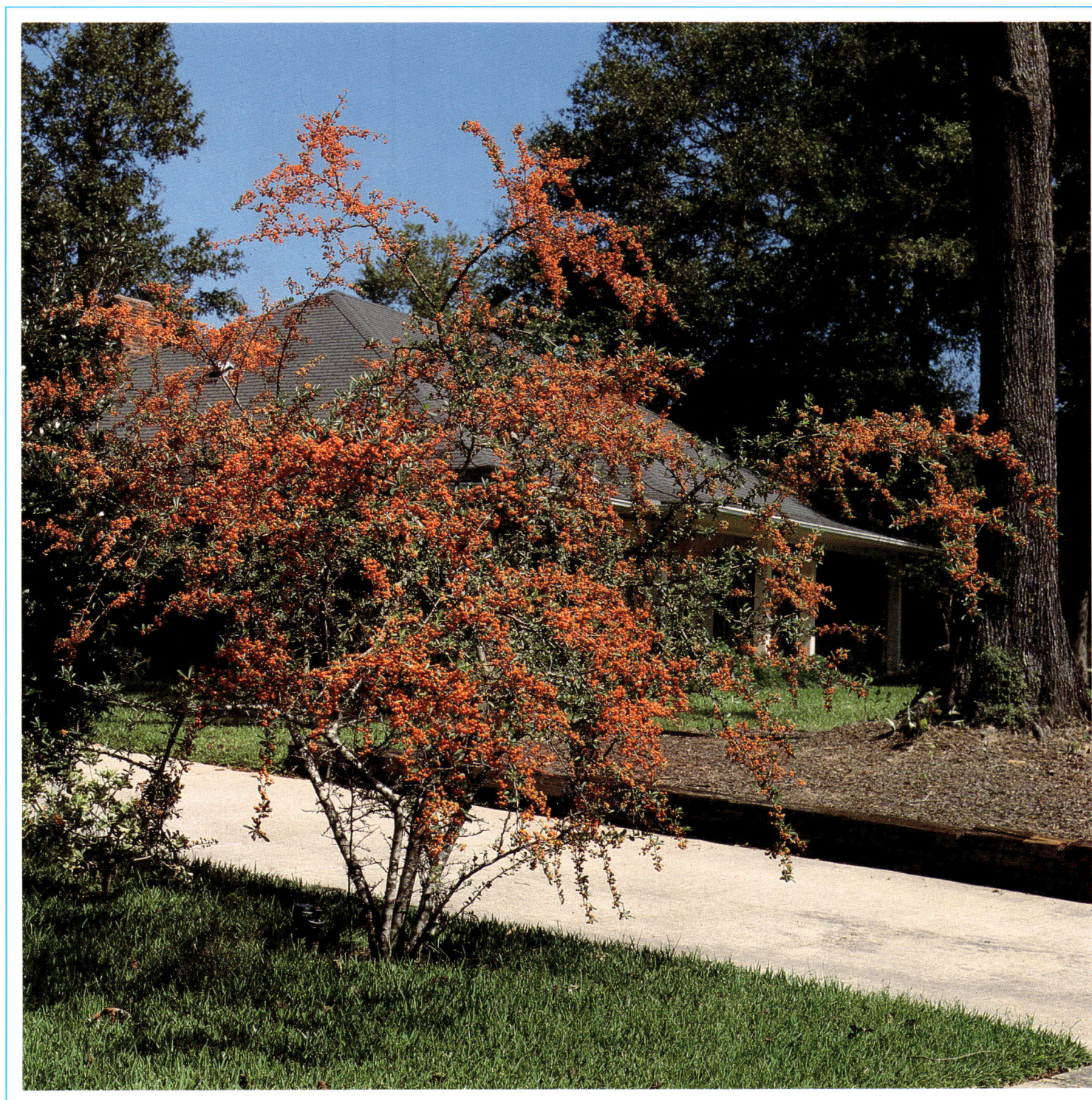

61

INDIAN HAWTHORN *Raphiolepis indica*

This spreading, open, evergreen shrub grows to a height and spread of 5′ (1.5m). It is prized for its striking foliage and flower display.

Profuse, white or pink flowers appear at branch ends, late fall or early summer (April in colder areas). Small black fruit follow the flowers.

The 2-3″ (5-8cm) leaves are a thick, leathery, glossy dark green which turn purple-green for winter interest.

Soil: *Raphiolepis* tolerates most soils but does best in a medium-textured, slightly neutral (pH 6.0-7.0) soil with moderate drainage, moisture and fertility.

Light: Plant in full sun. It is more leggy with fewer blooms when planted in light shade. It is tolerant of wind and salt spray.

Pruning: Prune from youth on, for dense, compact plants. Pinch back tips once a year after flowering.

Uses: Use as a foundation, background, high ground cover or as an informal hedge.

This densely-branching, wide-spreading evergreen shrub has vigorous growth to about 10′ x 10′ (3m x 3m).

Fragrant, white, 3/4″ (1.9cm) flowers appear in the spring and bloom intermittently throughout the summer.

This variety has round, leathery, dark green leaves that are 1-3″ (2.5-8cm) long.

Soil: *Rhapiolepis* tolerates most soils but does best in a medium-textured, slightly acid to neutral (pH 6.0-7.0) soil with moderate drainage, moisture and fertility.

Light: Full sun encourages a thick, bushy form.

Pruning: Prune from youth on, for dense, compact plants. Pinch back tips once a year after flowering.

Uses: Use as a foundation, background, high ground cover or as an informal hedge.

RHODODENDRON
Glen Dale, Gable, Belgian and Rutherford Hybrids

Glen Dale Hybrids (e.g. *R.* 'Snow Clad', upper left) are highly variable in form, from low compact to tall and open. They have a wide color range with many stunning variations. They are hardy in Zones 7 & 8.

Gable Hybrids (e.g. *R.* 'Louise Gable', upper right) are hardy evergreen shrubs that can be grown from Zone 6-8. They show a beautiful display of color from April-May.

Belgian Hybrids (e.g. *R.* 'Red Wings', lower left) are rather tender, but are recommended with reservation for Zones 9 & 10.

Rutherford (American developed Belgians) Hybrids (e.g. *R.* 'Albert-Elizabeth', lower right) are also tender, with some cultivars recommended for Zones 8 & 9.

Soil: Plant in a good well-drained soil that is rich in organic matter. Add peat moss, leaf mold or compost if necessary. Water well during hot dry spells. Fertilize with commercial acid plant food during and following bloom. Keep roots cool with a 2″ (5cm) mulch. See Appendix D for details of soil preparation.

Light: Plant Gable Hybrids in shade; others in partial shade, depending on specific cultivar cultural directions.

Pruning: Pinch back tips after flowering to assure a compact form. Prune old gangly stems to restore desired shape. Remove faded flower heads.

Uses: Use as a foundation planting, group planting, border or in a woodland setting.

RHODODENDRON *Kurume Hybrids*

Kurume semi-evergreen, semi-dwarf hybrids are hardier and more adaptable than Southern Indicas. Shapely and dense, the average height is 3′ (9m), with some 4-6′ (1.2-1.8m) in height and spread.

The compact plants have small leaves and a profusion of 1½-2″ (3.8-5cm) flowers with exquisite colors from white to pink, scarlet, lavender and salmon with many additional variations.

Soil: Plant rhododendrons in a good well-drained soil that is rich in organic matter. Add peat moss, leaf mold or compost if necessary. Water well during hot dry spells. Fertilize with commercial acid plant food during and following bloom. Keep roots cool with a 2″ (5cm) mulch. See Appendix D for details of soil preparation.

Light: Plant in partial shade.

Pruning: These plants are particularly attractive when kept in mounds or tiers.

Uses: Use as a foundation planting, group planting, border or in a woodland setting.

Southern Indica Hybrids may have rapid, open growth or slow, low, spreading growth. Different varieties may bloom early, mid or late season.

Large, showy flowers may be single, semi-double or double. Colors range from white through pink, orchid-pink, lavender, violet-red, red and orange. Blossoms may be variegated, streaked or blotched.

Evergreen rhododendrons have spring leaves that drop off by fall, and summer leaves that are more leathery and remain throughout winter into spring.

Soil: Plant rhododendrons in a good well-drained soil that is rich in organic matter. Add peat moss, leaf mold or compost if necessary. Water well during hot dry spells. Fertilize with commercial acid plant food during and following bloom. Keep roots cool with a 2″ (5cm) mulch. See Appendix D for details of soil preparation.

Light: Plant in full sun. Southern Indicas are most suitable to high light areas.

Pruning: Pinch back tips after flowering to assure a compact form. Prune old gangly stems to restore desired shape. Remove faded flower heads.

Uses: Use as a foundation planting, group planting, border or in a woodland setting.

LAVENDER COTTON *Santolina chamaecyparissus*

This dense, mounding, dwarf evergreen shrub will reach 2' (60cm), but is most effective when kept to 1' (30cm) or less.

Bright yellow flowers in little rounded heads appear throughout the summer.

Rough, finely-divided silver-gray leaves occur all along stiff, woody stems. Foliage is aromatic if bruised.

Soil: *Santolina* will thrive in almost any soil. Water use is low in cool areas, moderate in hot situations.

Light: Plant in full sun.

Pruning: Prune to desired shape and cut back in early spring. Remove faded flowers.

Uses: *Santolina* is well suited as a foreground planting, border, edge or ground cover.

HAWAIIAN ELF SCHEFFLERA *Schefflera arboricola*

Zone: 10

Schefflera arboricola is a large, evergreen plant that may reach 20 x 20' (6 x 6m). It can be kept smaller with careful pruning.

The intense, dark green leaves have 3" (8cm), broad leaflets with rounded tips.

Soil: Plant in a good, well-drained garden soil, high in organic matter with moderate moisture-holding capacity. Add peat moss or leaf mold to improve the soil.

Light: Plant in filtered sun or light shade. Schefflera thrives in high humidity.

Pruning: Prune to desired shape and size. If stems are planted at an angle, the plant will have a striking multi-layered effect.

Uses: Use as a foundation planting or near a pool or patio. It is well suited as a container planting when the smaller size is desired.

This evergreen shrub or small tree grows to 3-6′ x 4-8′ (.9-1.8 x 1.2-2.4m). It makes an attractive complement when positioned with camellias and azaleas.

Creamy yellow, fragrant flowers bloom all summer.

The distinctive foliage has glossy, leathery, oval 1½-3″ (4-8cm) leaves on red stems. New leaves are bronze-red, but the mature leaves will have red tints all year. Full sun brings out the red colors.

Soil: *Ternstroemia* needs acid soil and ample moisture, particularly in a sunny location.

Light: Plant in full sun in cooler areas or in partial shade in hot inland areas.

Pruning: Pinch back tip growth to promote roundness of form.

Uses: Use as an accent, specimen, hedge, screen or foundation.

GERMANDER *Teucrium chamaedrys*

This low, slow-growing evergreen sub-shrub reaches 1-2′ (30-60cm) with the same spread.

Pale to dark purple-rose flowers bloom in loose spikes late in the summer.

The 3/4″ (1.9cm) leaves are dark green and deeply toothed.

Soil: *Teucrium* will tolerate poor rocky soils, but not poor drainage. Ordinary garden watering is suitable.

Light: Plant in full sun. It will tolerate heat and some drought when well established.

Uses: Use as a dwarf hedge, border, edge or small-scale ground cover. For most uses, set 2′ (60cm) apart.

GIANT THEVETIA *Thevetia thevetioides*

Thevetia is an evergreen shrub or small tree with rapid growth to 12 x 12 ' (3.6 x 3.6m). It may be trained to a single-stemmed specimen.

Brilliant yellow 4″ (10cm) flowers bloom in large clusters, mainly during June and July. Intermittent bloom occurs throughout the winter.

Dark green 3-6″ (8-15cm), wrinkled leaves are white-pubescent beneath. All plant parts are poisonous.

Soil: Plant in good garden soil with ample moisture-holding capacity. Mulch up to 1′ (30cm) around the stem base to cool the roots and improve anchorage, as the plant is shallow rooted.

Light: *Thevetia* thrives in heat and full sun. It must be protected from wind.

Pruning: Prune to desired shape.

Uses: Use the shrub form as a hedge, screen or background planting. The small tree form makes an attractive specimen or accent.

PRINCESS FLOWER or
GLORY BUSH *Tibouchina urvilleana (T. semidecandra)*

Zones: 9 & 10

This evergreen shrub or small tree has open growth to about 15′ (4.5m). Foliage color is outstanding.

Stunning 3″ (8cm), deep purple flowers appear at branch ends from May through August, and intermittently to January.

The velvety green, oval, 3-6″ (8-15cm) leaves are often edged in red. New growth on buds, leaves and stem tips is orange or reddish; older leaves are red, yellow and orange, adding considerable winter interest.

Soil: *Tibouchina* does best in a well-drained, slightly acid soil, with roots in the shade and foliage in the sun. Water regularly and protect from wind. Feed after each bloom period.

Light: Plant in full sun among low, spreading species.

Pruning: Pinch branch tips to encourage fullness.

Uses: Use as an accent, foundation, hedge or border.

JAPANESE VIBURNUM *Viburnum japonicum*

Zones: 7-9

Viburnum japonicum is an upright, 10-12′ (3-3.6m) evergreen shrub that is valued for its attractive foliage.

White flowers in 4″ (10cm) fragrant clusters bloom in the spring. Showy red fruit follow the flowers.

The 6″ (15cm) long leaves are a dark leathery green.

Soil: Viburnum does well in medium to heavy textured, rich soils with moderate water-holding capacity.

Light: Plant in sun or light shade. Protect from direct sun where summers are long, hot and dry.

Pruning: Prune according to desired shape.

Uses: *Viburnum* is suitable as a hedge, screen, foundation or background planting.

73

SANDANKWA VIBURNUM *Viburnum suspensum*

This beautiful, medium size, evergreen shrub grows to 5-6′ (1.5-1.8m) with an equal spread.

Fragrant, showy, white flowers produce an attractive display in the spring. Red fruit in summer.

The large, oval, shiny bright green leaves densely clothe the slender branches.

Soil: Plant in a rich, medium-textured soil with an ample moisture-holding capacity.

Light: This viburnum does well in sun or partial shade.

Pruning: Prune to desired shape.

Use: Use as an accent, specimen, foreground planting or screen.

Coniferous Evergreens

BUNYA-BUNYA or
FALSE MONKEY PUZZLE TREE   *Araucaria bidwillii*

Araucaria bidwillii is a tall, coniferous, evergreen tree that grows to about 80′ (24m), and has a narrow, pyramidal form.

The glossy, juvenile leaves are long, stiff and spread out in a 2-row pattern. The dark green, oval, sharply-pointed mature leaves are spirally arranged on drooping branches. The tree bears large, heavy cones at an older age.

Soil: Plant in a good, well-drained garden soil with ample moisture-holding capacity. Water thoroughly during long, dry periods.

Light: Plant in full sun.

Uses: This large, unique tree needs considerable room and makes an excellent specimen, accent or shade tree.

NORFOLK ISLAND PINE *Araucaria heterophylla*

Zone: 10

This coniferous evergreen tree has a pyramidal shape and grows to about 100′ (30m).

Small, bright green needles densely clothe branches that are arranged in graceful, horizontal planes.

Soil: Plant in a good, well-drained garden soil with ample moisture-holding capacity. Water thoroughly during the period of establishment, and during long, hot dry periods.

Light: Plant in full sun.

Uses: Use as a stately specimen, accent or shade tree. Give it plenty of room to mature.

NORFOLK ISLAND PINE *Araucaria heterophylla*

ATLAS CEDAR *Cedrus atlantica*

This fast-growing, broad, pyramidal tree has graceful branches that curve upwards. Mature height can reach 40-60' (12-18m) in 30-50 years. The tree becomes rather flat-topped with maturity.

Silvery or light green 1-2" (2.5-5cm) long needles retain their color all year. Erect, 2-5" (5-13cm) cones appear on upper branches.

Soil: *Cedrus* does well in a medium-coarse to medium tex-tured, well-drained soil with moderate fertility and moisture-holding capacity.

Light: Plant in full sun and protect from frost in Zones 6 and 7.

Pruning: Pruning is rarely needed. If desired, clip individual branches to shape young trees.

Uses: *Cedrus* makes a beautiful accent or specimen tree.

This fast-growing, broadly conical evergreen tree has horizontal branches with pendulous tips. It will grow 2' (60cm) each year when young, and matures at 40-60' (12-18m) in 30-40 years.

The needles are a soft bluish green throughout the year. Four-inch (10cm) long, erect cones add beauty and landscape interest.

Soil: *Cedrus* does well in a medium-coarse to medium textured soil that is well drained and has moderate fertility and moisture-holding capacity.

Light: Plant in full sun. Protect from frost in Zones 6 and 7.

Pruning: Pruning is rarely needed. If desired, clip individual branches to shape young trees.

Uses: Use as an attractive accent or specimen tree.

DWARF HINOKI FALSE CYPRESS *Chamaecyparis obtusa 'Nana'* Zones: 6-8

This dwarf, very slow-growing conifer matures at about 3′ (.9m) tall with a spread greater than its height. Layers of dense, flattened branches produce a flat topped, mounded form.

The dark green foliage may have a bronze tinge in winter.

Soil: *Chamaecyparis* does best in a sandy to light loamy soil with excellent internal drainage. Heavy soils with poor drainage contribute to a serious root rot problem.

Light: Plant in sun or light shade.

Pruning: Lightly prune dead central branches if needed.

Uses: 'Nana' is excellent in rock gardens, as a mass planting on slopes or for borders and edges.

DWARF BLUE CYPRESS
or SAWARA CYPRESS   *Chamaecyparis pisifera 'Cyanoviridis' (C.p. 'Boulevard')*   Zones: 6-8

'Cyanoviridis' is a beautiful, dwarf evergreen with an irregular cone shape. A slow grower, it will reach 5-8′ (1.5-2.4m) in height with a spread of 3-4′ (.9-1.2m). The distinct color and texture complement other evergreens in the landscape.

The fine-textured, plumelike foliage is a light, silvery blue-green. Turns bronze in winter.

Soil: *Chamaecyparis* does best in a sandy to light loamy soil with excellent internal soil drainage. Heavy soils with poor drainage contribute to a serious root rot problem.

Light: Plant in sun or light shade.

Pruning: Lightly prune dead central branches if needed.

Uses: Use *Chamaecyparis* as an accent, foreground or border planting. It may be shaped as an effective low hedge. In any situation, it makes a sharp contrast when planted with other evergreens.

LEYLAND CYPRESS   x *Cupressocyparis leylandii*

x *Cupressocyparis leylandii* is a fast-growing hybrid ever-green that may reach 10-15' (3-4.5m) in 5 years.

It has a stiff, narrow, pyramidal form in youth, but may become more open and loose beyond age 10 or earlier when grown in a very warm climate.

Long, slender, upright, flattened branches have gray-green foliage sprays and small, scaly cones.

Soil: x *Cupressocyparis* does well in almost any soil that is well- to moderately-well drained. It needs average water and withstands strong wind.

Light: Plant in full sun or light shade.

Pruning: Prune to contain desired shape.

Uses: Use as a screen, accent or background planting.

SMOOTH ARIZONA CYPRESS or ARIZONA CYPRESS
Cupressus glabra (C. arizonica)

Cupressus glabra is a medium tall, fast-growing conifer with a pyramidal form that reaches 40′ (12m). It thrives in hot, inland interior climates and makes an excellent windbreak or tall screen.

The scalelike foliage varies in color and form from bright to gray-green, with small, scaly cones.

Soil: Plant in a sandy to light loamy, well-drained soil.

Cupressus needs only average water and is considerably drought tolerant.

Light: Plant in full sun.

Pruning: Prune to desired shape.

Uses: Use an an accent, specimen, hedge, screen or windbreak.

BLUE ITALIAN CYPRESS   *Cupressus sempervirens 'Glauca'*   Zones: 7-10

This is the classic, conical cypress of historical Greek and Roman writers. It has very short branches that form a dense, narrow column that reaches to 65' (20m) or more. 'Glauca' makes an excellent formal planting due to its stiff, picturesque outline.

The stout branchlets have outstanding dark, grayish blue-green scalelike leaves.

Soil: Plant in a medium coarse to medium-textured soil that is well drained and has a moderate fertility and moisture-holding capacity.

Light: Plant in full sun.

Pruning: Shear lightly to maintain the ideal cone form.

Uses: Use in a classic, formal planting or as a distinctive specimen or accent anywhere in the landscape.

BLUE ITALIAN CYPRESS

ARMSTRONG JUNIPER *Juniperus chinensis 'Armstrongii'*

'Armstrongii' is a compact, spreading conifer, 3-4′ (.9-1.2m) high and up to 4′ (1.2m) across.

Dense, lacy-textured, gray-green foliage is striking on gracefully arching branches.

Soil: Junipers do well in almost any soil that is well drained. Avoid placing near lawn sprinkling systems. They are quite drought hardy when well established.

Light: Plant in full sun in cool summer climates, or in partial shade in hot, dry inland areas.

Pruning: Prune or trim to desired shape.

Uses: This juniper is excellent sheared as a globe or hedge.

ARMSTRONG JUNIPER

GREEN PFITZER JUNIPER   *Juniperus chinensis 'Pfitzerana'*

'Pfitzerana' is a fast-growing spreader that reaches 5′ (1.5m) high and 10′ (3m) wide.

The bright green foliage densely clothes the broadly-spreading, ascending branches. *Juniperus chinensis* 'Aureo-Pfitzerana', GOLDEN PFITZER JUNIPER, (shown in the inset) makes a striking, golden contrast against other dark green evergreens.

Soil: Junipers do well in most any soil that is well drained.

Avoid planting near lawn sprinkling systems. They are quite drought hardy when well established.

Light: Plant in full sun in cool summer climates, or in partial shade in hot, dry inland areas.

Pruning: Prune or trim to desired shape.

Uses: Use as a specimen, foundation, hedge/screen or as a bank cover. Utilize 'Aureo-Pfitzerana' where color contrast would be maximized.

HOLLYWOOD JUNIPER *Juniperus chinensis 'Torulosa'*

Zones: 6-9

'Torulosa' is a broad pyramidal juniper that grows to 20′ (6m) high. The branches are irregular, and produce a twisted effect.

The rich green foliage is soft to the touch.

Soil: Junipers do well in almost any soil that is well drained. Avoid planting near lawn sprinkling systems. They are quite drought hardy when well established.

Light: Plant in full sun in cool summer climates, or in partial shade in hot, dry inland areas.

Pruning: Prune or trim to desired shape.

Uses: 'Torulosa' makes a beautiful accent in any landscape situation.

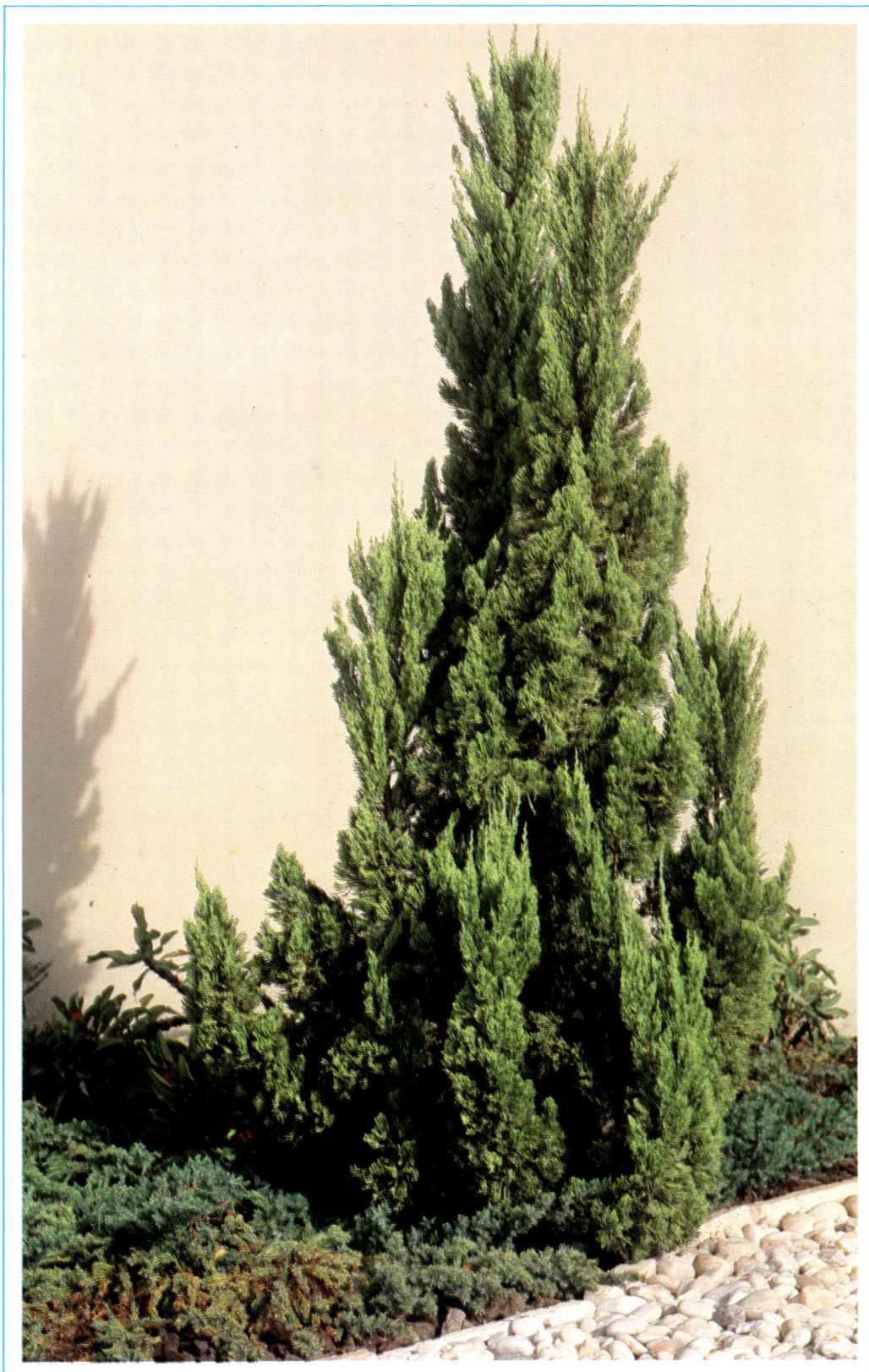

BLUE PACIFIC or SHORE JUNIPER   *Juniperus conferta 'Blue Pacific'*   Zones: 6-10

This low, creeping juniper reaches only 1' (30cm) high and spreads 6-8' (1.8-2.4m) across.

The soft, dense, ocean blue-green foliage is very salt tolerant.

Soil: Junipers do well in most any soil that is well drained. Avoid planting near lawn sprinkling systems. They are quite drought hardy when well established.

Light: Plant in full sun in cool summer climates, or in partial shade in hot, dry inland areas.

Pruning: Prune or trim to desired shape.

Uses: 'Blue Pacific' makes an excellent ground or bank cover, particularly along the seacoast.

TAMARIX JUNIPER
Juniperus sabina 'Tamariscifolia'

Zones: 6-8

'Tamariscifolia' is a low spreading juniper that grows to no more than 1½' (45cm) high, but spreads 10-20' (3-6m) wide in symmetrical mounds.

The dense foliage is blue-green. *Juniperus sabina* 'Tamariscifolia New Blue' has the same growth habit with distinctively bluer color.

Soil: Junipers do well in almost any soil that is well drained.

Avoid planting near lawn sprinkling systems. They are quite drought hardy when well established.

Light: Plant in full sun in cool summer climates, or in partial shade in hot, dry inland areas.

Pruning: Prune or trim to desired shape.

Uses: Use as a bank or wall cover or as an effective foreground planting.

ROCKY MOUNTAIN JUNIPER or
COLORADO RED CEDAR *Juniperus scopulorum cvs.*

Juniperus scopulorum cultivars have beautiful, scalelike, green, blue-green or silvery-toned foliage. They are available in compact, pyramidal, upright, mounding and low-growing forms. *Juniperus scopulorum* 'Welchii' (shown here) is a silvery green, upright, cone-shaped evergreen with a densely branched habit. It matures in a narrow, pointed spike at 15-20' (4.5-6m).

Soil: Junipers do well in almost any soil that is well drained.

Avoid planting near lawn sprinkling systems. They are quite drought hardy when well established.

Light: Plant in full sun in cool summer climates, or in partial shade in hot, dry inland areas.

Pruning: Prune or trim to desired shape.

Uses: Use as an accent, foundation, hedge/screen or as a ground cover, depending on variety.

SKY ROCKET JUNIPER *Juniperus virginiana 'Skyrocket'*

'Skyrocket' is a very narrow columnar juniper that grows to 20-25' (6-7.5m) high. It provides a stately, classical, Italian cypress effect in the landscape.

The foliage is silver-blue, with a tight, compact branching habit.

Soil: Junipers do well in most any soil that is well drained. Avoid planting near lawn sprinkling systems. They are quite drought hardy when well established.

Light: Plant in full sun in cool summer climates, or in partial shade in hot, dry inland areas.

Pruning: Prune or trim to desired shape.

Uses: Use as an accent or specimen, particularly in a stately entranceway.

SKY ROCKET JUNIPER *Juniperus virginiana 'Skyrocket'*

SLASH PINE *Pinus elliottii*

Pinus elliottii is a fast growing, upright coniferous tree that will reach 50-75´ (15-22.5m) in height and more than 1´ (30cm) in diameter with maturity.

Stiff, dark, blue-green, 8-10˝ (20-25cm) needles are in bundles of two or three. Cones are 3-6˝ (8-15cm). Reddish brown bark occurs in irregular, scaly plates on the trunk.

Soil: This pine does well in a moist soil and may be posi-tioned where internal soil drainage is less than perfect.

Light: Plant in full sun.

Pruning: The tree will lose its lower branches with age.

Uses: Use as a tall, stately tree along roadways or as a beautiful specimen or shade tree, given ample room.

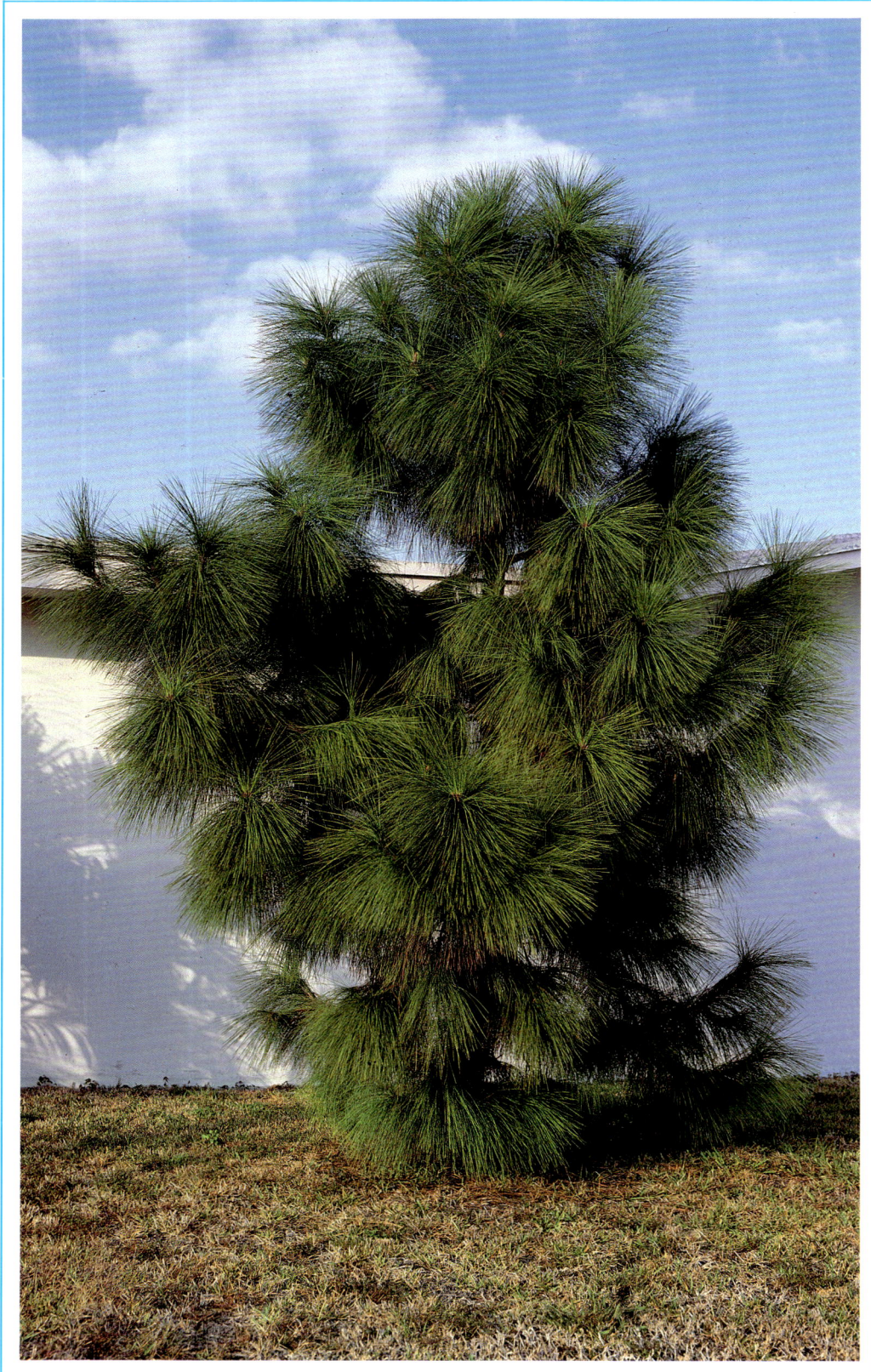

SPRUCE PINE or CEDAR PINE *Pinus glabra*

Zones: 8 & 9

Pinus glabra is a tall, upright, coniferous tree that matures at 75-80′ (21-24m) high, with a diameter of 1′ (30cm) or larger. Growth rate is slower than that of *P. elliottii*.

The blue-green, 3″ (8cm) needles are slender, flexible and in bundles of two. Cones are 2-3.5″ (5-9cm) long and rounded. Bark is a furrowed, dark gray.

Soil: *Pinus glabra* does well in almost any coarse to medium-textured soil that is moderately or well drained.

Light: Plant in full sun.

Uses: Use as a tall tree along roadways or driveways, or as a beautiful specimen, given ample room.

This broad, tall conifer has a moderate growth rate to about 50' (15m). It developes an irregular, open crown with many short, ascending branches.

The soft, light green, 4" (10cm) needles are in bundles of two or three. Oval, reddish brown 3½" (9cm) cones bend backward toward the trunk.

Soil: This pine will grow in poor soils with excessive in-ternal soil drainage, but it will produce the best specimen on a fertile soil with good moisture-holding capacity. It will tolerate heat, some drought and seaside conditions.

Light: Plant in full sun.

Uses: Use as a specimen, screen, windbreak or position in a small group planting.

This slow-growing, shrubby, symmetrical pine reaches 3-4′ (.9-1.2m) in height and 5-6′ (1.5-1.8m) in width in 15-20 years.

The needles are a 1-1½″ (2.5-3.8cm) long, dark green, in bundles of two. Cones are 1″ (2.5cm) oval, medium to dark brown.

Soil: Plant in a medium-coarse to medium-textured soil that is well drained, with a moderate fertility and moisture-holding capacity.

Light: Plant in full sun.

Uses: This pine is one of the most widely used for its low growth habit. Use as a foreground planting, as a border, or as a rock garden specimen.

Pinus nigra is a beautiful, upright growing pine that matures at about 50-60' (13.5-18m). It is symmetrical when young, but loses its lower branches with greater height and age.

Very dark green needles in bundles of two, contrast with the yellow-green of the new growth each spring. Eyecatching white buds precede the new growth.

Soil: Plant in a medium-coarse to medium-textured soil that is well drained, with a moderate fertility and moisture-holding capacity.

Light: Plant in full sun. The tree is quite salt tolerant.

Uses: Use as a screen, windbreak, specimen or accent planting.

ITALIAN STONE PINE or UMBRELLA PINE *Pinus pinea*

This globular or flat-topped conifer has a moderate growth rate to about 80′ (24m). Stout, bushy and globe-shaped when young, it takes on an umbrella form with age.

The long, dark green, 2″ (5cm) needles are in bundles of two. The 5″ (12.5cm) cones (greenish when young and chestnut brown when mature) produce edible seeds called Pignolia nuts.

A Mediterranean type climate with hot days and cool nights, dry summers and rainy winters suits *Pinus pinea* best.

Soil: Plant in a medium-coarse to medium-textured soil that is well drained, with a moderate fertility and moisture-holding capacity.

Light: Plant in full sun. The tree is quite salt tolerant.

Uses: Use as an accent, specimen or foundation planting.

Pinus radiata is a fast growing, symmetrical tree that reaches 80′ (24m) at maturity. It is an excellent choice for windy seashore conditions.

Rich green 6″ (15cm) needles are in bundles of three.

Soil: Plant in a medium-coarse to medium-textured soil that is well drained, with a moderate fertility and moisture-holding capacity.

Light: Plant in full sun.

Uses: This pine makes an excellent windbreak or tall hedge/screen.

EASTERN WHITE PINE *Pinus strobus*

Pinus strobus is a fast-growing, pyramidal conifer when young, but loses its lower branches with age. It reaches 15-25' (4.5-7.5m) in 15 years, then matures to over 100' (30m).

Soft, blue-green needles are in bundles of five.

Soil: Plant in a medium-coarse to medium-textured soil that is well drained, with a moderate fertility and moisture-holding capacity.

Light: Plant in full sun.

Uses: *Pinus strobus* makes a beautiful specimen, accent screen or windbreak. It is not well suited as a street tree because it is very intolerant of atmospheric pollution.

EASTERN WHITE PINE *Pinus strobus*

JAPANESE BLACK PINE *Pinus thunbergiana*

Pinus thunbergiana is a broadly pyramidal conifer with a bold, irregular, wide-spreading, branching habit. Mature height is about 75′ (22.5m).

Rich green, 4″ (10cm) long needles are in bundles of two. Striking whitish gray buds precede the new growth. Three-inch cones are sharply pointed and medium brown.

Soil: Plant in a medium-coarse to medium-textured soil that is well drained, with a moderate fertility and moisture-holding capacity.

Light: Plant in full sun.

Uses: This pine is an excellent choice for a Japanese garden setting. It also makes an effective specimen or screen.

WEEPING PODOCARPUS or
AFRICAN FERN PINE *Podocarpus gracilior*

Zone: 10

This beautiful, bushy, pyramidal evergreen grows to 40-50′ (12-15m) and forms a broad crown.

Long, bright green, very narrow, dense leaves give a very fine-textured effect on graceful, pendant branches.

Soil: *Podocarpus* does well in a coarse, sandy soil with a moderate fertility and moisture-holding capacity.

Light: Plant in full sun or light shade.

Pruning: *Podocarpus* makes an excellent espalier or it may be trained as a tree with single or multiple stems, as shown in the inset.

Uses: Use as an accent, specimen, hedge or screen.

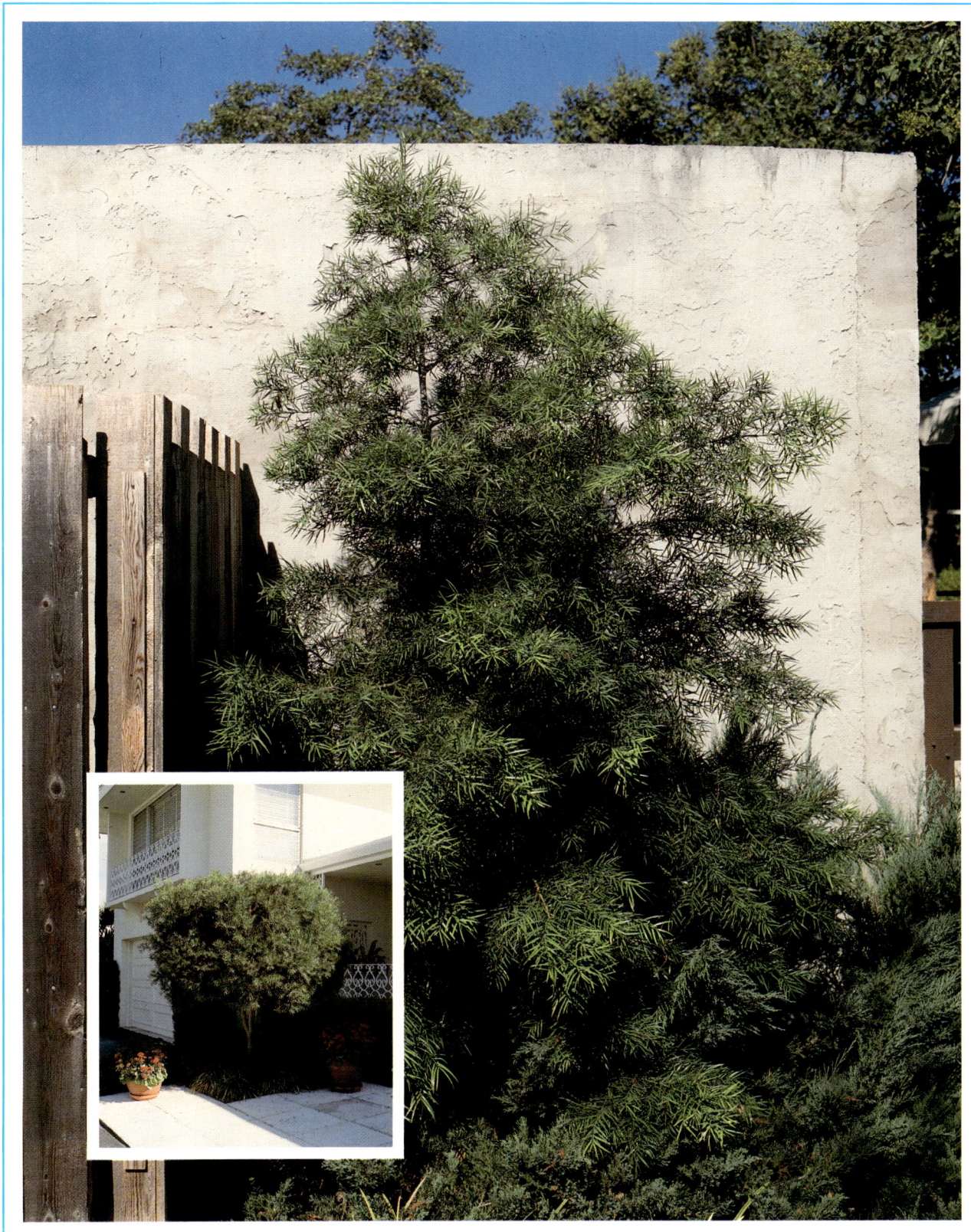

YEW PINE or YEW PODOCARPUS *Podocarpus macrophyllus*

Zones: 8-10

This upright, evergreen shrub or tree grows to 8-12′ (2.4-3.6m) in height and spreads 3-5′ (.9-1.5m).

The deep green, leathery, 3-4″ (8-10cm) leaves are yewlike in appearance.

Soil: *Podocarpus* does well in a coarse, sandy soil with a moderate fertility and moisture-holding capacity.

Light: Plant in full sun or light shade.

Pruning: *Podocarpus* is easily trained to desired shape. It makes a stunning topiary, as shown in the inset.

Uses: Use as a large shrub, street or lawn tree, accent, specimen or screen.

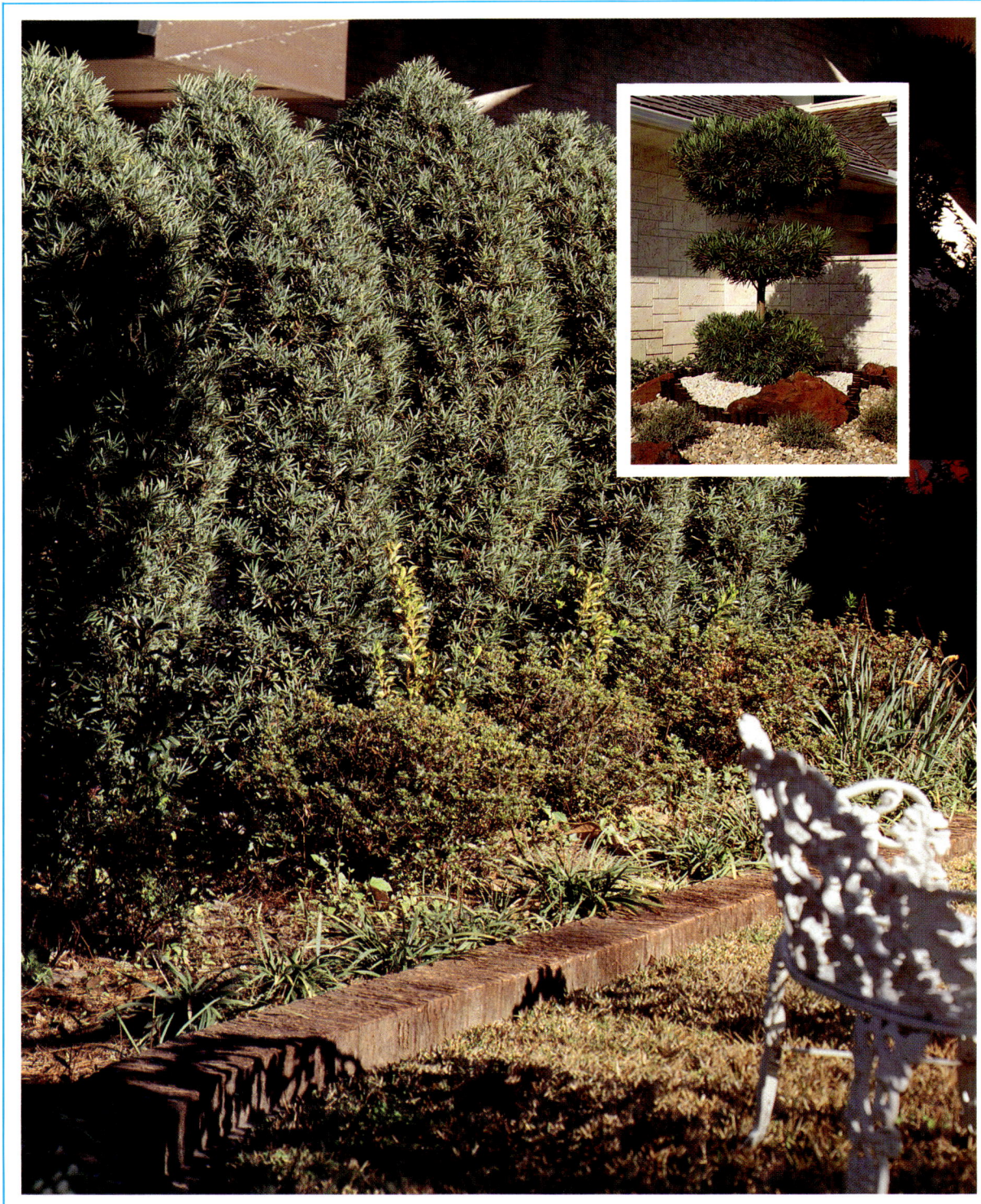

YEW PINE or YEW PODOCARPUS *Podocarpus macrophyllus*

102

This slow-growing, pinelike evergreen tree will mature at between 25-40′ (7.5-12m) high. Horizontal branches have graceful, ascending tips.

Glossy dark green, needlelike leaves are whorled around the stems and bunched at branch ends. Long, woody, 3-5″ (8-13cm) cones appear with age.

Soil: Plant in a rich, slightly acid to neutral pH 5.5-7.0) soil.

Light: Position in full sun along the coast, and in partial shade in hot inland areas.

Pruning: Prune to retain oriental shape if desired.

Uses: Use as an accent, specimen or bonsai.

BALD CYPRESS   *Taxodium distichum*

Zones: 7-10

This deciduous conifer thrives in wet areas and grows to 100′ (30m) tall. Young trees are pyramidal, but become broad-topped with maturity. Mature shredded bark adds landscape interest, as shown in the inset.

The leaves are ½″ (1.3cm) long, in a delicate, yellow-tinged foliage spray. The sprays turn bright orange-brown in the fall before dropping off.

Soil: *Taxodium* thrives in any wet soil that is acid (pH 7.0 or lower). It may be planted in wet lawn conditions.

Light: Place in full sun or light shade.

Pruning: Remove dead or unwanted branches.

Uses: This makes an outstanding specimen by a stream, lake or pond.

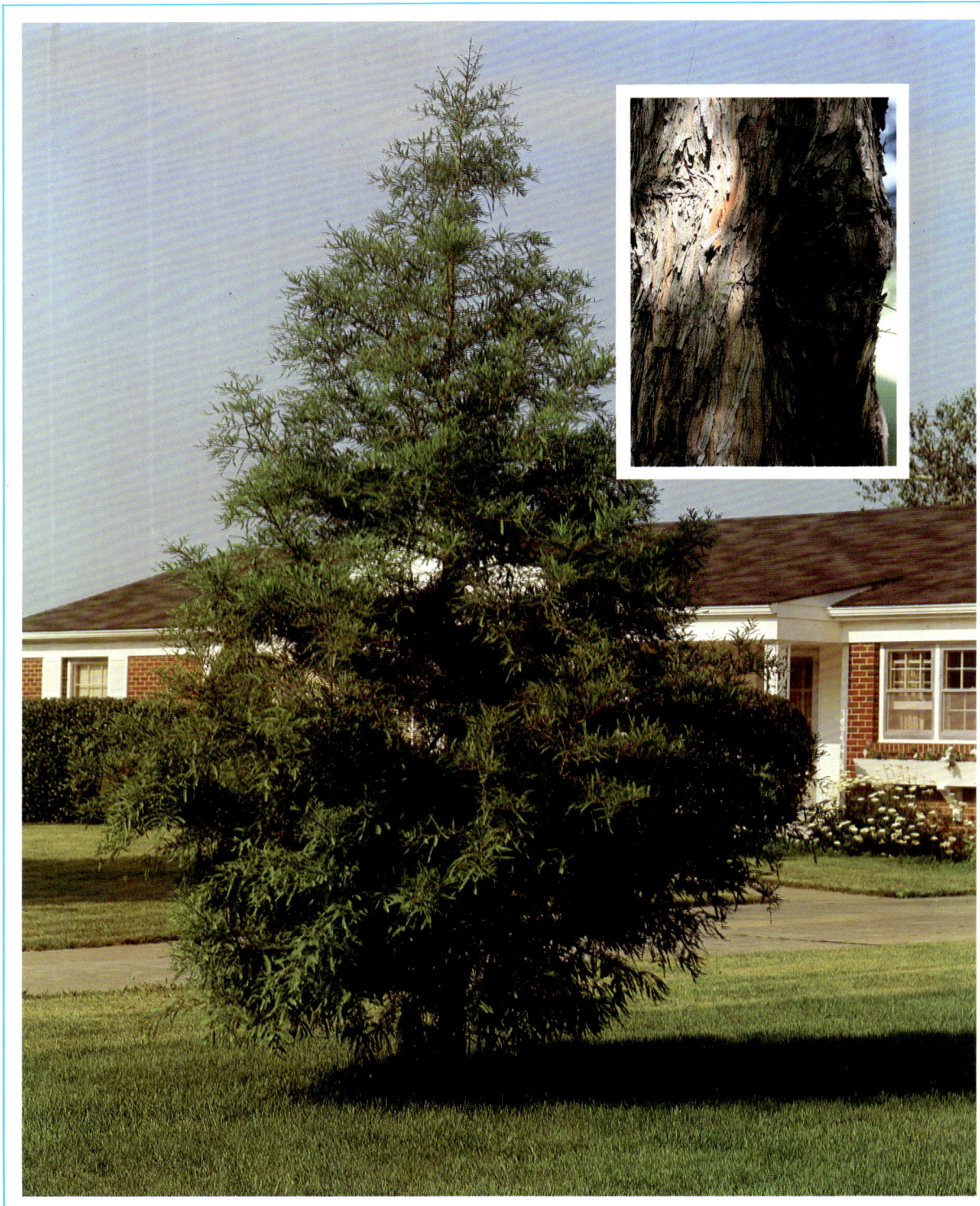

Thuja occidentalis 'Hetz Midget'

'Hetz Midget' is a small globe-shaped arborvitae with striking foliage.

The dark green, scalelike foliage densely clothes tight, flattened branchlets.

Soil: *Thuja* does well in most any soil that is well drained.

Avoid placing near lawn sprinkling systems.

Light: Plant in full sun.

Pruning: Prune to maintain globe shape if needed.

Uses: Use as a specimen, accent or hedge.

HETZ MIDGET ARBORVITAE *Thuja occidentalis 'Hetz Midget'*

DARK GREEN ARBORVITAE *Thuja occidentalis 'Nigra'*

This beautiful pyramidal shaped, upright arborvitae matures at 12-18′ (3.6-5.4m).

The dark green foliage holds its beautiful color all through the winter.

Soil: *Thuja* does well in most any soil that is well drained.

Avoid placing near lawn sprinkling systems.

Light: Plant in full sun.

Pruning: Prune to maintain pyramidal shape if needed.

Uses: Use as a specimen, accent, hedge or screen.

Deciduous Shrubs

BOTTLE BRUSH BUCKEYE *Aesculus parviflora*

Zones: 6-8

This wide-spreading shrub or small tree grows up to 10-15′ (3-4.5m) high.

Numerous 8-12″ (20-30cm), bottlebrush-shaped clusters of white blossoms bloom in the summer. Fruit are smooth capsules containing non-edible, poisonous nuts.

Medium green, palmate leaves have 10″ (25cm) leaflets.

Soil: Plant in a rich, moist, well-drained soil.

Light: *Aesculus* does best in full sun, but will tolerate light shade.

Pruning: Prune according to desired size and shape.

Uses: Use as an accent for a large area or as a big natural planting.

Berberis thunbergii 'Aurea' is a deciduous shrub that will reach 8' (2.4m) in height and 5-8' (1.5-2.4m) in width if left unpruned. Single spines line the arching branches.

Profuse light yellow flowers bloom all along the stems in the spring. Red fruit follow the flowers.

Leaves ½-1½" (1-4cm) long are golden yellow all summer, turning yellow-orange in the fall.

Soil: Plant in any average, well-drained garden soil. *Berberis* thrives with very little care.

Light: Plant in full sun. 'Aurea' is tolerant of heat and drought.

Pruning: Prune to shape. Shear several times each season to maintain the dense, formal appearance.

Uses: Use as a low hedge, specimen, accent or foundation planting.

'Kobold' is a bright green, very dwarf Japanese barberry cultivar. It is similar to *B.t.* 'Crimson Pigmy' but more dense and round.

The small, round, deep green leaves are ½-1½" (1-3.8cm) long.

Soil: Plant in an average, well-drained garden soil. *Berberis* thrives with very little care.

Light: Place in full sun to light shade.

Pruning: Prune to maintain desired dwarf shape if needed.

Uses: Use as a specimen, accent, low hedge or border planting.

ROSE GLOW BARBERRY

Berberis thunbergii 'Rose Glow'

'Rose Glow' is a compact, densely branched deciduous shrub with outstanding fall color that lasts longer than that of any other shrub.

New growth leaves are a light variegated pink, then become a dark rose-red at maturity.

Soil: Plant in any average, well-drained garden soil. *Berberis* thrives with very little care.

Light: Place in full sun to develop the intense rose-red color.

Uses: 'Rose Glow' makes an excellent specimen or accent against other green shrubs. It also makes a beautiful hedge or screen.

Berberis thunbergii 'Rose Glow'

JAPANESE FLOWERING QUINCE *Chaenomeles japonica (C. speciosa)* Zones: 6-9

Chaenomeles japonica is a small, showy deciduous shrub that reaches 8-10′ (2.4-3m) in height. Numerous varieties are available in upright or spreading forms.

Apple blossomlike flowers in apricot, pink, rose-pink, orange-red or red are clustered along the branches from early spring through summer. Greenish yellow quincelike fruit follow the blossoms.

Shiny green, oblong leaves may be red tinged when young.

Soil: *Chaenomeles* does well in light, medium or heavy soils that are well- or moderately well drained. Add iron chelate or iron sulfate if soil pH is above 7.5.

Light: Place in full sun.

Pruning: Prune in bud or bloom season. The branches make stunning floral arrangements.

Uses: Use as a shrub border, foundation planting, hedge, espalier, barrier planting or unique specimen.

SILVER EDGED TATARIAN DOGWOOD   *Cornus alba 'Argenteo-marginata'*   Zones: 6-8

This upright, deciduous shrub reaches an unpruned height of 7-9' (2.1-2.7m). It should be pruned to encourage new growth for bright red stem color and greater vigor.

Whitish, fragrant flowers in 2" (5cm) clusters bloom in early June. White fruit follow the flowers and ripen in late summer.

Showy dark green leaves have white edges.

Soil: Plant in any soil that is moist and well drained. *Cornus* thrives in damp places, especially near ponds or streams.

Pruning: Prune in early spring before new growth starts. Cut away the oldest stems right to the ground to encourage a succession of new shoots; remove about one-third each year.

Light: Position in light to full shade.

Uses: Use as a specimen or accent, singly or in groups. Stem color adds winter interest and leaf color is striking in the summer.

RED TWIG DOGWOOD *Cornus sericea Baileyi*

This upright, deciduous shrub reaches an unpruned height of 8-10′ (2.4-3m). It should be pruned to encourage new growth, for bright wine-red stem color (upper left), and greater vigor.

Small white blossoms appear in May, followed by white fruit which ripen in late summer.

The 5″ (13cm) long, bright green leaves turn brilliant red in the fall. *Cornus sericea* 'Flaviramea', YELLOW TWIG DOGWOOD (lower right), has vibrant yellow twigs and branches.

Soil: Plant in any soil that is moist and well drained. *Cornus* thrives in damp places, especially near ponds or streams.

Light: Position in full sun or light shade.

Pruning: Prune in early spring before new growth starts. Cut away the oldest stems right to the ground to encourage a succession of new shoots; remove about one-third each year.

Uses: Use as a specimen or accent, singly or in groups. Stem color adds winter interest.

SMOKE TREE *Cotinus coggygria*

This rounded, deciduous shrub or tree reaches a height of 10-12′ (3-3.6m) in 5-8 years, and then matures to about 25′ (7.5m) if left unpruned. Spread at maturity will be 10-15′ (3-4.5m).

Cotinus flowers in early summer on the new season's growth. Sterile flower parts extend and become covered with hairs, giving a pinkish, smoky appearance by late summer.

The rounded or oval, dark green leaves turn yellow to brilliant orange in the fall.

Soil: Plant in a medium coarse to medium-textured soil that is well drained. *Cotinus* requires only low to medium fertility and moisture.

Light: Position in full sun.

Pruning: Pruning is rarely required. Remove straggly growth and shape in early spring before new growth starts.

Uses: Use as a unique specimen in shrub or tree form.

CRANBERRY COTONEASTER   *Cotoneaster apiculatus*

Cotoneaster apiculatus is a mounded, spreading deciduous shrub that reaches 2-4' (.6-1.2m) in height and spreads 5-10' (1.5-3m). It is semi-evergreen in milder climates.

Small pinkish white flowers appear in the spring, followed by bright red berries that look like cranberries. The fruit persist through the winter.

The ½-1" (1.3-2.5cm) long, glossy green leaves have gray undersides. Fall color is a deep crimson.

Soil: *Cotoneaster* does best in poor garden soil and requires very little care. It may be used effectively for erosion control on dry slopes and banks.

Light: Plant in full sun for best color and berry production.

Pruning: Pruning is rarely needed.

Uses: Use as a low hedge, foundation planting or ground cover.

WARMINSTER BROOM *Cytisus x praecox*

This fast-growing, deciduous shrub has slender upright branches which curve outward to a height of 5-6' (1.5-1.8m) with an equal spread.

Abundant pea-shaped, fragrant, light yellow flowers appear on the previous season's growth before the leaves unfurl. Dry, flat pods ripen in late summer, rattle in the wind and explode noisily as they dry.

Soil: Plant in a sandy to loamy, well-drained soil with a pH of 6.5 or greater.

Light: Position in full sun. *Cytisus* is tolerant of wind and seacoast conditions.

Pruning: Prune immediately after flowering. Trim off two-thirds of the previous season's growth.

Uses: Use as an accent, screen, hedge or as a group planting.

SLENDER DEUTZIA *Deutzia gracilis*

Zones: 6-8

Deutzia gracilis is an upright, deciduous shrub with slender, arching branches. It reaches 2-4′ (.6-1.2m) in height with a spread of 4-6′ (1.2-1.8m).

Profuse clusters of snow white flowers bloom over the young leaves (on last year's growth) in late spring. Small brown seed pods follow the flowers.

Soil: Plant in a good well-drained garden soil with moderate moisture and fertility.

Light: Position in full sun or light shade. Protect from strong winds.

Pruning: Prune after flowering to encourage new growth for next year's flowers. If any shoots are winterkilled, remove in the spring.

Uses: This makes an excellent group planting, specimen, accent, patio shrub or low, informal hedge. For a hedge, plant 24-27″ (60-69cm) apart.

SLENDER DEUTZIA

118

RED-VEINED ENKIANTHUS

Enkianthus campanulatus

Enkianthus campanulatus is a slow-growing, deciduous shrub or tree that reaches 20′ (6m) at maturity.

Bellshaped, light yellow to light orange flowers have distinctive red veins and hang in terminal clusters in late spring. *Enkianthus campanulatus* 'Palibinii' (shown in inset) is a showy variety with deep red blooms.

The bright green leaves occur in whorls, or are concentrated at branch ends. Fall color is brilliant red.

Soil: Plant in a rich, well-drained soil which has been conditioned with ample peat moss, humus or ground bark. The soil pH should be slightly acid (5.0-6.0).

Light: Position in light shade.

Pruning: Prune only to remove dead or broken branches.

Uses: Use as a stunning specimen or accent.

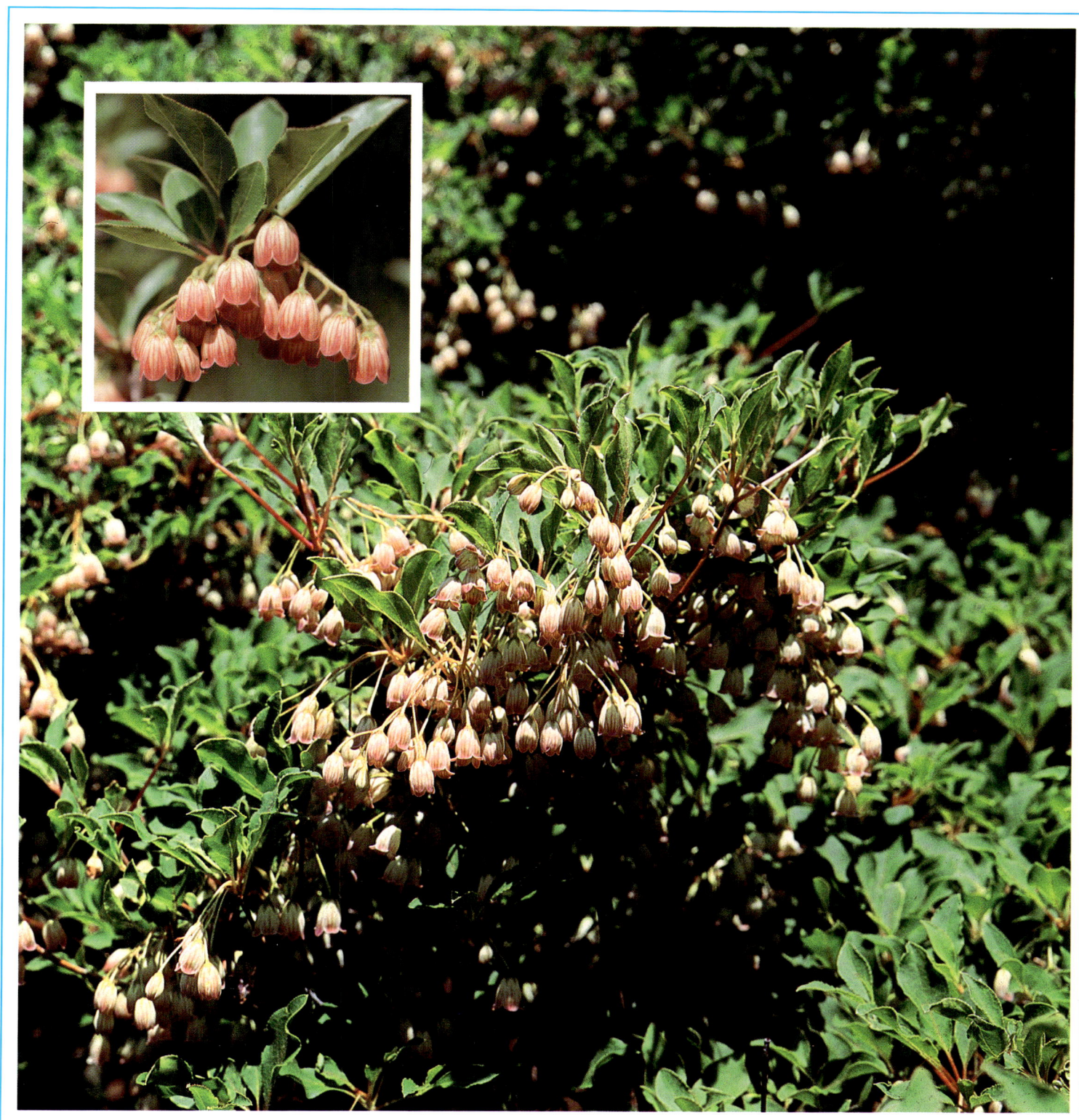

This small, deciduous shrub reaches 4-6' (1.2-1.8m) in height, forming a flat topped mound of dense, slender stems. The branches are corky with "winged" projections.

Inconspicuous flowers are followed by a light crop of bright, orange-red fruit.

The dark green leaves turn a brilliant rose-red in the fall. The color is stunning against other dark green evergreens.

Soil: Plant *Euonymus* in almost any soil and give it moderate watering until it is well established.

Light: The species must have full sun and good air circulation in areas of high humidity, as it is highly susceptible to mildew. Light shade is suitable in a dry climate.

Pruning: Pruning is not necessary.

Uses: Use this *Euonymus* as a spectacular accent or specimen. 'Compacta' makes a beautiful unclipped hedge or screen as well.

PEARL BUSH *Exochorda x macrantha 'The Bride'*

'The Bride' is a vigorous, compact, deciduous shrub that reaches 4 ′ (1.2m) in height with an equal spread.

A profusion of white, 1½-2 ″ (4-5cm) wide flowers open from pearlike buds, forming showy, spikelike clusters.

The 1½-2 ″ (4-5cm) long, medium green leaves appear with the flowers.

Soil: Plant in any good, well-drained garden soil. Give it moderate moisture.

Light: *Exochorda* does best in full sun. A south or west-facing position would be excellent.

Pruning: Prune after blossom period to control size and shape.

Uses: Use as an accent, specimen, hedge or screen.

These forsythias are hybrids between *F. suspensa* (Weeping F.) and *F. viridissima* (Greenstem F.). Most varieties reach 7-10′ (2.1-3m), with wide, arching branches.

All have a profusion of either light-, deep- or orange-marked, yellow blossoms on bare branches in early spring.

Medium green leaves clothe the stems after the blossom period.

Soil: Forsythia does well in any good, well-drained garden soil. Feed and water regularly throughout the growing season.

Light: Position in full sun.

Pruning: Prune after bloom by cutting one-third of the branches back to the ground.

Uses: Use as a specimen, background or screen.

CHINESE WITCH HAZEL *Hamamelis mollis*

Zones: 6-8

Hamamelis mollis is a spreading deciduous shrub or small tree that grows to 15-20′ (4.5-6m) high and spreads 8-10′ (2.4-3m). It is valued for its early spring flowers and beautiful fall color.

Bright yellow flowers with four ribbonlike petals appear during February and March, before the leaves unfurl. The fruit are brown with black seeds.

Medium green leaves 4-7″ (10-18cm) long, turn bright yellow in the fall.

Soil: Plant in a medium-coarse to medium textured soil with ample organic matter. Give it moderate to high moisture.

Light: Position in full sun or light shade.

Pruning: Prune to desired shape after flowering.

Uses: Use as an informal border, woodland edge planting or as a showy specimen with dark green evergreens.

HILLS OF SNOW HYDRANGEA

Hydrangea arborescens 'Grandiflora'

Zones: 6-9

This hydrangea is a dense, upright deciduous shrub that reaches up to 10′ (3m) in height.

'Grandiflora' has very large clusters of sterile white flowers from June throughout the growing season.

The 4-8″ (10-20cm) long, oval leaves are grayish green. Fall color is bronze-red.

Soil: Plant in a rich, well-drained soil that has been conditioned with peat moss or leaf mold. Water and feed throughout the period of bloom.

Light: Position in full sun.

Pruning: Prune to control size and form. Cut out stems that have flowered. Reduce the overall number of stems to produce bigger flower clusters.

Uses: Use as a foreground planting, shrub border or specimen.

HILLS OF SNOW HYDRANGEA *Hydrangea arborescens 'Grandiflora'*

BIGLEAF HYDRANGEA *Hydrangea macrophylla hybrids*

Zones: 7-9

Hydrangea macrophylla hybrids are symmetrical, round topped, deciduous shrubs that vary from 4-l0′ (1.2-3m) in height. Large, showy, terminal flower clusters bloom in early summer. Color may vary with soil acidity.

The flowers are white, pink, red or blue. Pink and red forms often turn blue or purple in an acid soil.

Leaves are a coarsely toothed, 8″ (20cm) long, rich green.

Soil: Plant in a rich, well-drained soil that has been condi-tioned with peat moss or leaf mold. Water and feed throughout the period of bloom.

Light: Position in full sun or partial shade.

Pruning: Prune to control size and form. Cut out stems that have flowered. Reduce the overall number of stems to produce bigger flower clusters.

Uses: Use these showy shrubs as foundation plantings, as an accent or for a stunning hedge or screen.

PEEGEE (PG) HYDRANGEA *Hydrangea paniculata 'Grandiflora'*

This fast-growing, deciduous shrub will grow 3-5′ (.9-1.5m) in one season and reach an unpruned height of 15-20′ (4.5-6m). It may be easily trained into a small tree.

Flowers on the current season's growth are in showy, erect clusters in August and September. Creamy white blossoms turn pink, then bronze, when mature; they are beautiful when dried for winter decoration.

The oval, 3-6″ (8-15cm) leaves turn from green to dull bronze in the fall.

Soil: Plant in a rich, well-drained soil that has been conditioned with peat moss or leaf mold. Water and feed throughout the period of bloom.

Light: Position in full sun.

Pruning: Prune to control size and form. Cut out stems that have flowered. Reduce the overall number of stems to produce bigger flower clusters.

Uses: Use 'Grandiflora' as an outstanding accent or specimen.

OAK-LEAVED HYDRANGEA *Hydrangea quercifolia*

Hydrangea quercifolia is a deciduous shrub that grows 4-6′ (1.2-1.8m) tall, and forms a large clump.

Erect clusters of white flowers appear on last year's growth during the summer.

The deep green, 6-12″ (15-30cm) long leaves are lobed and sharply pointed. Fall color is bright red or red-purple.

Soil: Plant in a rich, well-drained soil that has been conditioned with peat moss or leaf mold. Water and feed throughout the period of bloom.

Light: Position in full sun or partial shade.

Pruning: Pruning is rarely needed. Remove winterkilled stems in the spring. To shape, cut back to one-half the size in fall.

Uses: Use as an accent for a large area or as a big, natural planting.

JAPANESE ROSE   *Kerria japonica 'Pleniflora'*

Kerria japonica 'Pleniflora' is a graceful, arching, rounded deciduous shrub that grows 8′ (2.4m) high and 5-6′ (1.5-1.8m) wide. The cut green branches make beautiful Japanese arrangements.

'Pleniflora' has double yellow, 1″ (2.5cm) flowers from March through May.

Bright green, 2-4″ (5-10cm) long leaves are triangular with toothed edges. Fall color is yellow.

Soil: Plant in a good, well-drained garden soil and water frequently during the growing season.

Light: Position in partial shade.

Pruning: Prune dead wood after bloom period.

Uses: Use as an accent or specimen. *Kerria* is also well suited as a screen, hedge or foundation planting.

BEAUTY BUSH *Kolkwitzia amabilis*

This graceful, upright deciduous shrub reaches 10′ (3m) high with arching branches if grown in partial shade. It will be lower and more compact if grown in full sun.

Profuse clusters of pink, yellow-throated flowers bloom in the spring. Prickly, pinkish tan fruit follow the blossoms.

The leaves are gray-green. Brown flaky bark on the stems gradually peels, adding winter interest.

Soil: Plant in good, rich garden soil and give it moderate water.

Light: Position in full sun or light shade.

Pruning: Prune lightly after bloom and before the fruit appears.

Uses: *Kolkwitzia* makes an excellent accent or specimen. The flowers are spectacular.

CREPE MYRTLE
Lagerstroemia indica

Lagerstroemia indica is a large, upright, multi-stemmed shrub or small tree that grows up to 15-20' (4.5-6m) high. Dwarf forms are 3-6' (.9-1.8m) high. Deciduous bark on the trunk plus long, spectacular period of bloom gives year long landscape interest.

Flowers with crinkled (crepelike) petals form dense 6-10" (15-25cm) clusters at branch ends. Colors include rose (main illustration), pink, lavender (inset) and red.

Small, light green leaves turn yellow, red or rusty red in the fall. Light brown bark flakes off exposing light, rosy inner bark.

Soil: *Lagerstroemia* does well in a sandy loam to a loam with good drainage, moderate fertility and ample moisture. Feed regularly through the season of bloom. Mulch in a mound around the stem for winter protection.

Light: Plant in full sun. This shrub may need to be sprayed for mildew in areas of high humidity.

Pruning: Prune when dormant to increase flowering wood for the next year, or lightly in the spring just after new growth to shape and remove dead wood.

Uses: Use as an outstanding specimen, accent, hedge, screen or yard tree.

130

MINIATURE WEEPING CREPE MYRTLE

Lagerstroemia indica 'Dixie Series'

Zones: 7-9

'Dixie Series' *Lagerstroemia* cultivars are deciduous shrubs that mature at 3-4' (.9-1.2m), with graceful branches that arch downward. They make excellent patio plantings or hanging basket specimens.

Profuse clusters of showy blooms are stunning from early May into October. Colors include red, pink, rose, lavender, white and bicolors.

Small, light green leaves turn yellow, red or rusty red in the fall. Light brown bark flakes off exposing light, rosy inner bark.

Soil: *Lagerstroemia* does well in a sandy loam to a loam soil with good drainage, moderate fertility and ample moisture. Feed regularly through the season of bloom. Mulch in a mound around the stem for winter protection.

Light: Plant in full sun. This shrub may need to be sprayed for mildew in areas of high humidity.

Pruning: Prune when dormant to increase flowering wood for the next year, or lightly in the spring just after new growth to shape and remove dead wood.

Uses: Use these miniatures for borders, ground cover, patio plantings, small accents or in baskets.

131

VARIEGATED AMUR RIVER SOUTH PRIVET
Ligustrum sinense 'Variegatum' Zones: 7-10

Ligustrum sinense 'Variegatum' is a distinctly southern privet that will retain much of its foliage in the winter under mild conditions. Mature height will be about 8-10' (2.4-3m).

The leaves are a beautiful green with cream highlights.

Soil: Plant in almost any soil that has a moderate moisture-holding capacity. Water frequently throughout the growing season.

Light: Position in full sun or light shade.

Pruning: Clip or shear to desired shape for a hedge. Leave unpruned for a natural barrier planting.

Uses: Use as an accent, formal hedge or informal screen.

VARIEGATED AMUR RIVER SOUTH PRIVET *Ligustrum sinense 'Variegatum'* Zones: 7-10

STAR MAGNOLIA *Magnolia stellata*

Magnolia stellata is a densely-branched, deciduous shrub or small tree that grows up to 10-12′ (3-3.6m) and spreads 8-10′ (2.4-3m).

Creamy white flowers with straplike petals bloom very early, before the leaves unfurl.

Leathery, oval, 2-4″ (5-10cm) leaves turn yellow and brown in the fall.

Soil: Plant in a rich soil with good drainage, moderate fertility and a high moisture-holding capacity.

Light: Plant this magnolia in full sun.

Pruning: Prune only when absolutely necessary, and right after flowering. Remove entire stem back to the base and paint the wound with tree seal.

Uses: It is slow growing and shrubby, so use for borders, entryways, companion plantings or in a woodland setting.

FRANGIPANI *Plumeria rubra cvs.*

Plumeria rubra is a deciduous shrub or small tree with an open, spreading form that grows to 25′ (7.5m) high. Several varieties with stunning blossoms are available.

Large, fragrant clusters of waxy flowers may be rose (upper right) or white with yellow highlights (lower left, *P.r.* 'Acutifolia'). The stunning variety featured as the main illustration is also a *P.r.* 'Acutifolia' cultivar.

Thick, leathery, pointed leaves which can reach lengths of up to 20″ (50cm) are clustered near branch ends.

Soil: Plant in a good, well-drained soil that is high in organic matter, with moderate moisture-holding capacity. Add peat moss or leaf mold to improve the soil.

Light: Plant in full sun near the coast and in light shade in hot, inland areas. Protect from frost.

Uses: Use as a beautiful, tropical-looking accent or specimen.

SHRUBBY CINQUEFOIL *Potentilla fruticosa*

Potentilla fruticosa is a compact, tightly branched shrub that grows to a height of 4' (1.2m).

Several varieties are available that have beautiful, roselike floral displays. 'Abbotswood' has white flowers and makes a beautiful hedge. 'Dark Gold-Digger' is a golden yellow spreader. 'Gold Star' is a low dwarf shrub with 2" (2.5cm) wide, golden yellow blooms.

The distinctive green leaves are gray beneath and divided into 3-7 leaflets.

Soil: *Potentilla* thrives in a medium-coarse to medium textured soil with moderate moisture-holding capacity.

Light: Plant in full sun in all but the hottest inland areas where the plants will need light shade.

Uses: Use as an accent, specimen, hedge or ground/ bank cover, depending on variety.

RHODODENDRON *Ghent Hybrids*

Ghent hybrids are genetic crosses between the European *R. flavum* and any of several North American species. Most have a tall, upright form reaching 6-10' (1.8-3m) high, with an equal spread. Ghents flower early to midseason.

Flowers are both single and double, 1½-2½" (3.7-6cm) wide and may be white, yellow, orange or red.

The oval, green leather leaves turn brownish in the fall.

Soil: Plant in a good well-drained soil that is rich in organic matter. Add peat moss, leaf mold or compost if necessary. Water well during hot, dry spells. Fertilize with commercial acid plant food during and following bloom. Keep roots cool with a 2" (5cm) mulch. See Appendix D for details of soil preparation.

Light: Plant Ghent hybrids in light or partial shade, depending on specific cultivar planting directions. Protect Rhododendrons from strong winds.

Pruning: Pinch back tips after flowering to assure a compact form. Prune old gangly stems to restore desired shape. Remove faded flower heads.

Uses: Use as a foundation planting, group planting, border or in a woodland setting.

RHODODENDRON *Mollis Hybrids*

Mollis hybrids are genetic crosses between *R. japonicum* x *R. molle* and native swamp azaleas. They are less hardy than the Ghent hybrids, but may be more heat resistant.

The 2½-4″ (6-10cm), single or double flowers may be white, yellow, orange, red or bicolored.

Leaves are an oval, glossy, bright green during the growing season and then turn brownish in the fall.

Soil: Plant in a good well-drained soil that is rich in organic matter. Add peat moss, leaf mold or compost if necessary. Water well during hot, dry spells. Fertilize with commercial acid plant food during and following bloom.

Keep roots cool with a 2″ (5cm) mulch. See Appendix D for details of soil preparation.

Light: Plant Mollis hybrids in light or partial shade, depending on specific cultivar planting directions. Protect rhododendrons from strong winds.

Pruning: Pinch back tips after flowering to assure a compact form. Prune old gangly stems to restore desired shape. Remove faded flower heads.

Uses: Use as a foundation planting, group planting, border or in a woodland setting.

ROSESHELL AZALEA *Rhododendron roseum*

Rhododendron roseum is a native plant found in the open woods and mountains and grows to 8' (2-4m) tall.

The beautiful rose-pink to deep pink flowers have a spicy clove scent.

Glossy green, oval pointed leaves have a soft pubescence underneath.

Soil: Plant in a good well-drained soil that is rich in organic matter. Add peat moss, leaf mold or compost if necessary. Water well during hot, dry spells. Fertilize with commercial acid plant food during and following bloom.

Keep roots cool with a 2" (5cm) mulch. See Appendix D for details of soil preparation.

Light: Plant *R. roseum* in light or partial shade, depending on specific cultivar planting directions. Protect Rhododendrons from strong winds.

Pruning: Pinch back tips after flowering to assure a compact form. Prune old gangly stems to restore desired shape. Remove faded flower heads.

Uses: Use as a foundation planting, group plantings, border or in a woodland setting.

ROSESHELL AZALEA *Rhododendron roseum*

CUTLEAF STAGHORN SUMAC   *Rhus typhina 'Laciniata'*   Zones: 6-8

This deciduous shrub is an upright grower that is smaller than the species and matures at about 6-12′ (1.8-3.6m) with a wider spread. The branches are covered with short, brown hairs resembling deer antlers "in velvet".

Inconspicious flowers in 4-8″ (10-20cm) clusters are followed by clusters of velvety, orange-red fruit that persist all winter.

The leaves of 'Laciniata' are deep green above, grayish beneath, very deeply cut and they turn bright red in the fall.

Soil: *Rhus* grows in almost any soil except alkaline (pH greater than 7.0-7.5). It is well suited to banks or slopes where erosion control could be a problem.

Pruning: Prune to remove dead or damaged stems. Root prune if suckering becomes invasive to neighboring plants.

Uses: Use as an accent, border, specimen or as a mass planting.

AMERICAN ELDERBERRY *Sambucus canadensis*

This fast-growing deciduous shrub grows to about 12´ (3.6m) with an equal spread. Early growth is rapid at 3´ (90cm) each year.

Small white blossoms in flat, 6-8″ (15.2-20.3cm) clusters appear in late spring and early summer. Delicious blue-black, edible berries grow in clusters, and are suitable for pies, preserves and wines.

The coarse, green compound leaves have 5-9 leaflets. *Sambucus canadensis* 'Aurea' (shown in the inset) has golden yellow leaves and bright red berries that are poisonous if eaten by humans, however.

Soil: *Sambucus* thrives in a moist, well-drained soil.

Light: Plant in full sun for best flower and berry production. The gold color of 'Aurea' is intensified in full sun.

Pruning: Prune in early spring to maintain desired size and shape.

Uses: Use as an effective screen or woodland edge planting.

This fast-growing deciduous shrub with a graceful, spreading habit reaches 4-6′ (1.2-1.8m) at maturity.

Profuse clusters of double white flowers appear in June and remain through July.

The oval, bluish green leaves are lighter underneath, and turn red in the fall.

Soil: Plant in any well-drained garden soil with a moderate moisture-holding capacity.

Light: *Spiraea* does best in full sun.

Pruning: Prune immediately after flowering by cutting back or shearing flowered stems. Remove all older branches to encourage a succession of new basal shoots.

Uses: Use as a specimen, accent, shrub border or background planting.

RED JAPANESE SPIRAEA
Spiraea japonica 'Coccinea'

Spiraea japonica 'Coccinea' is a broad, compact, densely-branched deciduous shrub that grows to about 3' (90cm).

Rich crimson flowers in 4" (10cm) clusters clothe erect stems throughout the summer.

The leaves are an oval, bluish green.

Soil: Plant in any well-drained garden soil with a moderate moisture-holding capacity.

Light: Spiraea does best in full sun.

Pruning: Prune immediately after flowering by cutting back or shearing flowered stems. Remove all older branches to encourage a succession of new basal shoots.

Uses: Use as a shrub border or background planting. For a hedge, plant 15-24" (38-60cm) apart and cut back to 6" (15cm) from the ground. Pinch back shoot tips to encourage branching and shear after flowering.

RED JAPANESE SPIRAEA *Spiraea japonica 'Coccinea'*

SHOE BUTTON SPIRAEA or BRIDAL WREATH
Spiraea prunifolia

This deciduous shrub has erect, gracefully curving stems and reaches a height of 5-8′ (1.5-2.4m).

Delicate, striking white blossoms appear all along the slender stems of last year's growth.

Dark green, glossy leaves unfurl after the flowers. Fall leaf colors are a brilliant orange and red.

Soil: Plant in any well-drained garden soil with moderate moisture-holding capacity.

Light: *Spiraea* does best in full sun.

Pruning: Prune immediately after flowering by cutting back flowered stems to strong, new growth. Remove all older branches to encourage a succession of new basal shoots.

Uses: Use as a specimen, accent, shrub border or background planting.

BRIDAL WREATH or VANHOUTTE SPIRAEA   *Spiraea x vanhouttei*   Zones: 6-8

This dense, deciduous shrub has long, arching stems that reach a mature height of 6-8′ (1.8-2.4m). *Spiraea* x *vanhouttei* is the most commonly-planted spiraea.

Snow white flowers in clusters clothe the stems of last year's growth just as new leaves begin to unfurl.

The oval, pointed leaves are a dark, blue-green. Fall color is bright orange-red.

Soil: Plant in any well-drained garden soil with a moderate moisture-holding capacity.

Light: *Spiraea* does best in full sun.

Pruning: Prune immediately after flowering by cutting back or shearing flowered stems. Remove all older branches to encourage a succession of new basal shoots.

Uses: Use as a shrub border or background planting. For a hedge, plant 15-24″ (38-60cm) apart and cut back to 6″ (15cm) from the ground. Pinch back shoot tips to encourage branching and shear after flowering.

DWARF LACESHRUB or
DWARF STEPHANANDRA

Stephanandra incisa 'Crispa'

Zones: 6-9

'Crispa' is a low, spreading deciduous shrub with long, slender, drooping branches. Mature height is 1½-3' (45-90cm) with a spread as wide or wider.

Small greenish white flowers in rounded clusters appear in June.

Fine-textured, bright green leaves turn red-purple in the fall.

Soil: Plant in a medium-coarse to medium-textured soil that is well drained. Add peat moss or leaf mold to improve soil fertility and moisture-holding capacity.

Light: Position in full sun along the coast or in light shade in hot inland areas. Protect from frost in colder areas.

Uses: Use 'Crispa' as a low border planting, ground/bank cover, mass planting or as an accent.

KOREAN LILAC or
MISS KIM LILAC *Syringa patula (S. palibiniana)*

Syringa patula is a compact, twiggy, deciduous shrub that will eventually reach 10′ (3m) but stays at about 3′ (90cm) for a long period. It may be kept at that height with selective pruning.

Five inch (13cm) clusters of pink to lilac flowers bloom in May.

The leaves are an oval, pointed, 4″ (10cm) medium green.

Soil: Plant in a medium-coarse to medium textured soil that is well drained, and has a near neutral (7.0) soil pH. Add peat moss or leaf mold to condition a poor soil.

Light: *Syringa* does best in full sun.

Pruning: Remove dead flower heads and cut out older, weaker stems. Prune to maintain desired size and shape.

Uses: Use as an accent or specimen. To use as a low screen or hedge, plant 2-3′ (60-90cm) apart.

Syringa x *prestoniae* hybrids are hardy, deciduous shrubs that grow to about 10′ (3m) high and bloom on new spring growth after other lilacs, thereby extending the bloom season.

A range of colors are available which include 'Elinor', a light pink to orchid-pink (featured here); 'Nocturne', blue and 'Royalty', purple to violet.

Oval, pointed, medium leaves are 4″ (10cm).

Soil: Plant in a medium-coarse to medium textured soil that is well drained, and has a near neutral (7.0) soil pH. Add peat moss or leaf mold to condition a poor soil.

Light: *Syringa* does best in full sun.

Pruning: Remove dead flower heads and cut out older, weaker stems. Prune to maintain desired size and shape.

Uses: Use as an accent or specimen. To use as a low screen or hedge, plant 2-3′ (60-90cm) apart.

COMMON LILAC *Syringa vulgaris cvs.*

These fast-growing, deciduous shrubs have beautifully arching branches, with a mature height of 8-15′ (2.4-4.5m) and spread of 5-10′ (1.5-3m).

Spring flowers are very fragrant, single or double and in 6-8″ (15-20cm) long clusters. Many named varieties offer a range of colors that include white, purple, pink and yellow.

The smooth-edged, oval, pointed, medium green leaves hold their color all season.

Soil: Plant in a medium-coarse to medium textured soil that is well drained and has a near neutral (7.0) soil pH. Add peat moss or leaf mold to condition a poor soil.

Light: *Syringa* does best in full sun.

Pruning: Remove faded flower heads and cut out older, weaker stems to ground level. To control overgrowth, cut back all shoots to about 4″ (10cm). Thin only the weak shoots from the new growth over the next 3-4 years. Continue successive shoot replacement by removing some older ones each year.

Uses: Use as a beautiful accent or specimen. To use as a screen or hedge, plant 2-4′ (.6-1.2m) apart.

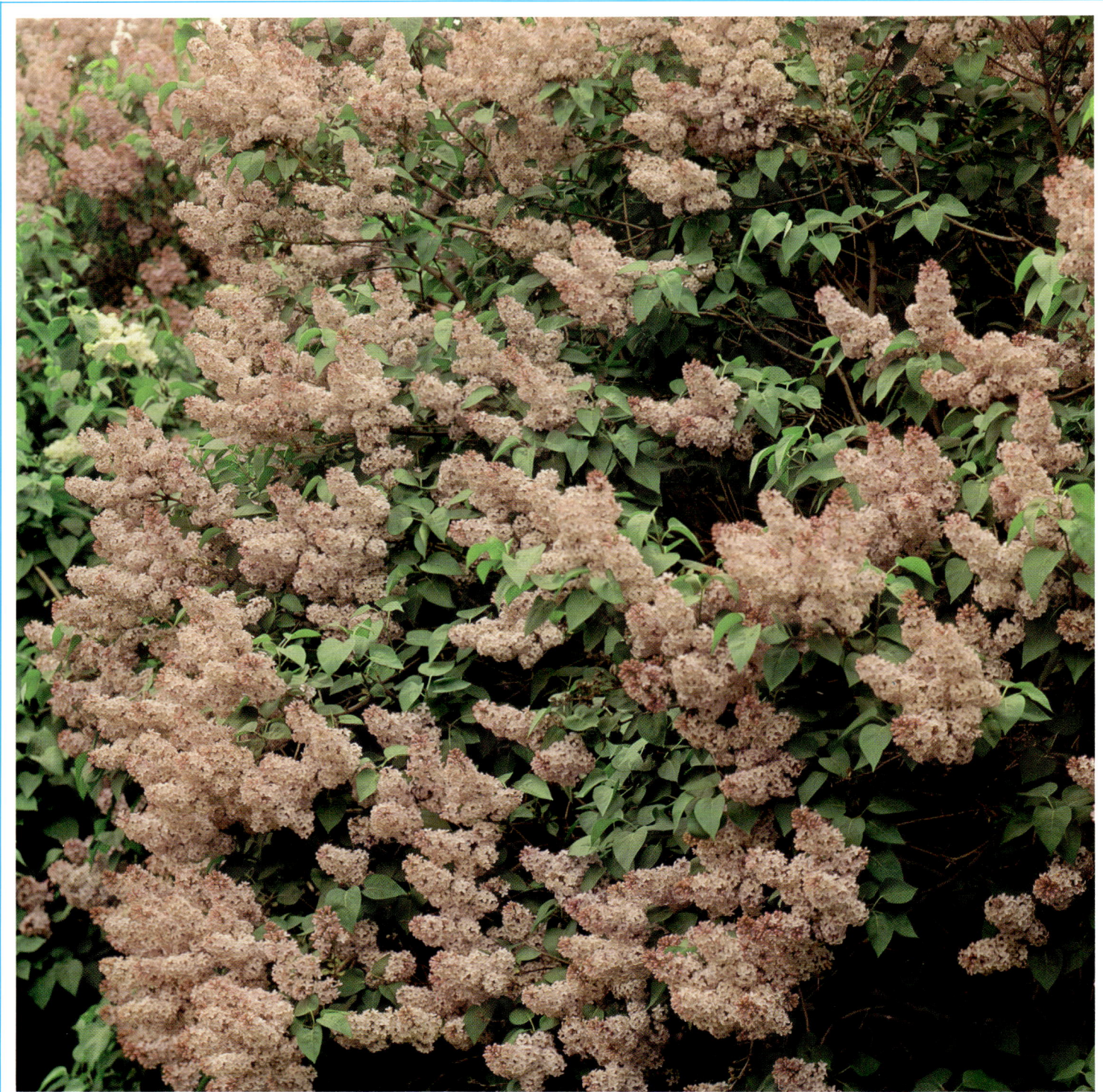

TAMARIX or ATHEL *Tamarix aphylla*

Zones: 8-10

This tamarix is an evergreen-appearing, deciduous shrub or small tree that grows 10-20′ (3-6m) high. It makes an outstanding windbreak due to its high wind tolerance.

Small pinkish flowers bloom in clusters at branch ends in late summer.

Foliage consists of grayish green, jointed branchlets that give a fine, feathery look.

Soil: Plant in most any soil that is neutral to alkaline (pH 7.0 or greater). Give ample water during the establishment period.

Light: Position in full sun.

Pruning: Prune to desired shape and size. Tamarix may be trained to a single-stemmed specimen.

Uses: Use as a windbreak, large screen or unique specimen in a hot, dry area.

FRAGRANT SNOWBALL *Viburnum x carlcephalum*

This hybrid viburnum is a deciduous shrub that grows 8-10′ (2.4-3m) tall and 4-5′ (1.2-1.2m) wide.

Waxy white flowers with a rose tinge bloom in 4-5″ (10-13cm), fragrant clusters and persist from spring through early summer. Fruit are not produced.

The 2-3½″ (5-9cm) long leaves are a dull grayish green, and turn brilliant orange-red in the fall.

Soil: Viburnums thrive in heavy, rich soils with an ample moisture-holding capacity. A good location would be near a swimming pool or pond.

Light: Position in sun or light shade.

Pruning: Prune to desired shape and size.

Uses: Use as an accent, specimen, screen or group planting.

FRAGRANT SNOWBALL *Viburnum x carlcephalum*

KOREAN SPICE VIBURNUM *Viburnum carlesii*

Viburnum carlesii is a medium-size, showy, deciduous shrub that grows 4-8′ (1.2-2.4m) tall and spreads 4-5′ (1.2-1.5m) wide. It has a loose, open habit.

Fragrant flowers are pink in the bud, and open white in 3″ (8cm) clusters throughout the spring season. Fruit are blue-black and appear during the summer.

The grayish green leaves provide brilliant fall color.

Soil: Viburnums thrive in heavy, rich soils with an ample moisture-holding capacity. A good location would be near a swimming pool or pond.

Light: Position in sun or light shade.

Pruning: Prune to desired shape and size.

Uses: Use as an accent, specimen, screen or group planting.

JUDD'S VIBURNUM *Viburnum x juddii*

This rapid-growing viburnum hybrid is similar to *V. carlesii*, but more spreading and bushy. It matures at about 8' (2.4m) high by 6' (1.8m) wide.

Clusters of delicate pink buds (inset) 3-4" (8-10cm) across open into fragrant white blossoms in the early spring. Reddish-black fruit are produced in the fall.

Deep green 2" (5cm) leaves are deeply veined with pubescent undersides.

Soil: Viburnums thrive in heavy, rich soils with an ample moisture-holding capacity. A good location would be near a swimming pool or pond.

Light: Position in sun or light shade.

Uses: Use as an accent, specimen or screen. The shrub is very attractive to birds.

Viburnum lantana is a deciduous shrub or small tree that grows up to 15′ (4.5m) tall.

Tiny white flowers bloom in 2-4″ (5-10cm) clusters in late spring or early summer. Showy, bright red fruit later turn black.

Wide, oval, 5″ (12.5cm) long, green leaves are pubescent top and bottom, and eventually turn bright red in the fall.

Soil: This viburnum does well in a medium-coarse to medium textured soil with moderate moisture-holding capacity. It will withstand some drought.

Light: Plant in full sun or light shade.

Pruning: Prune to desired shape and size.

Uses: Use as a background or woodland planting.

COMMON SNOWBALL   *Viburnum opulus 'Sterile' (V.o. 'Roseum')*   Zones: 6-8

This large, deciduous shrub grows to 10-15' (3-4.5m).

A profusion of sterile white flowers bloom in clusters that resemble snowballs. Fruit are not produced.

Lobed, maple leaf-shaped, 2-4" (5-10cm), dark green leaves have purple-red fall color.

Soil: This viburnum does well in a medium-coarse to medium textured soil with moderate moisture-holding capacity. It will withstand some drought.

Light: Plant in full sun or light shade.

Pruning: Prune to desired shape and size.

Uses: Use as a stunning accent, specimen or situate it as a background or woodland planting.

CHASTE TREE *Vitex agnus-castus*

This open, spreading, rounded deciduous shrub or tree usually has multiple stems. Mature height can be 10-20′ (3-6m), depending on length of warm, summer growing season.

Showy lavender-blue flowers in dense 1′ (30cm) spikes bloom summer and early fall.

Fanlike leaves with five to seven, 2-6″ (5-15cm) leaflets are dark green above and whitish beneath.

Soil: *Vitex* tolerates many soils, but best growth and blooms are produced on a rich, moist, well-drained soil.

Light: Plant in full sun. *Vitex* needs ample sun and summer heat to produce beautiful blooms.

Pruning: Support with stakes and train to a single stem if tree form is desired.

Uses: Use as a showy specimen, accent or border planting. The floral show is particularly beautiful when positioned with gray-green evergreen shrubs.

PINK WEIGELA *Weigela florida*

Weigela florida is a beautiful, showy, 6-10′ (1.8-3m) high deciduous shrub that has graceful, arching branches laden with fragrant blooms.

Stunning rose-pink, trumpet-shaped flowers bloom May through June, attracting bees and hummingbirds.

The leaves are stiff, medium green and coarse textured.

Soil: Plant in a good, rich, well-drained soil. Condition the soil with peat moss or leaf mold if necessary. Feed during bloom and give moderate water throughout the growing season.

Light: Position in full sun or partial shade.

Pruning: Cut back branches that have bloomed to favor shorter, new-growth stems. Cut oldest stems to the ground to stimulate suckering. Thin suckers to desired shape and density.

Uses: Use as a background planting, large screen or in a mixed shrub border.

Flowering Trees

RUBY HORSE CHESTNUT   *Aesculus x carnea 'Briotii'*   Zones: 6-10

This round-headed, deciduous tree reaches a height of 20′ (6m) in 10-15 years. It may be 30-40′(9-12m) at maturity with a spread of 20′ (6m). Flowering begins on a 6-8′ (1.8-2.4m), young tree.

Brilliant red, 5-7″ (13-18cm) flower spikes appear in May. Fruit are inedible brown nuts encased in spiked husks.

The palmate, glossy dark green leaves open in early spring. There is usually no fall color.

Soil: Plant in a fertile, well-drained soil with a moderate moisture-holding capacity. Water frequently during the summer months.

Light: Position *Aesculus* in full sun. Light shade is tolerated, but may lessen flower production.

Pruning: Prune in early spring if needed.

Uses: Use for a shade or accent tree. It is not well suited as a street tree.

SILK TREE OR MIMOSA *Albizia julibrissin*

This rapid growing, deciduous tree will reach 40′ (12m) with a spread wider than the height. It may be shaped to form a flat-topped umbrella at 10-20′ (3-6m).

Delicate, puffy pink flowers that resemble a pincushion bloom in the summer. Fruit are flat brown pods, and appear in late summer.

The light green, fernlike leaves fold inward at night.

Soil: Plant in a fertile, well-drained soil with ample moisture-holding capacity. It needs plenty of water during the growing season.

Light: Place in full sun. *Albizia* does best in areas of high summer heat.

Pruning: Stake and train the tree when young. Pinch off the lowest branch buds to ensure a clear stem for at least 4-6′ (1.2-1.8m).

Uses: Use as an interesting specimen or accent. The tree is particularly beautiful when viewed from slightly above.

SILK TREE OR MIMOSA *Albizia julibrissin*

DWARF POINCIANA or BARBADOS PRIDE   *Caesalpinia pulcherrima*   Zone: 10

This stunning, tropical-appearing tree has rapid early growth to about 10′ (3m) high with the same spread.

Brilliant orange-red flowers with striking 4-5″ (10-13cm) long stamens bloom in clusters all summer. Hummingbirds are very attracted to the flowers.

The beautiful, dark green, fernlike leaves have many tiny leaflets.

Soil: Plant in a sandy, well-drained soil and give infrequent, though ample, watering.

Light: Position in full sun. *Caesalpinia* does best in areas of high summer heat.

Pruning: This tree may be cut back right to the ground in early spring if a compact mound is desired.

Uses: Use as a showy accent, specimen or as a natural screen.

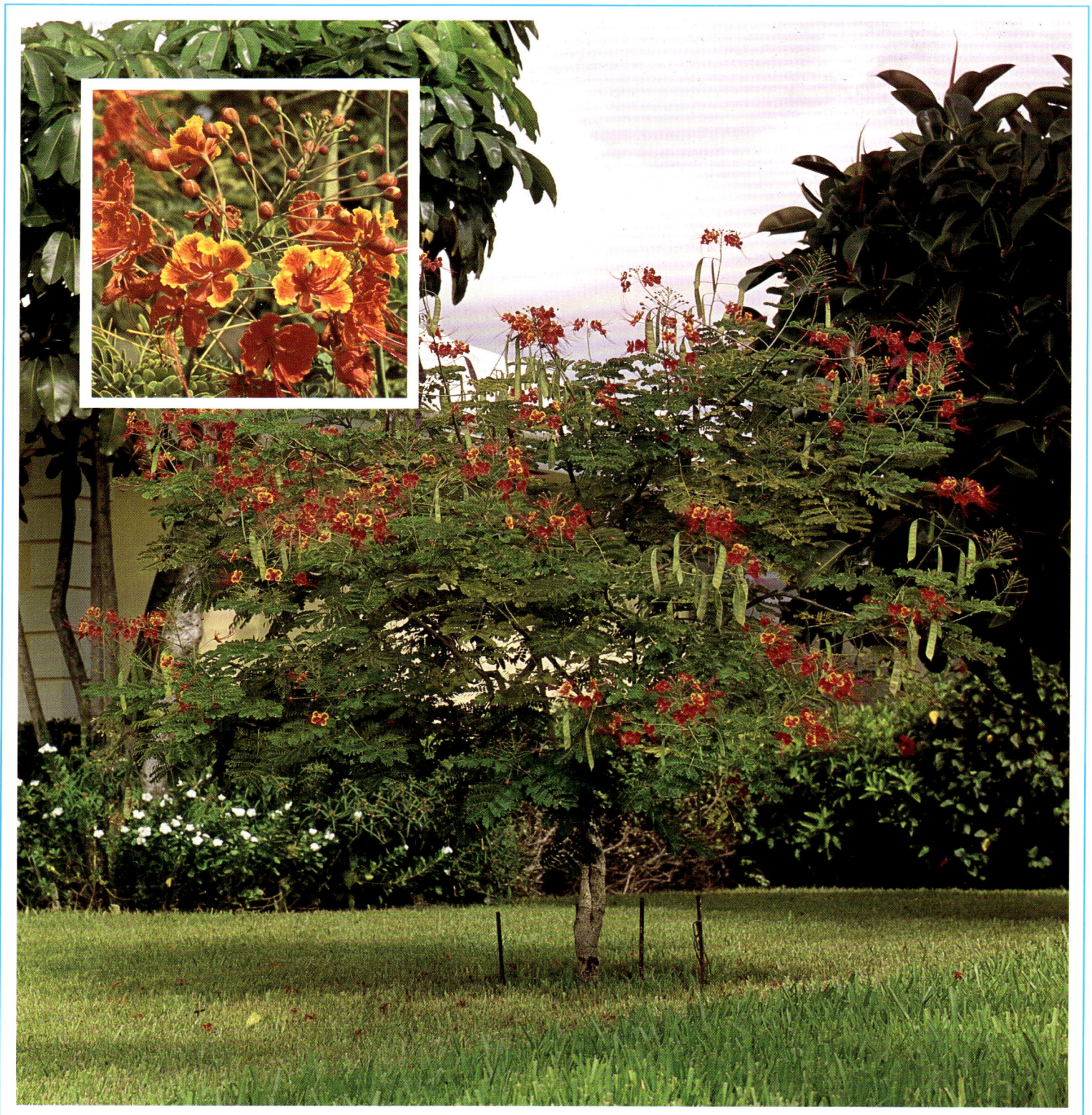

SCARLET OR LEMON BOTTLEBRUSH *Callistemon citrinus* Zones: 9 & 10

This medium size to 25′ (7.5m) flowering tree produces a stunning floral display.

Cylindrical, 6″ (15cm) flower spikes have masses of brilliant, crimson, brushlike stamens with dark yellow anthers. Hummingbirds are very attracted to the flowers.

The narrow, 3″ (8cm) long leaves have a bronze tinge when young, becoming bright green with age.

Soil: *Callistemon* does well on a wide range of soils that are moist yet well drained, with at least medium fertility. The tree is reasonably drought tolerant when well established.

Light: Position in full sun, but not in hot, dry areas. This tree may be damaged by cold spells.

Pruning: Stake and prune when young to form a round-headed tree. Prune lightly every three years for maximum flowering.

Uses: Use as an accent, specimen or as a natural screen.

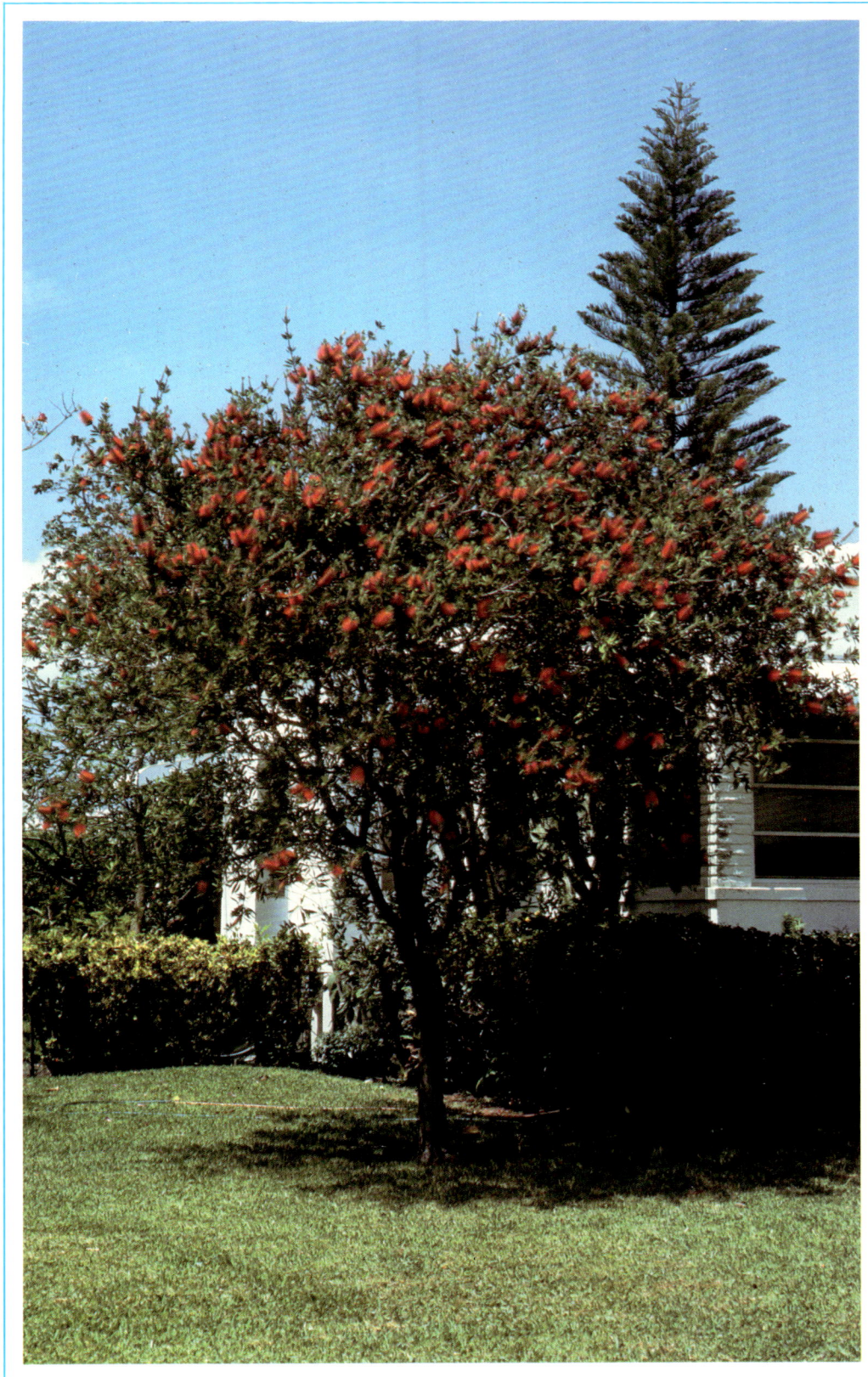

SCARLET OR LEMON BOTTLEBRUSH *Callistemon citrinus*

WEEPING BOTTLEBRUSH *Callistemon viminalis*

This subtropical, small tree has graceful, pendulous branches that produce a distinctive, weeping habit. Mature height is 25-30′ (7.5-9m).

The narrow, light green leaves are 6″ (25cm) long.

Bright red brushlike flowers bloom in the spring and fall with sporatic bloom the year around.

The 6″ (15cm) long, narrow leaves are a light green.

Soil: Plant in a moist yet well-drained soil with moderate fertility. Water generously throughout the season of bloom.

Light: Position in full sun, but not in hot, dry areas. This tree may be damaged by cold spells.

Pruning: Stake and prune when young, then little or no further shaping is needed.

Uses: Use as an accent or background planting. The tree may also be used as a patio container planting if held to a smaller size.

EASTERN REDBUD or JUDAS TREE *Cercis canadensis*

This irregular spreading, deciduous tree reaches a height of 10-15′ (3-4.5m) in 10-12 years. Mature height is 35′ (10.3m) with a spread equal or greater than the height. Flowering begins at 4-5 years of age.

Purplish pink blossoms appear before the leaves unfurl, providing an outstanding display. Long greenish pink seedpods turn brown when dry and persist into winter.

Heartshaped, 3-5″ (8-13cm) long leaves open in late spring.

Soil: Plant in a deep, well-drained sandy loam. Water frequently until it is well established (1-2 years). The tree is generally drought tolerant after establishment.

Light: Position in full sun or light shade.

Pruning: Pruning is rarely needed.

Uses: Use as an accent or in an informal group planting. Cercis is well suited to use as a bank cover where soil erosion could be a problem.

This slow growing, deciduous tree may have single or multiple stems, and will reach 12-15′ (3.6-4.5m) high, with an equal spread in 10-15 years. It matures at 25-30′ (7.5-9m), but flowers when only 2-4′ (.6-1.2m) tall.

The flowers are in 6-8″ (15-20cm) long, pendulous clusters of minute, individual, fragrant white blossoms which appear in late spring or early summer. Female trees have clusters of dark blue berries.

Oval, light green, 3-8″ (8-20cm) long leaves turn bright yellow in the fall.

Soil: Plant in a moist, deep, well-drained soil.

Light: Position in full sun or light shade.

Pruning: Prune and train to an individual stem if desired. Further pruning is rarely needed.

Uses: *Chionanthus* makes a showy specimen or accent.

FRINGE TREE

FLOSS SILK TREE *Chorisia speciosa*

Chorisia speciosa is a semi-deciduous or deciduous tree which grows to 50′ (15m) with a hairy trunk studded with large, stout spines.

Showy pink or rose, five-petaled flowers resemble hibiscus blooms.

Tropical-appearing leaves have leaflets that resemble the fingers of a human hand. Leaf drop occurs during the fall flowering or if the temperature goes below 27 F (-2°C).

Soil: Plant in a rich, sandy loam soil with excellent drainage. Give frequent, ample watering during establishment, then water regularly.

Light: Position in full sun.

Pruning: Pruning is rarely needed.

Uses: *Chorisia* makes a spectacular specimen or park tree.

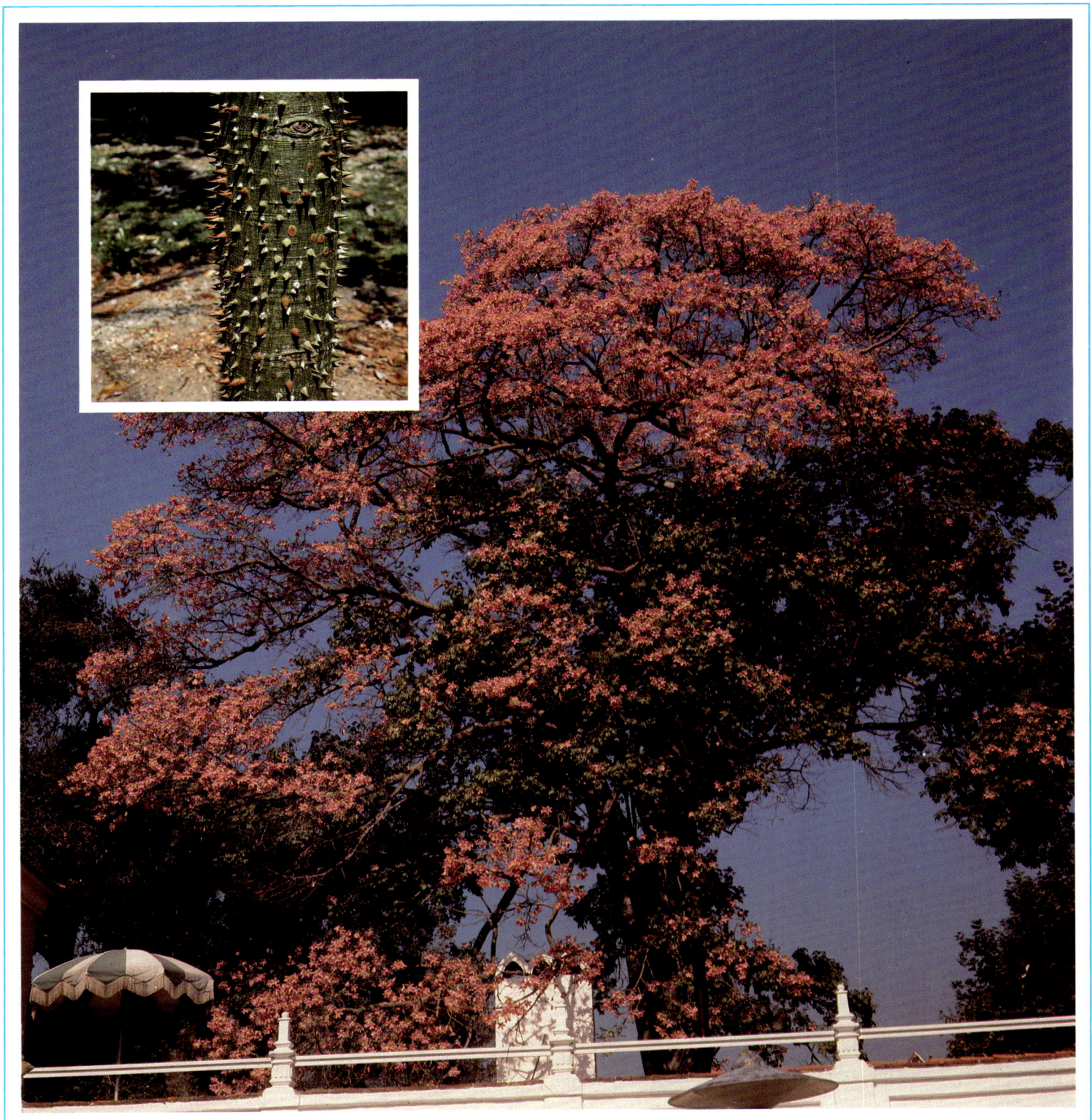

FLOWERING DOGWOOD *Cornus florida*

This spreading, flat-topped, deciduous tree may have single or multiple stems. It matures at 15-30′ (4.5-9m) high, with a spread of 15-20′ (4.5-6m). The bark is nearly black and deeply furrowed on mature trees.

Flowers with individual white bracts 3-5″ (8-13cm) across appear in early spring before the leaves unfurl.

Leaves are pinkish green when young, turning medium green in the summer. Fall color is red.

Soil: Plant in a moist, well-drained, acid (pH 5.5-6.5) soil.

Condition with leaf mold, peat moss or compost. Mulch in the spring after the soil has warmed. Water thoroughly in dry periods.

Light: Position in full sun in northern zones and in light shade in the deep south.

Pruning: Pruning is not usually recommended since dogwoods are slow to heal.

Uses: *Cornus* makes a beautiful specimen or group planting.

PINK FLOWERING DOGWOOD *Cornus florida 'Rubra'*

This spreading, flat-topped deciduous tree may have single or multiple stems. It matures at 15-30′ (4.5-9m) high and spreads to 15-20′ (4.5-6m) wide. The bark is nearly black and deeply furrowed on mature trees.

White or pink flowers with individual bracts 3-5″ (8-13cm) across appear in early spring before the leaves unfurl. Shiny red fruit follow the blossoms, and are eaten by birds.

The leaves are pinkish green when young, turning medium green in the summer. Fall color is red.

Soil: Plant in a moist, well-drained, acid (pH 5.5-6.5) soil. Condition with leaf mold, peat moss or compost. Mulch in the spring after the soil has warmed. Water thoroughly in dry periods.

Light: Position in full sun in northern zones and in light shade in the deep south.

Pruning: Pruning is not usually recommended since dogwoods are slow to heal.

Uses: *Cornus* makes a beautiful specimen or group planting.

KOREAN DOGWOOD *Cornus kousa*

This small, spreading, deciduous tree matures at 15-25′ (4.5-7.5m) high with a spread of 12-20′ (3.6-6m).

Flat, 3-5″ (8-13cm) sprays of white or pinkish white blossoms appear along branch tops in late spring or early summer after the leaves have expanded. Soft red berries follow the flowers, and are eaten by birds.

The 3″ (8cm) long leaves are a bright green. Fall color is reddish brown.

Soil: Plant in a moist, well-drained, acid (pH 5.5-6.5) soil. Condition with leaf mold, peat moss or compost. Mulch in the spring after the soil has warmed. Water thoroughly in dry periods.

Light: Position in full sun in northern zones and in light shade in the deep south.

Pruning: Pruning is not usually recommended since dogwoods are slow to heal.

Uses: *Cornus* makes a beautiful specimen or group planting.

168

HAWTHORN OR COCKSPUR THORN

Crataegus crus-galli

Zones: 6-8

This spreading, deciduous tree has dense, horizontal branches that persist to ground level if left unpruned. The tree will reach 20' (6m) in 10-15 years and mature at 25-35' (7.5-10.5m).

Clusters of white flowers appear all along the branches in May and June. Small red fruit follow blossoms and persist through winter.

The 2-3" (5-8cm) long leaves are a glossy medium green. Fall colors are orange and red.

Soil: Plant in a loam to clay loam, well-drained soil. *Crataegus* is tolerant of acid or alkaline conditions.

Light: Plant in full sun.

Pruning: Prune during winter to shape the top. Remove basal suckers at any time.

Uses: Use as an accent, street tree, roadside planting or barrier. This adaptable species tolerates urban pollution, cold or drought.

ENGLISH HAWTHORN *Crataegus laevigata 'Paulii'* Zones: 6-8

This thickly-branched, thorny tree has a moderate growth rate and matures at about 25′ (7.5m). It starts flowering about two years after planting.

Profuse clusters of deep red, pink, or white blossoms occur along the branches in the spring. Varieties may be single or double flowered. Small red fruit follow single flowers and persist through the winter.

The three- or five-lobed, 2½″ (6cm) leaves are medium to dark green. Fall color is yellow.

Light: Plant in full sun. This adaptable species tolerates urban pollution, cold or drought.

Pruning: Prune during winter to shape the top. Remove basal suckers at any time.

Uses: Use as an accent, street tree, roadside planting or barrier.

ROYAL POINCIANA *Delonix regia*

This stately, tropical flowering tree grows to 50′ (15m) high with a spread nearly as wide.

Brilliant, 3½-4″ (8.7-10cm), scarlet flowers are followed by 18″ (45cm) long, flat, woody black pods.

Fernlike leaves often fall before blossoms appear.

Soil: Plant in a rich, well-drained soil, high in organic matter with a moderate moisture-holding capacity. Add peat moss or leaf mold to improve the soil.

Light: Position in full sun.

Pruning: Pruning is rarely needed.

Uses: *Delonix* makes an outstanding specimen or park tree.

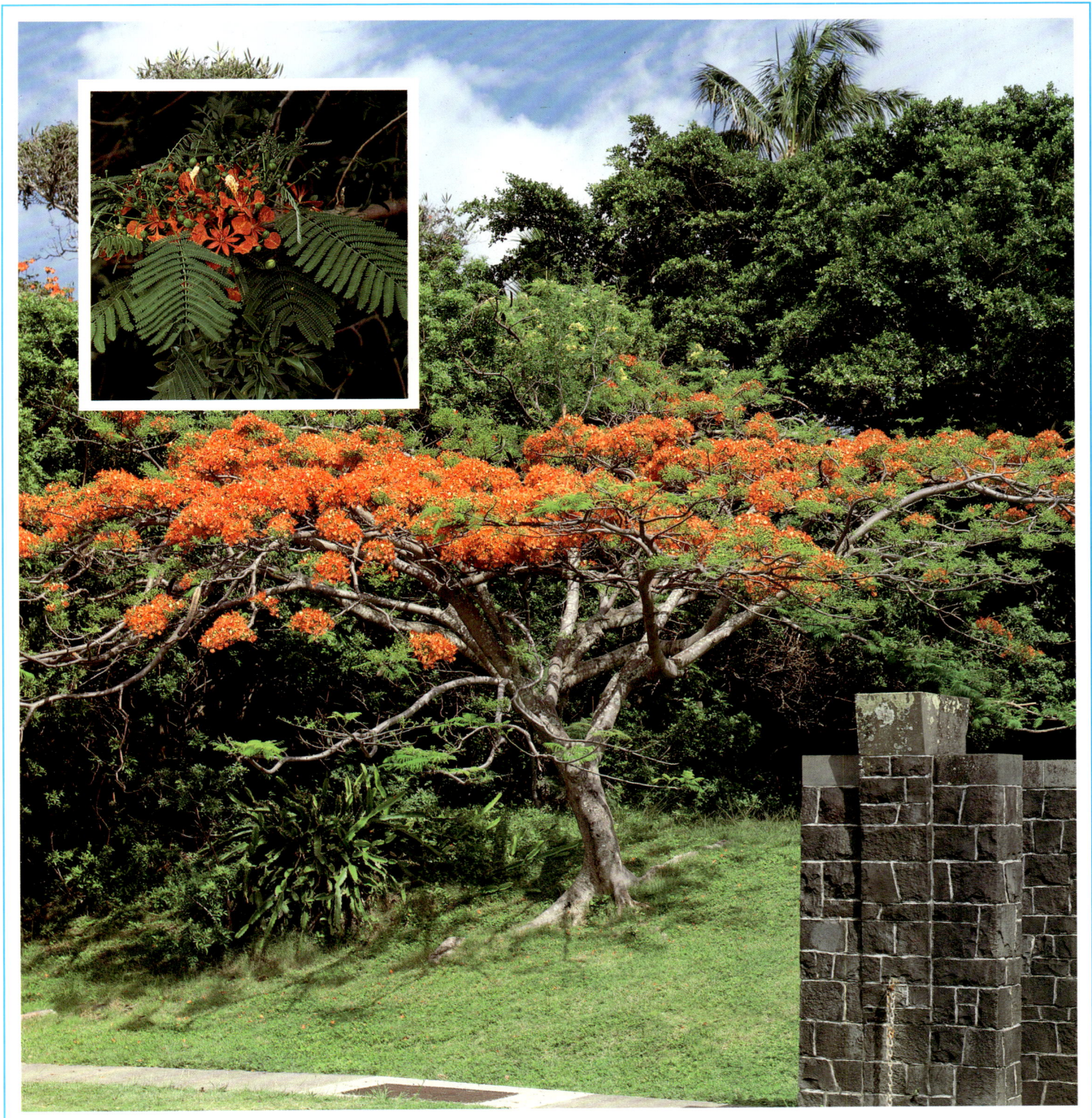

WILD OLIVE or SILVER BELL TREE *Halesia carolina*

Halesia carolina grows to about 40′ (12m) with a spread of 15-20′ (4.5-6m).

Showy clusters of snow white, bell-shaped flowers hang from pendular branches as the leaves appear.

Soil: Plant in a deep, humus-rich, well-drained soil with ample water holding capacity.

Light: Position in full sun or part shade.

Pruning: Pruning is rarely needed.

Uses: *Halesia* makes a stunning accent, specimen or woodland edge planting. It is also striking when positioned with rhododendrons.

GOLDEN-RAIN TREE *Koelreuteria paniculata*

This deciduous tree reaches 8-10′ (2.4-3m) in 5-10 years, and matures at 20-30′ (6-9m) with a spread of 10-20′ (3-6m).

Large, open, 12-15″ (30-38cm) clusters of small yellow flowers appear in early summer. Green, 2″ (5cm) bladder-like seedpods turn pink, then brown when ripe.

The compound, 8-15″ (20-38cm) leaves are reddish in the spring, maturing blue-green in the summer and yellow in the fall.

Soil: Plant in any well-drained garden soil. *Koelreuteria* tolerates alkaline conditions.

Light: Plant in full sun.

Pruning: Prune young trees in the spring; mature trees rarely need pruning.

Uses: Use as a specimen, accent, shade or street tree.

GOLDEN CHAIN TREE *Laburnum x watereri*

This vase-shaped, deciduous tree matures at a height of 12-15′ (3.6-4.5m). Multiple trunk specimens spread 9-12′ (2.7-3.6m) while single trunk trees grow 6-8′ (1.8-2.4m) wide.

Hanging clusters of yellow, pealike blossoms appear in the spring starting at age 1-2 years.

The 1-3″ (2.5-8cm) leaves are in groups of three.

Soil: *Laburnum* does well in sandy or even rocky soils.

Light: Position in full sun to light shade. Prefers light shade.

Pruning: Pruning is rarely needed.

Uses: Use as a showy accent or specimen. The tree is too narrow to use for shade. Protect from strong wind.

SAUCER MAGNOLIA *Magnolia x soulangiana*

Magnolia x soulangiana is a deciduous tree or shrub that may have single or multiple trunks with smooth, gray bark. Height at maturity is 25′ (7.5m) with a spread equal to or exceeding the height.

Candle-shaped buds open to large, rose-tinted, fragrant white blossoms in early spring before the leaves unfurl. Coarse green fruit mature red in the fall and open to reveal red, inedible seeds.

The broad, oval, 6″ (15cm) long, medium green leaves are slightly downy underneath, and turn brown in the fall.

Soil: Plant in a deep, well-drained, acid (pH 5.0-6.0) soil. Condition with peat moss or compost. Plant no deeper than it was in its previous position. Apply mulch to within 3″ (8cm) of, but not touching, the stem in early spring.

Light: Plant in full sun in northern zones and in light shade in the deep south.

Pruning: Pruning is rarely needed.

Uses: Use as a showy specimen or accent.

175

ALMEY CRAB APPLE   *Malus 'Almey'*

This fast growing, ornamental tree matures at 12-15′ (3.6-4.5m) high with an equal spread.

Purplish red buds open to large crimson or pink flowers with a white star at the base of each petal. Flowering begins before the leaves unfurl in the first or second season after planting. Fruit ripen to maroon over an orange base color.

Young, pinkish purple leaves turn glossy green in the summer.

Soil: Plant in a moist, well-drained, acid (pH 5.0-6.5) soil.

Condition with peat moss, leaf mold or compost. Eliminate weed or grass competition around the young tree. Mulch lightly after the soil has warmed in the spring.

Light: Position in full sun.

Pruning: Stake newly planted trees until established in 2-4 years. Prune young trees in winter or early spring to shape as desired. Prune mature trees only to eliminate dead or straggly shoots.

Uses: Use as a specimen, accent or roadside tree.

JAPANESE FLOWERING CRAB APPLE *Malus floribunda*

Malus floribunda is a small, deciduous, ornamental, gracefully-arching tree that grows to 15-25′ (4.5-7.5m).

Deep pink buds open in a profusion of pinkish white flowers.

Small, 5″ (13cm) reddish yellow fruit add interest from August through October.

The dense, deep green leaves are fine textured.

Soil: Plant in a moist, well-drained, acid (pH 5.0-6.5) soil. Condition with peat moss, leaf mold or compost.

Eliminate weed or grass competition around the young tree. Mulch lightly after the soil has warmed in the spring.

Light: Position in full sun.

Pruning: Stake newly planted trees until established in 2-4 years. Prune young trees in winter or early spring to shape as desired. Prune mature trees only to eliminate dead or straggly shoots.

Uses: Use as a specimen, accent or roadside tree.

RADIANT CRAB APPLE *Malus 'Radiant'*

Malus 'Radiant' is a small, deciduous ornamental tree that matures at 15-25' (4.5-7.6m) with a spread of 10-20' (3-6m). It has a round, spreading crown with irregular or horizontal branching.

Deep red buds open to deep pink flowers in the spring.

Small ½" (1.3cm), bright red fruit persist into late fall.

The 1-3" (3-8cm) leaves are medium green.

Soil: Plant in a moist, well-drained, acid (pH 5.0-6.5) soil. Condition with peat moss, leaf mold or compost.

Eliminate weed or grass competition around the young tree. Mulch lightly after the soil has warmed in the spring.

Light: Position in full sun.

Pruning: Stake newly planted trees until established in 2-4 years. Prune young trees in winter or early spring to shape as desired. Prune mature trees only to eliminate dead or straggly shoots.

Uses: Use as a specimen, accent or roadside tree.

RED JADE CRABAPPLE *Malus 'Red Jade'*

Malus 'Red Jade' is a small, deciduous, ornamental tree that grows to 15′ (4.5m) and has long, slender, weeping branches. It makes an outstanding specimen.

Single white flowers appear in early spring.

Bright red ½ ″ (1.3cm) fruit persist long after leaf drop, and are very showy on weeping branches.

The dark green leaves precede the blossoms.

Soil: Plant in a moist, well-drained, acid (pH 5.0-6.5) soil. Condition with peat moss, leaf mold or compost.

Eliminate weed or grass competition around the young tree. Mulch lightly after the soil has warmed in the spring.

Light: Position in full sun.

Pruning: Stake newly planted trees until established in 2-4 years. Prune young trees in winter or early spring to shape as desired. Prune mature trees only to eliminate dead or straggly shoots.

Uses: Use as a specimen, mass planting or as a natural screen.

BIRD CHERRY or EUROPEAN BIRD CHERRY *Prunus padus*

This rounded, deciduous, ornamental tree reaches 30-40′ (9-12m) and has attractive, peeling bark on the main stems.

Abundant, fragrant white flowers appear in clusters from July through August. Small, black oval fruit follow the blossoms.

Sharply-toothed, elliptic, 2-4″ (5-10cm) leaves are medium green.

Soil: Plant in a medium coarse to medium-textured, well-drained soil with a medium fertility and moisture-holding capacity.

Light: Position in full sun.

Pruning: Prune lightly in early spring to maintain desired shape.

Uses: Use as a striking accent, specimen or woodland edge planting. *Prunus padus* is beautiful when placed with solid green evergreen species.

ORNAMENTAL FLOWERING PEACH *Prunus persica cvs.*

Identical to fruiting peach in growth habit and height, *Prunus persica* ornamental cultivars are more widely adapted to various sites. They have spectacular blooms, and are either nonfruiting or have only insignificant fruit. Early flowering varieties should only be planted in Zones 8 or 9. Mid- to late season varieties are well suited to Zones 6 or 7.

Early to late flowering varieties are available in double pink, white and red. Midseason 'Peppermint Stick' has red, white and red/white striped blossoms on the same tree. Smaller varieties with weeping branches are available in double pink, white or red. All make gorgeous cut flower bouquets.

Soil: Plant in a well-drained, sandy loam to loam soil. Give moderate watering during the growing season.

Light: Position in full sun.

Pruning: Prune as little as possible. Pinch back gangly shoots to maintain desired form.

Uses: Use these flowering peaches as a stunning accent behind evergreens or along a wall or fence.

KWANZAN FLOWERING CHERRY

Prunus serrulata 'Kwanzan'

'Kwanzan' has stiffly upright branches that form an inverted cone. Mature height is 30′ (9m) with a spread of 20′ (6m).

Large, double, deep rose-pink flowers bloom in pendant clusters in late spring.

Young leaves are reddish and some may appear with the flowers. Mature color is medium green.

Soil: Plant in a well-drained, coarse, well-aerated soil. Water frequently during long dry periods.

Light: Position in full sun.

Pruning: Prune as little as possible. Remove awkward or crossing branches. Pinch back gangly shoots.

Uses: Use as a beautiful accent or specimen near a garden, patio, woodland edge or with dark green evergreens.

BRADFORD CALLERY   *Pyrus calleryana 'Bradford'*

This medium-sized, deciduous tree grows to about 20′ (6m), and is highly prized as a stunning foundation planting.

The rich green leaves with wavy edges turn a striking burgundy color in cold fall areas (upper inset).

Clusters of delicate white blossoms appear in early spring. (lower inset).

Soil: Plant in a well-drained sandy or loamy soil. If the soil is heavy clay, plant in raised beds.

Light: Position in full sun.

Pruning: Prune only where needed.

Uses: 'Bradford' makes an excellent accent, specimen or foundation planting. It is also well suited to espaliering.

GOLDEN TRUMPET TREE *Tabebuia chrysotricha*

This spreading, rounded, open branched, semi-deciduous tree grows to 40′ (12m). It is one of the showiest trees available for use in hot, subtropical areas.

Clusters of bright yellow, trumpet shaped flowers bloom in terminal clusters in late winter or early spring.

The finely divided leaves with five leaflets are 4″ (10cm) long.

Soil: *Tabebuia* tolerates many well-drained soil types if given frequent feeding and watering. It is reasonable drought tolerant after the first couple of years.

Light: Plant in full sun or partial shade.

Pruning: Stake when young and train to a single shoot until 8′ (2.4m). Prune to manage shape.

Uses: *Tabebuia* makes an outstanding accent, specimen, or street tree.

184

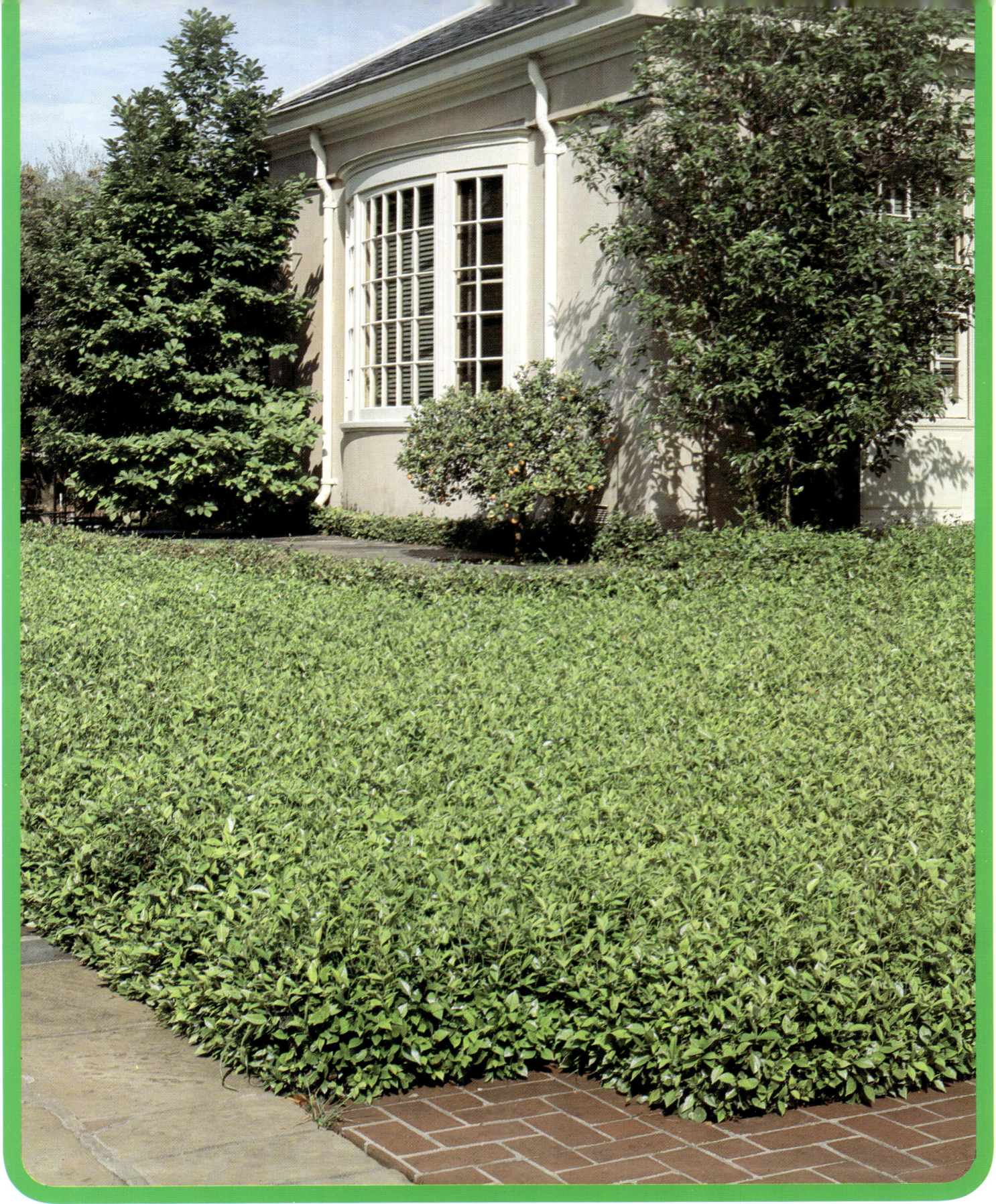

Ground Covers

PROSTRATE WHITE ABELIA *Abelia x grandiflora 'Prostrata'*

Abelia x grandiflora 'Prostrata' is a low-growing, semi-evergreen shrub that makes an excellent ground or bank cover.

Clusters of small, delicate white, bell-shaped flowers cover the shrub from June through fall.

Small, 1″ (2.5cm), showy bright green leaves have a red tinge when young.

Soil: Abelia does best in a medium-coarse to medium textured, well-drained soil that has been enriched with leaf mold or compost.

Light: Plant in full sun or light shade.

Pruning: Prune to shape in early spring if needed.

Uses: 'Prostrata' is used primarily for a ground or bank cover, or as a border/edge planting.

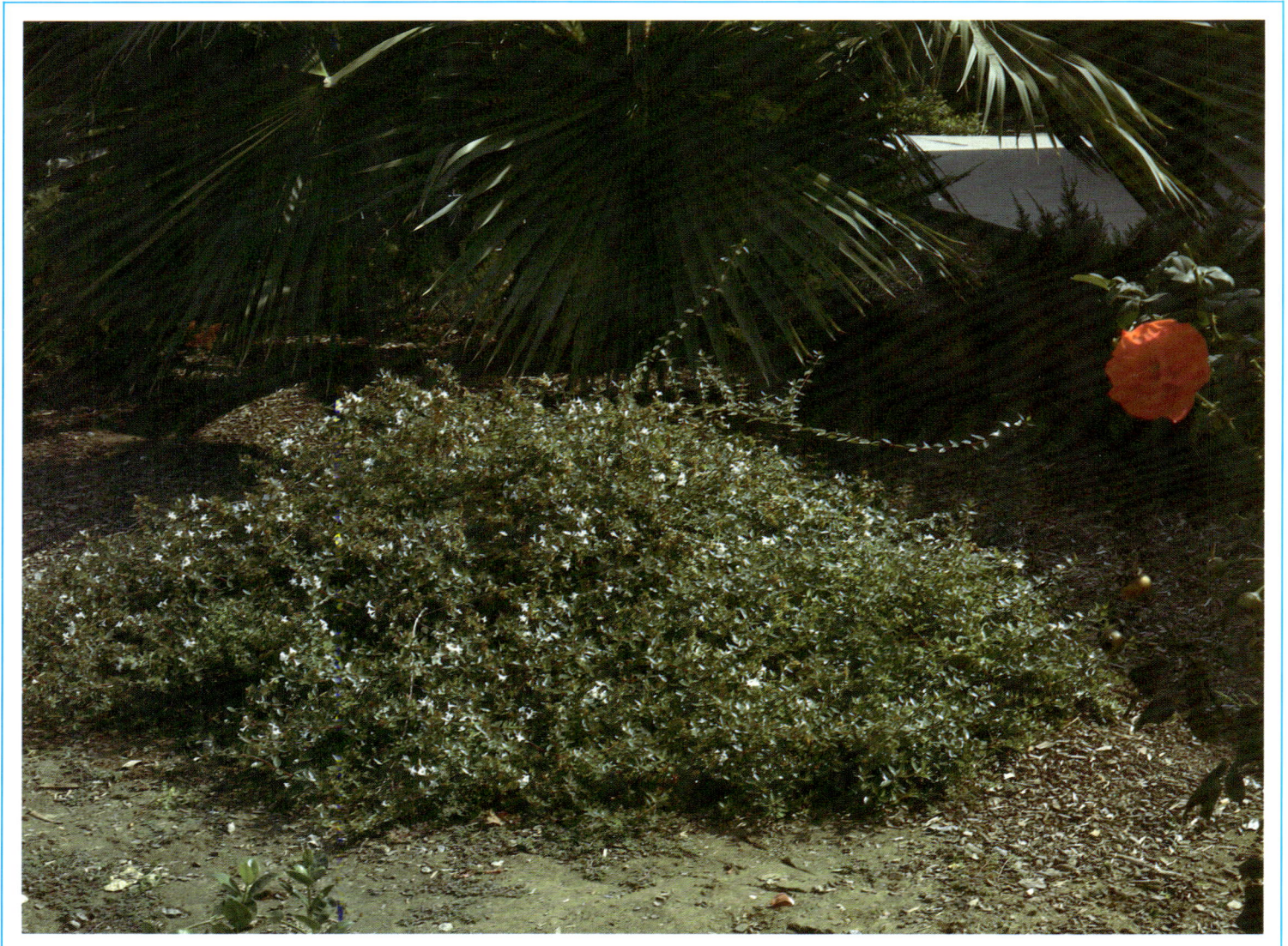

BUGLEWEED or CARPET BUGLE *Ajuga reptans cvs.*

These low-growing, spreading herbaceous perennials develop mounds up to 6″ (15cm) high, and spread rapidly by stolons (an overground stem that produces a new plant at its tip).

Six-inch (15cm), compact flower spikes bloom in May and June. Colors include blue, white, pink and purple.

The 4″ (10cm), rounded leaves show distinctive color variation, and may be green, purple, bronze or variegated. *Ajuga reptans* 'Jungle Bronze' (lower left) is vibrant in a sunny position and *A. r.* 'Burgundy Glow' (lower right) is striking in combination with evergreens. Green leaved varieties turn reddish bronze in the fall. Leaves of all varieties may be held through the winter.

Soil: *Ajuga* does well in a fertile, well-drained soil. Damp, humid conditions tend to encourage rot. Fertilize regularly for active healthy growth.

Light: Plant in full sun to accent bronze or metallic tints.

Uses: Use as a ground cover or as an edging for borders and along walks. Plant 6-12″ (15-30cm) apart.

SCOTCH HEATHER *Calluna vulgaris cvs.*

Calluna vulgaris cultivars are spreading evergreen plants that range in height from 8-24″ (20-60cm).

Tiny blossoms in spikes at the shoot tips bloom from late summer into fall, and may be white, pink or purple.

The tiny leaves are scalelike and dark green.

Soil: *Calluna* does well in any coarse, well-drained, slightly acid (pH 5.5-6.5) soil. Low fertility is not a problem.

Light: Plant in full sun. Light shade will contribute to fewer flowers.

Pruning: Shear plants back to one-half their height in early spring, just before the new growth begins.

Uses: Use as a ground cover, border, or low hedge. *Calluna* is also well suited for a rock garden or patio planting.

GREEN CARPET NATAL PLUM   *Carissa grandiflora 'Green Carpet'*   Zones: 9 & 10

'Green Carpet' is a low-growing, spiny, evergreen shrub that grows to a height of 1-1½′ (30-45cm) and spreads laterally to 4′ (1.2m) or more.

Attractive star-shaped, white flowers with a delicate fragrance bloom throughout the year, followed by deep, red, plum-shaped fruit.

Abundant 1½-2″ (4-5cm), dark, shiny, deep green oval leaves create a dense appearance.

Soil: Plant in a medium-coarse to medium textured soil with good drainage.

Light: Plant in full sun and a warm, south or west-facing position.

Pruning: Pruning is not needed.

Uses: 'Green Carpet' makes an excellent ground cover, border or edge planting.

Cotoneaster adpressus is a low-growing, deciduous, semi-prostrate shrub that spreads slowly and mounds to about 10″ (25cm) high.

Pinkish blooms appear in early summer, followed by ½″ (1.3cm), bright red berries.

The small, bright green leaves have brilliant red fall color.

Soil: Cotoneaster does best in poor garden soil and requires very little care. It may be used effectively for erosion control on dry slopes and banks.

Light: Plant in full sun.

Pruning: Pruning is rarely needed.

Uses: Use in rock gardens, as a ground cover, or on banks and walls. Space plants 3-4′ (.9-1.2m) apart.

BEARBERRY COTONEASTER *Cotoneaster dammeri cvs.*

This low-growing, evergreen shrub spreads horizontally and creates mounds by taking root wherever the stems touch the ground. Mature height is 1-2' (30-60cm) depending on cultivar. *Cotoneaster dammeri* 'Skogsholem' (featured here) matures at 12-18" (30-45cm) and spreads 2' (60cm) each year. 'Coral Beauty' and 'Royal Beauty' are not quite as tall.

White spring flowers are followed by a profusion of brilliant red, ½" (1.3cm) berries.

The 1" (2.5cm) leaves are a glossy dark green with lighter undersides.

Soil: Cotoneaster does best in poor garden soil and requires very little care. It may be used effectively for erosion control on dry slopes and banks.

Light: Plant in full sun.

Pruning: Pruning is rarely needed.

Uses: Use in rock gardens, as a ground cover or on banks and walls. Space plants about 4' (1.2m) apart.

ROCK COTONEASTER *Cotoneaster horizontalis*

Zones: 6-8

This low-growing, wide-spreading deciduous shrub reaches 2-3′ (.6-.9m) in height, and up to 15′ (4.5m) in width.

The unique branch pattern of this shrub forms a flat, herringbone pattern.

Pinkish spring flowers are followed by shiny, bright red berries.

Small, round, glossy bright green leaves are lighter underneath. Fall color is orange and red.

Soil: *Cotoneaster* does best in poor garden soil and requires very little care. It may be used effectively for erosion control on dry slopes and banks.

Light: Plant in full sun.

Pruning: Pruning is rarely needed.

Uses: Use as a ground or bank cover. Give it plenty of room so that branch ends don't need pruning.

192

CROWN-OF-THORNS *Euphorbia milii*

Zone: 10

Euphorbia milii is a broadly-spreading, woody subshrub that grows 1-2′ (30-60cm) high. Shrubby lateral stems stretch out 3-4′ (.9-1.2m) and have sharp thorns.

Blossoms are clusters of bright pink to red bracts, and are present nearly all year.

The thin, roundish, light green, 2″ (5cm) leaves are clustered at branch ends, and are found, singly, all along the stems. A reddish tinge is developed if grown in full sun.

Soil: Plant in a medium-coarse, well-aerated, sandy soil. Water regularly.

Light: Plant in full sun.

Pruning: Pinch branch ends to promote fullness. Stems contain a white, milky sap which extrudes on cutting.

Uses: Use as a ground cover or train on a frame or trellis up against a wall.

ALGERIAN IVY or CANARY IVY *Hedera canariensis*

Hedera canariensis is a vigorous, woody evergreen vine that makes an excellent ground cover for large areas.

The shiny, dark green, large leathery leaves are 5-8″ (13-20cm) wide, with 3-5 shallow lobes. The leaves are more widely spaced than on *H. helix*.

Soil: Plant in a well-drained, humus-rich soil with a good moisture-holding capacity. *Hedera canariensis* requires more water than other Hedera species. Make sure the soil is moist at planting time. Water frequently during establishment and regularly thereafter.

Light: Position in sun along the coast or in partial shade in hot, dry inland areas.

Uses: *Hedera canariensis* makes an excellent ground cover. Plant 12-18″ (30-45cm) apart. It is equally effective on a trellis or fence.

ENGLISH IVY   *Hedera helix cvs.*

Hedera helix cultivars are hardy, spreading, woody evergreen vines that make an excellent ground cover for areas smaller than where *H. canariensis* would be used.

The dark, dull green, 3-5 lobed, 2-4″ (5-10cm) wide leaves have pale leaf veins.

Soil: Plant in a well-drained, fertile garden soil with at least a moderate moisture-holding capacity. Make sure the soil is moist at planting time. Water frequently during establishment and regularly thereafter.

Light: Position in full sun along the coast or in partial shade in hot, dry inland areas.

Uses: Use as a ground or bank cover. It is equally effective on a wall, trellis or fence.

SOUTHERN SWORD FERN   *Nephrolepis exaltata (N. cordifolia)*

Nephrolepis exaltata is a finely-toothed, tufted fern that matures at 2-3′ (.6-.9m) tall and spreads by thin, hairy runners. When clusters of these ferns are planted, they give a stunning woodsy effect.

The fronds (leaves) are narrow, closely spaced and bright green.

Soil: *Nephrolepis* is tolerant of poor soils as long as they are well drained. Infrequent watering is sufficient.

Light: Plant in light or heavy shade.

Pruning: This fern can be invasive if not controlled. It is easily moved, however.

Uses: Use as a ground cover for a woodland planting or position immediately behind a low border/edge in a shaded area.

JAPANESE SPURGE *Pachysandra terminalis*

Pachysandra terminalis is an evergreen perennial that forms dense, creeping mats, 6-8″ (15-20cm) high.

Tiny spikes of fragrant white flowers appear in the spring; white fruit follow the blossoms.

The 2-4″ (5-10cm) leaves are a rich dark green, clustered on top of the stems. The leaves become yellowish in full sun. *Pachysandra terminalis* 'Variegata' (shown in the inset) has leaves edged with white.

Soil: Plant in a good, well-drained garden soil with a pH no higher than 7.0. Position 6-12″ (15-30cm) apart and water frequently until well established. Feed during the growing season.

Light: Plant in full sun or light to full shade.

Uses: Use as a ground cover or for an edge or border along lawns or walkways.

BEACH NAUPAKA *Scaevola frutescens (S. plumieri)*

Zone: 10

Scaevola frutescens is a spreading, tropical shrub that reaches 5′ (1.5m) if left unpruned. It is useful as a ground cover or screen in coastal areas where soil erosion could be a problem.

Small white flowers bloom within whorls of leaves during the spring and summer.

The fleshy, spatula-shaped, 6″ (15cm) leaves are medium green.

Soil: Plant in coastal sand wherever a soil binder is needed, or in any well drained soil.

Light: Position in full sun or partial shade.

Uses: Use as a ground cover, screen, low hedge, or windbreak.

ASIAN STAR JASMINE   *Trachelospermum asiaticum (Rhynchospermum asiaticum)*   Zones: 8-10

This evergreen shrub or vine crawls and spreads over the ground, and sends erect branchlets upward.

Small, fragrant yellowish white flowers bloom April through June.

The leaves are smaller than *T. jasminoides,* and are very dark, dull green.

Soil: Plant in a fertile, well-drained garden soil. Space 2-3′ (.6-.9m) apart.

Light: Position in full sun in cooler areas and in light shade in hot dry areas.

Pruning: Cut back older shoots about one-third each year to keep interior growth from becoming gangly and bare.

Uses: Use as a bank or ground cover. Feed in the spring and early fall. Water regularly throughout the growing season.

DWARF PERIWINKLE or MYRTLE *Vinca minor*

This low-growing evergreen creeper has trailing stems, spreads rapidly and forms a dense ground cover. Mature height is about 6″ (15cm).

Lavender 1″ (2.5cm) blossoms appear in early spring (see upper right inset). *Vinca minor* 'Alba' (lower right) has white blossoms.

The small, oblong leaves are a glossy dark green.

Soil: Plant in a good, fertile, well-drained garden soil. Water frequently and feed regularly throughout the growing season.

Light: Position in light or full shade.

Uses: Use as a ground cover for shady areas. Plant 12-18″ (30-45cm) apart.

Hedges & Screens

ACACIA or PRICKLY MOSES *Acacia verticillata*

Zones: 9 & 10

This evergreen shrub has a beautiful open form with spreading, twisting branches if left unpruned. Mature height and width are about 15′ (4.5m). When sheared to a specific height and width, it becomes very dense and full.

Pale yellow flowers in 1″ (2.5cm) spikes bloom from April through May.

Coniferlike, dark green leaves in whorls give *Acacia* a delicate, airy appearance.

Soil: Plant in a sandy, well-drained soil. Give infrequent but thorough watering during the growing season. *Acacia* performs well in coastal areas and along beaches. It is wind and salt tolerant.

Light: Position in full sun.

Pruning: Pinch lead shoots to promote dense, lateral branching. Shear to desired height and width.

Uses: Use as a screen or unpruned hedge.

CRIMSON PYGMY BARBERRY
Berberis thunbergii 'Crimson Pygmy' ('Atropurpurea Nana') Zones: 6-8

'Crimson Pygmy' is a semi-evergreen, miniature form of Red Leaf Barberry. Mature height is usually only 1½-2' (45-60cm) and width about 2½' (75cm). Branches are slender, arching and spiny.

The rounded, 1" (2.5cm) leaves are bright red when young, and turn a deep bronze-red with age.

Soil: *Berberis* does best in any well-drained garden soil. It will grow in most soil extremes as well, including those with high lime content.

Light: Position in full sun to bring out the stunning red color. It will tolerate heat and drought, but not strong wind.

Pruning: Very little pruning is needed.

Uses: Use as a low hedge, border or edge planting.

TUTTLE NATAL PLUM *Carissa grandiflora 'Tuttlei'*

Zones: 9 & 10

This evergreen shrub has compact, dense foliage, and grows to 2-3′ (.6-.9m) high by 3-5′ (.9-1.5m) wide. It produces abundant flowers and fruit.

Delicate 2″ (5cm), star-shaped, white flowers have a light, sweet fragrance, and bloom throughout the year. Red plum-shaped fruit follow the blooms.

Dark, shiny deep green, oval, 3″ (8cm) leaves give a dense, rounded appearance to the shrub.

Soil: Plant in a medium-coarse to medium textured soil with good drainage.

Light: Position in full sun and in a warm, south or west-facing position.

Pruning: Prune lightly for a screen or heavily for a fomal hedge.

Uses: 'Tuttlei' makes an excellent low hedge or screen.

204

Coccoloba uvifera is a wide-spreading shrub or tree which reaches 15-20' (4.5-6m) if left unpruned. It is a good specimen for dry, sandy coastal areas where wind induced soil erosion could be a problem.

Yellowish white flowers in dense racemes are followed by purple fruit that resemble bunches of grapes. The fruit may be used for jelly.

The 8" (20cm) leaves are leathery and glossy with prominent red veins.

Soil: Plant in any dry, sandy soil. *Coccoloba* tolerates a high soil pH (above 7.0) and withstands salt spray as well. It is an excellent soil binder.

Light: Position in full sun or light shade.

Pruning: Shear to desired height and width.

Uses: Use as a natural barrier or screen along the coast.

SEA GRAPE *Coccoloba uvifera*

GARDEN CROTON   *Codiaeum variegatum*

Codiaeum variegatum is an open, spreading shrub that reaches 4-6′ (1.2-1.8m) in height. It has brilliantly colored ornamental foliage.

The showy leaves differ in color by variety, and may be any combination of yellow, green, red, purple, orange or pink. Some may be spotted, blotched, bicolored or prominently veined. Leaf margins may be smooth, wavy, twisted or lobed.

Soil: Plant in almost any well-drained soil.

Light: Position in full sun or partial shade. Full sun accents the red tints. Protect from strong wind.

Pruning: Little pruning is needed when used as a natural screen.

Uses: *Codiaeum* makes a stunning screen, hedge or group planting.

PAMPAS GRASS *Cortaderia selloana*

Cortaderia selloana is a large, fast-growing ornamental grass that can grow 8′ (2.4m) in height each year. It will reach a mature height of 20′ (6m).

Whitish or pinkish flower plumes rise out of soft, fountainlike, gray-green leaves. These stunning plumes are 1-3′ (30-90cm) long and appear in late summer.

Soil: *Cortaderia* will grow in any soil, with any drainage. It is tolerant of either acid or alkaline conditions, as well as dry winds or coastal fog.

Light: Plant in full sun or light shade.

Pruning: Trim back to the ground when new growth is desired. Remove expansive, unwanted seedlings as they appear.

Uses: This makes an excellent windbreak or large, natural screen. It is also attractive in a small group planting.

WILLOWLEAF COTONEASTER *Cotoneaster salicifolius*

This vigorous, semi-evergreen shrub has upright growth to an unpruned height of 15′ (4.5m). Arching branches will spread to 15-18′ (4.5-5.4m).

The willowlike, 2-3″ (5-8cm) long leaves are a wrinkled dark green with grayish undersides. Bright red, ¼″ (.6cm) berries appear in 2″ (5cm) clusters.

Soil: These plants do best in poor garden soil and require very little care. They may be used effectively for erosion control on dry slopes and banks.

Light: Plant in full sun.

Pruning: Prune out undesirable upright branches and shear to desired height and width.

Uses: Use as a large screen or background planting.

BURKWOOD BROOM *Cytisus scoparius 'Burkwoodii'*

'Burkwoodii' is a medium-sized, deciduous shrub that grows to 5-8' (1.5-1.8m) and forms dense clumps of erect, slender stems.

Long sprays of beautiful garnet-red, gold-tipped flowers appear all along the branches in early spring.

The leaves are tiny, bright green and divided into leaflets.

Soil: For best foliage and flowers, plant in average, moist garden soil. However, Cytisus will grow in an infertile, rocky soil IF it is well drained.

Light: Plant in full sun.

Pruning: Control the size and form by pruning after bloom.

Uses: This shrub is excellent for erosion control on dry, difficult sites or it is suitable as an accent, foundation, hedge or screen.

Elaeagnus angustifolia (usually shown as a small tree) can be sheared into an attractive, effective, medium-sized hedge. The deciduous shrub has a trunk and branches with peeling brown bark that add winter interest.

Small, fragrant, greenish yellow flowers appear in early summer, followed by green, olivelike fruit.

The 2″ (5cm) leaves are a distinctive, willowlike silvery green.

Soil: Plant in any moderately- or well-drained soil.

Elaeagnus tolerates air pollution, heat, wind, seaside conditions and reasonable drought. It is highly effective for erosion control in problem areas.

Light: Position in full sun.

Pruning: Shear to desired height and width.

Uses: This makes an effective clipped hedge, natural screen/barrier or bank cover.

BARBADOS CHERRY or SURINUM CHERRY *Eugenia uniflora* Zone: 10

Eugenia uniflora is a compact evergreen shrub with slow, open growth to about 6-8′ (1.8-2.4m). It can be sheared into a hedge or used as a natural unpruned screen.

Fragrant white brushlike flowers are followed by distinctive grooved fruit that change from green to deep red. The fruit are edible and make a fine jam or jelly.

Soil: Plant in a rich, well-drained soil with a good moisture-holding capacity. Water regularly.

Light: Position in a protected spot in the sun or in light shade. *Eugenia* does not do well in a hot, dry, windy situation.

Pruning: Shear to desired size and shape.

Uses: Use as a formal hedge (this will reduce flowering and fruiting) or as a natural screen.

BARBADOS CHERRY or SURINUM CHERRY *Eugenia uniflora*

GALPHIMIA or THRYALLIS *Galphimia gracilis*

Zone: 10

Galphimia gracilis is an upright, spreading shrub that reaches 4-6′ (1.2-1.8m) in height.

Yellow, ½″ (1.3cm) flowers bloom in loose, terminal racemes.

The leaves are a 2-3″ (5-8cm), medium green.

Soil: Plant in a rich, well-drained soil with a good moisture-holding capacity. Water regularly.

Light: *Galphimia* likes full sun or light shade. Protect from strong wind.

Pruning: Prune to desired size and shape.

Uses: Use as a showy, clipped hedge, natural screen or in a group planting.

JUNGLE-FLAME *Ixora spp.*

Zone: 10

Ixora spp. are showy, upright shrubs that reach 6-8′ (1.8-2.4m) in height at maturity. Their bright colored flowers and attractive foliage make them especially ornamental.

Brilliant flowers in compact clusters may be red, yellow or orange. *Ixora duffii* 'Superking' is featured here.

The leaves are a leathery, 5-6″ (13-15cm) long, shiny dark green.

Soil: Plant in a fertile, well-drained, acid (pH 5.5-6.5) soil, high in organic matter. Condition with peat moss or leaf mold if necessary.

Light: Place in full sun.

Pruning: Prune to desired shape and height.

Uses: Use as a showy clipped hedge, natural screen or group planting.

DWARF YELLOW CAMARA

Lantana camara 'Dwarf Yellow'

'Dwarf Yellow' is an upright, evergreen or semi-deciduous shrub that is broadly spreading and reaches a mature height of only 1-2' (30-60cm).

Bright yellow flowers in 2" (5cm) clusters bloom profusely for most of the year.

The leaves are a rough-textured, dark green.

Soil: *Lantana* does well in most any well-drained soil.

Water thoroughly but infrequently. This species is excellent where soil erosion could be a problem.

Light: Place in full sun. It thrives in a dry situation.

Pruning: Shear to desired shape and size. Prune hard in the spring to remove dead wood.

Uses: Use as a low hedge or foundation planting.

Ligustrum japonicum is a heavily branched, upright growing shrub that matures at 6-9′ (1.8-2.7m). It is easily sheared into many desired shapes.

Fragrant white flowers bloom in the spring.

The leaves are a glossy, heavily textured deep green. The cultivar *L.j.* 'Aureum' (shown in the inset) has stunning gold-tipped and solid gold leaves.

Soil: *Ligustrum* does best in a fertile, well-drained soil.

Light: Plant in full sun or partial shade.

Pruning: Shear or shape into desired size and form.

Uses: Use as a hedge, screen or barrier planting.

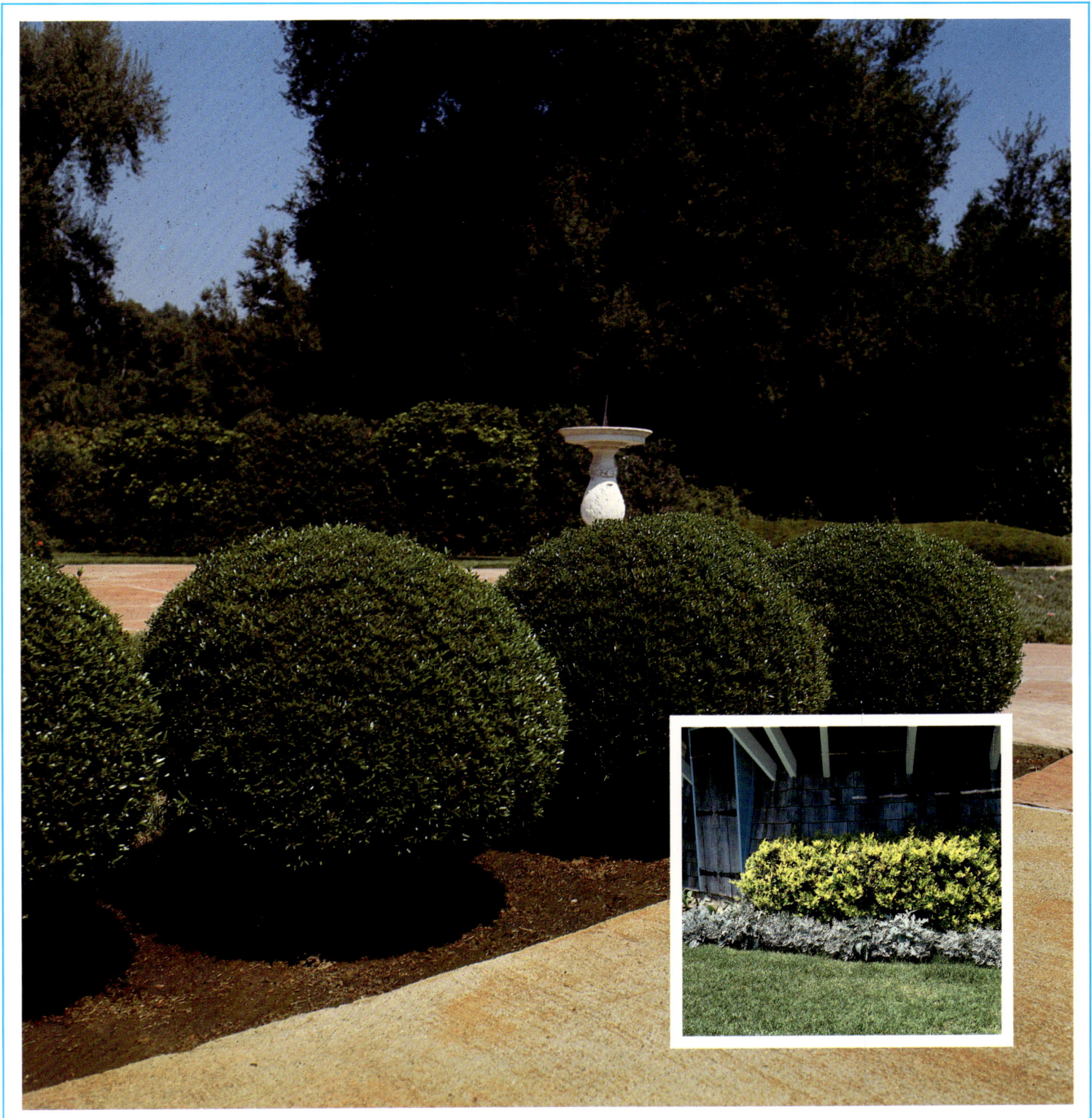

WAXLEAF PRIVET *Ligustrum japonicum*

HOWARD WAXLEAF PRIVET

Ligustrum japonicum 'Howardii'

Zones: 6-8

'Howardii' has all the qualities and form of *L. japonicum* (p. 215) with showy, gold foliage.

New leaves are a bright golden yellow and remain colorful until cool weather.

Soil: *Ligustrum* does best in a fertile, well-drained soil.

Light: Plant in full sun or partial shade.
Pruning: Shear or shape into desired size and form.
Uses: Use as a hedge, screen or barrier planting.

CLAVEY'S DWARF HONEYSUCKLE *Lonicera 'Clavey's Dwarf'*

Zones: 6-10

'Clavey's Dwarf' is a low, dense, spreading deciduous shrub that grows 3-5′ (.9-1.5m) high with an equal spread.

Small white flowers are inconspicious.

The small, oval leaves are bluish green.

Soil: Plant in a well-drained, fertile garden soil. Water moderately during the growing season.

Light: Position in full sun in coastal areas or in light shade in hot, dry inland areas.

Pruning: Prune to desired shape and size.

Uses: Use as a low, clipped hedge or informal, natural screen. It is equally well suited as a foundation planting.

CLAVEY'S DWARF HONEYSUCKLE *Lonicera 'Clavey's Dwarf'*

ORANGE JESSAMINE or SATINWOOD   *Murraya paniculata*   Zone: 10

This upright, open, evergreen shrub has dense, graceful, pendulous branches. Mature height is 8-10′ (2.4-3m) with an equal spread.

Waxy white, bell-shaped flowers have a citruslike fragrance. Bloom period may occur several times including late summer, fall and early spring. Attractive red, non-edible fruit follow the flowers.

The glossy, dark green leaves are divided into 3-9 oval, 1-2″ (2.5-5cm) leaflets.

Soil: Plant in a rich soil with high organic matter content. Condition with peat moss or compost. Water regularly.

Light: Position in light to full shade.

Pruning: Prune to desired size and shape.

Uses: Use as an outstanding ornamental hedge, screen or group planting. Ideal container plant.

ORANGE JESSAMINE or SATINWOOD

AFRICAN BOXWOOD   *Myrsine africana*

Zone: 10

This evergreen shrub has a loose branching habit when young, but becomes a stiff, rounded specimen, 3-8' (.9-2.4m) high at maturity if left unpruned. It can easily be held to 3-4', (.9-1.2m). The upright, dark red stems are closely set.

Flowers are inconspicious.

The round, dark green glossy leaves are ½" (1.3cm) long and are beautiful in cut floral arrangements.

Soil: *Myrsine* does well in any soil that is moderately or well drained. It is quite drought tolerant.

Light: Position in full sun or partial shade.

Pruning: Clip into desired shape and size.

Uses: This shrub is excellent in formal shapes, as a low hedge, foundation, background or in a narrow bed.

219

Myrtus communis 'Compacta' is a small, slow-growing, dense, tightly branched shrub. Mature height may only be 2-3' (60-90cm).

Creamy white, lightly fragrant flowers appear in the summer. Small, bluish black, ½" (1.3cm) fruit follow the flowers.

The small, glossy dark green leaves have a pungent scent when bruised.

Soil: Plant in a medium coarse to medium-textured soil. Good drainage is ESSENTIAL or chlorosis will occur.

Light: *Myrtus* does well in full sun or partial shade.

Pruning: Prune according to desired shape.

Uses: 'Compacta' is outstanding as a low, compact formal hedge.

SWEET OLIVE   *Osmanthus fragrans*

Osmanthus fragrans is a large evergreen shrub or small tree that becomes wide and dense as it matures. It can reach 10′ (3m) or more.

Tiny white flowers emit a strong apricotlike fragrance in the spring.

The 4″ (10cm), oval, leathery medium green leaves may be toothed or smooth edged.

Soil: *Osmanthus* does well in almost any soil including heavy clay.

Light: Position in full sun or light shade. Young plants grow best when lightly shaded and will thrive in full sun as they mature.

Pruning: Train or prune to desired shape and size.

Uses: Use *Osmanthus* as a hedge, screen, background or espalier.

PURPLE CHINESE HOLLY or
HOLLY-LEAF OSMANTHUS *Osmanthus heterophyllus 'Purpureus'*

Zones: 8-10

'Purpureus' is a dense, tightly branched evergreen shrub with striking purple tints to the foliage. It makes an excellent hedge or screen.

Tiny, fragrant white flowers bloom throughout the summer.

The hollylike leaves are spiny and leathery. New growth is dark purple while mature leaves are dark green with purple tints.

Soil: Osmanthus does well in almost any soil including heavy clay.

Light: Position in full sun or light shade. Young plants grow best when lightly shaded and will thrive in full sun as they mature.

Pruning: Train or prune to desired shape and size.

Uses: Use *Osmanthus* as a hedge, screen, background or espalier.

GOLDEN NINEBARK

Physocarpus opulifolius 'Luteus'

This deciduous shrub grows to 4-5' (1.2-1.5m) tall and is very hardy in areas with cold winters. Branches with peeling bark give added landscape interest.

Clusters of white flowers bloom in the spring and early summer.

The deeply lobed leaves are yellow in the sunlight and yellow-green in the shade.

Soil: Plant in average garden soil that is well-drained and has at least a moderate moisture-holding capacity.

Light: Plant in sun or shade. Full sun accents the yellow colors.

Pruning: Shear overlong branches to maintain correct form.

Uses: Use 'Luteus' as a beautiful natural screen or barrier. It may be pruned into a more formal hedge.

YEW PINE or YEW PODOCARPUS *Podocarpus macrophyllus* Zones: 9 & 10

This evergreen shrub has foliage that resembles that of *Taxus* (English and Japanese Yew). The species is particularly heat and drought tolerant. Unpruned it can reach heights of 20′ (6cm).

The leaves are broad, leathery, bright green and about 4″ (10cm) long.

Soil: Plant in any well-drained garden soil.

Light: Position in sun or partial shade.

Pruning: *Podocarpus* is easily pruned to any desired shape.

Uses: Use as a clipped hedge, screen or topiary.

YEW PINE or YEW PODOCARPUS *Podocarpus macrophyllus*

ENGLISH LAUREL *Prunus laurocerasus*

Prunus laurocerasus is a large evergreen shrub or small tree that reaches its best potential in the cooler areas with cold winters. It is recognized for its beauty as a clipped, formal hedge.

Creamy white flowers in 3-5″ (8-13cm) long spikes bloom among the leaves during the summer. Small black fruit appear in late summer and fall.

The glossy dark green leaves have a leathery texture and may be 3-6″ (8-15cm) long.

Soil: Plant in any well-drained garden soil. Regular watering and feeding speeds growth and produces vibrant foliage color.

Light: Position in partial shade where summers are very hot and in full sun in other areas.

Pruning: Prune and clip to maintain desired size and shape.

Uses: *Prunus laurocerasus* makes a stunning formal hedge or screen.

TALL HEDGE BUCKTHORN *Rhamnus frangula 'Columnaris'*

Zones: 6-8

This large, erect deciduous shrub reaches a height of 10-12′ (3-3.6m) with a spread of only 4′ (1.2m).

Small greenish yellow blossoms bloom in early summer, followed by small berries that ripen from green through red to black in late summer.

The 1¼-3″ (3-8cm) long leaves are dark green and very glossy. Fall color is yellow and is retained up to early winter.

Soil: Plant in any well-drained garden soil. Space 2½′ (75cm) apart for a tight, upright form.

Light: *Rhamnus* does best in full sun.

Pruning: This shrub is easily sheared to desired shape, and is commonly kept to a height of 4′ (1.2m).

Uses: Use as a quick-growing, temporary screen or windbreak. Maximum life is 25-30 years.

Roses

ROSES, Border *Rosa spp.*

Border roses are very hardy, compact, low-growing plants that have large clusters of small flowers. They are ideal along borders and in areas where colorful mass plantings enhance the landscape. The stunning mini-hybrid Floribundas shown here have beautifully shaped buds and open flowers which literally cover the plant.

Soil: Plant in a medium-coarse to medium textured, WELL-DRAINED soil. Avoid heavy clay by planting in raised beds. Mix one-half the soil from the planting hole (2-2½′ or .6-.75m deep) with equal amounts of peat moss, ground bark and/or compost. Add manure or complete fertilizer at the same time. Water continuously during the growing season. Feed regularly until six weeks before the first expected frost.

Light: Roses do best in full sun. Protect from midday sun in hot summer areas.

Pruning: Cut back previous year's growth by one-third in early spring. Mulch up to 12″ (30cm) with soil and straw in cold winter areas.

Uses: Use wherever an edge or foreground planting is desirable. Small to medium size mass plantings provide an incredible floral show.

ROSES, Climbing and Rambling *Rosa spp.*

Climbing roses may be either large-flowered natural climbers or varieties of bush roses. Large-flowering roses have 2-6″ (5-15cm) blooms on upright or arching, 6-15′ (1.8-4.5m) canes. Flowering may be in early spring or intermittent with a heavy fall crop.

Rambling roses have slender, flexible canes that may grow to 10-20′ (3-6m) each year. Small, 2″ (5cm) flowers in dense clusters bloom in late spring or early summer. Colors are deep red, pink, yellow or white.

Soil: Plant in a medium-coarse to medium textured, WELL-DRAINED soil. Avoid heavy clay by planting in raised beds. Mix one-half the soil from the planting hole (2-2½′ or .6-.75m deep) with equal amounts of peat moss, ground bark and/or compost. Add manure or complete fertilizer at the same time. Water continuously during the growing season. Feed regularly until six weeks before the first expected frost.

Light: Roses do best in full sun. Protect from midday sun in hot summer areas.

Pruning: Cut back previous year's growth by one-third in early spring. Mulch up to 12″ (30cm) with soil and straw in cold winter areas.

Uses: Use these roses on walls, fences or trellises.

ROSES, Floribunda *Rosa spp.*

Floribunda roses are vigorous, bushy plants, and smaller than most Hybrid Teas. Many varieties are available, including showy climbers.

Most have beautiful, high-centered, 2-4″ (5-10cm) blossoms with long, pointed buds. The single, double, or semi-double flowers may be white, cream, yellow, apricot, orange, coral, pink, red or lavender. Height and spread of these plants is 2-3′ (60-90cm).

Soil: Plant in a medium-coarse to medium textured, WELL-DRAINED soil. Avoid heavy clay by planting in raised beds. Mix one-half the soil from the planting hole (2-2½′ or .6-.75m deep) with equal amounts of peat moss, ground bark and/or compost. Water continuously during the growing season. Feed regularly until six weeks before the first expected frost.

Light: Roses do best in full sun. Protect from midday sun in hot summer areas.

Pruning: Cut back previous year's growth by one-third in early spring. Mulch up to 12″ (30cm) with soil and straw in cold winter areas.

Uses: Use as a mass planting or position in front of taller roses. An informal hedge or screen would be excellent as well.

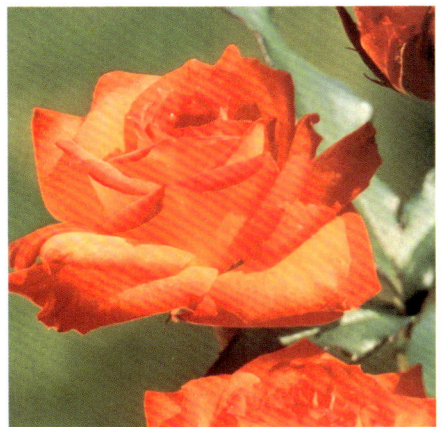

ROSES, Grandiflora *Rosa spp.*

Grandiflora roses are a cross between hardy, free-flowering Floribundas and large-flowered, long-stemmed Hybrid Teas. They flower from spring to frost in Zones 6-8, and continuously (with a brief dormancy) in Zones 9 & 10.

Their stately, double blossoms are 3-5″ (8-13cm) wide and resemble Hybrid Teas. Grandifloras have a color range of white, pink, yellow, orange and dark red. Height of these bushy plants may reach 8-10′ (2.4-3m).

Soil: Plant in a medium-coarse to medium textured, WELL-DRAINED soil. Avoid heavy clay by planting in raised beds. Mix one-half the soil from the planting hole (2-2½′ or .6-.75m deep) with equal amounts of peat moss, ground bark and/or compost. Water continuously during the growing season. Feed regularly until six weeks before the first expected frost.

Light: Roses do best in full sun. Protect from midday sun in hot summer areas.

Pruning: Prune during short dormant season to maintain desired shape and size. Cut back previous year's growth by one-third in early spring. Mulch up to 12″ (30cm) with soil and straw in cold winter areas.

Uses: These roses are excellent for tall mass plantings or as a natural screen or barrier.

ROSES, Hybrid Tea *Rosa spp.*

Hybrid Teas are the most popular class of roses on the market today. Thousands of varieties are grown and new ones are bred and featured each year. The vigorous plants range from 2-6' (.6-1.8m) in height, depending on variety.

The distinctively shaped flowers may be up to 8" (20cm) across, and are usually produced one to a stem. Stunning colors range from white to red, pink, orange, yellow, lavender, bicolored, blends and multicolors.

Soil: Plant in a medium-coarse to medium textured, WELL-DRAINED soil. Avoid heavy clay by planting in raised beds. Mix one-half the soil from the planting hole (2-2½' or .6-.75m deep) with equal amounts of peat moss, ground bark and/or compost. Add manure or complete fertilizer at the same time. Water continuously during the growing season. Feed regularly until six weeks before the first expected frost.

Light: Roses do best in full sun. Protect from midday sun in hot summer areas.

Pruning: Cut back previous year's growth by one-third in early spring. Mulch up to 12" (30cm) with soil and straw in cold winter areas.

Uses: Feature in a specimen planting, mass planting or use as an informal hedge or border.

ROSES, Miniature *Rosa spp.*

Miniature roses are low-growing, continuously blooming plants from 4-18″ (10-45cm) high. One foot (30cm) is average. A few climbing varieties are available which sprawl to 5′ (1.5m).

Vibrant clusters of ½-2″ (1.3-5cm) blossoms may be white, peach, yellow, pink, orange, red, lavender, bicolored or striped.

Soil: Plant in a medium-coarse to medium textured, WELL-DRAINED soil. Avoid heavy clay by planting in raised beds. Mix one-half the soil from the planting hole (2-2½′ or 6-.75m deep) with equal amounts of peat moss, ground bark and/or compost. Add manure or complete fertilizer at the same time. Water continuously during the growing season. Feed regularly until six weeks before the first expected frost.

Light: Roses do best in full sun. Protect from midday sun in hot summer areas.

Pruning: Cut back previous year's growth by one-third in early spring. Mulch up to 12″ (30cm) with soil and straw in cold winter areas.

Uses: Use as a small mass or border planting. Miniatures are charming in rock gardens, window boxes, hanging baskets or in containers.

ROSES, Tree *Rosa spp.*

Tree roses look like small trees and are derived from almost any rose variety. This 'man-built' plant is the product of a sturdy rootstock with one or two budded-on parts. Hybrid Teas make the most popular tree roses but climbers create a graceful, drooping form similiar to a miniature weeping willow.

Standard Trees are 5' (1.5m), Patio Trees 4' (1.2m) and Miniature Trees 1½' (45cm). A beautiful range of colors is available.

Soil: Plant in a medium-coarse to medium textured, WELL-DRAINED soil. Avoid heavy clay by planting in raised beds. Mix one-half the soil from the planting hole (2-2½' or .6-.75m deep) with equal amounts of peat moss, ground bark and/or compost. Water continuously during the growing season. Feed regularly until six weeks before the first expected frost.

Light: Roses do best in full sun. Protect from midday sun in hot summer areas.

Pruning: Prune during short dormant season to maintain a striking, rounded crown.

Uses: Use as an accent or specimen. Tree roses are striking in formal gardens. Tree roses are not hardy in cold winter areas.

Shade & Ornamental Trees

GOLDEN MIMOSA or FERN LEAF ACACIA *Acacia baileyana*   Zones: 9 & 10

This spectacular evergreen tree will grow to 20-30′ (6-9m) in height and 20-40′ (6-12m) in width. It has a relatively short life span of 20-30 years.

Profuse clusters of bright yellow flowers bloom very early in the spring.

The leaves are a feathery, blue-green.

Soil: Plant in a sandy, well-drained soil. Give infrequent, but thorough, watering during the growing season.

Light: Position in full sun.

Pruning: Stake the trunks of young trees until they have become well anchored. Prune large trees to open the interior crown and reduce dieback from shading. Remove branches back to the trunk.

Uses: Use this acacia as a stunning shade or ornamental tree. When allowed to form multiple trunks, it is excellent as a soil builder on banks.

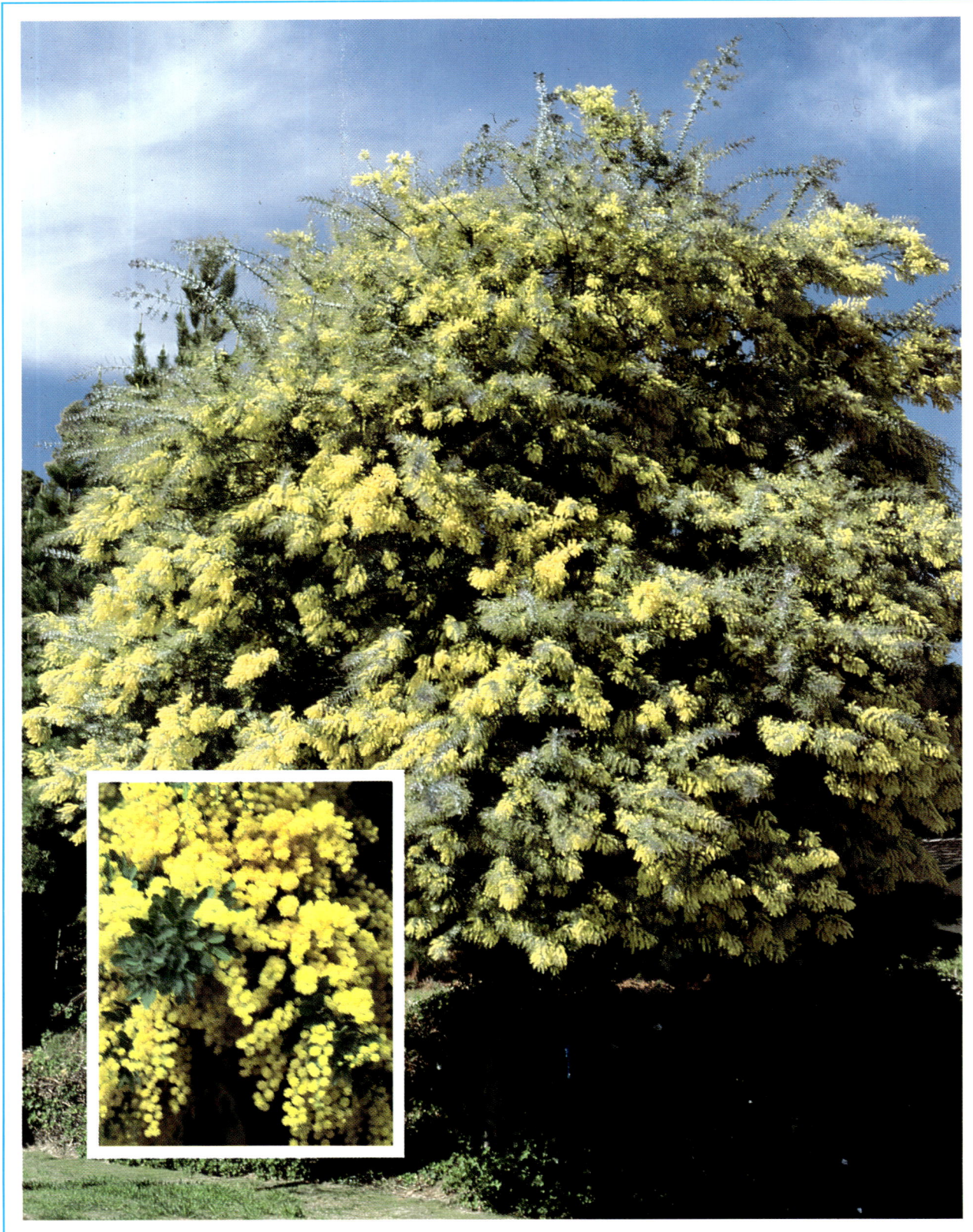

AMUR MAPLE *Acer ginnala*

This multistemmed shrub may be trained to a small single stem ornamental tree. Height at 10 years may be 20' (6m), with mature height about 30-35' (9-10.5m).

Tiny white blossoms in early spring are followed by bright red, winged fruit in midsummer.

The smooth lobed leaves are pale green in the spring and turn dark green in summer. Fall colors are brilliant yellow, orange and scarlet.

Soil: Plant in average garden soil with at least moderate drainage.

Light: Position in full sun to light shade.

Pruning: Stake and train to a single stem and prune late summer and fall to desired shape and form.

Uses: Use as a small accent or specimen tree.

RED MAPLE *Acer rubrum*

This rounded or oval deciduous tree will reach 20' (6m) in 5-10 years, then mature at 50-70' (15-21m) high with a spread of 30-50' (9-15m). The branches, buds and flowers are red, and form an attractive contrast with the mature gray bark of trunk and stems.

The dark green leaves have silvery undersides. Fall color may be orange to deep red in frost areas.

Soil: *Acer rubrum* does best in a moist, well-drained soil.

It will tolerate reduced soil drainage or a high water table. Surface roots take the nourishment from topsoil beneath and around the tree.

Light: Position in full sun or light shade.

Pruning: Thin branches in late summer and fall. Excessive sap bleed could be a problem if pruned in winter or spring.

Uses: Use as an accent, specimen or shade tree.

SOUTHERN SCARLET MAPLE *Acer rubrum 'Drummondii'*

Zones: 8-10

Acer rubrum 'Drummondii' is a fast-growing, deciduous tree with a narrow, rounded crown and brilliant fall color in warmer climates. Mature height is about 40-50′ (12-15m).

Flowers and fruit are red. The leaves are more deeply cut than those of *A. rubrum,* and fall color is brilliant scarlet.

Soil: *Acer rubrum* 'Drummondii' does best in a moist but well-drained soil.

Light: Position in full sun or light shade.

Pruning: Thin branches in late summer and fall. Excessive sap bleed could be a problem if pruned in winter or spring.

Uses: Use as an accent, specimen or shade tree.

SILVER MAPLE *Acer saccharinum*

Zones: 6-9

This large, rapid-growing, wide-spreading deciduous tree may reach 20′ (6m) in 5-8 years. It matures at 60-100′ (18-30m) with a spread of 40-50′ (12-15m). The silver-gray bark of youth becomes deeply furrowed with age. Brittle branches often break off in high winds.

Leaves are light green with silver undersides, and are more deeply cut than those of *A. saccharum* (pg. 241). Fall color may be brilliant yellow, orange or red in frost areas.

Soil: This tree thrives in a good moist soil, but will grow almost anywhere. Surface roots spread to find water and may clog drains.

Light: Plant in full sun or light shade. It tolerates urban pollution and coastal conditions.

Pruning: Thin branches in late summer and fall. Excessive sap bleed could be a problem if pruned in winter or spring.

Uses: Use as an accent, specimen or shade tree.

SUGAR or HARD MAPLE *Acer saccharum*

This stately, upright, oval-headed deciduous tree has a moderate growth rate and may reach 20' (6m) in 10-12 years. It matures at about 75' (22.5m) high with a spread of 40-50' (12-15m).

Leaves are medium green above and lighter below. Fall colors are outstanding and may be yellow, orange and red in frost areas.

Soil: *Acer saccharum* needs a deep, moist, well-drained soil. Surface roots take the nourishment from topsoil beneath and around the tree. This tree is easily injured by ice-melting chemicals and salt used on highways. Air pollution from traffic can be harmful as well. Plant away from roads.

Light: Position in full sun.

Pruning: Thin branches in late summer and fall. Excessive sap bleed could be a problem if pruned in winter or spring.

Uses: Use as an accent, specimen or shade tree.

PAW PAW *Asimina triloba*

Asimina triloba is a small, sometimes shrubby, deciduous tree that reaches a mature height of 35-40′ (10.5-12m) with a narrow, oval crown.

Purplish 1½-2″ (3.7-5cm) flowers appear in early June before the leaves.

The oblong, irregular-shaped leaves may be 6-10″ (15-25cm) long. They hang down and slightly under, giving the tree a weeping appearance.

The 5″ (13cm) long fruit are green when young and yellow-brown with a whitish to yellow, edible pulp at maturity.

Soil: *Asimina triloba* thrives in a rich soil, high in organic matter and moisture-holding capacity. Condition the soil with peat moss or compost if necessary. Water frequently.

Light: Plant in full sun.

Pruning: Train to a single stem if necessary.

Uses: Use as an ornamental accent or specimen tree.

RIVER BIRCH *Betula nigra*

This fast-growing, loose-headed, upright deciduous tree may be single- or multiple-trunked. Height in 10 years is about 20′ (6m), with a mature height of 60-70′ (18-21m). The showy bark is red-brown, and becomes torn or shredded.

Oval, pointed, pale green young leaves become medium green with light undersides. Fall color is golden yellow.

Soil: *Betula* does best in a moist sandy to loam soil.

Betula nigra will tolerate thin, sandy, acid conditions as well.

Light: Position in full sun. The tree will tolerate heat and drought when well established.

Pruning: Prune in summer and fall if needed.

Uses: Use as an accent or specimen tree. A small group planting is also attractive.

This fast-growing, loose-headed deciduous tree may have single or multiple trunks. Height may be 20′ (6m) in 10 years and 60-70′ (18-21m) at maturity. A single trunk specimen spreads one-half its height. Distinctive white, papery bark peels after 4-5 years.

Oval, pointed leaves are light yellow-green when young, becoming medium green with lighter undersides. Fall color is golden yellow.

Soil: This tree does best in a moist, medium-coarse to medium textured, moderately- or well-drained soil.

Light: Position in full sun.

Pruning: Prune in summer and fall if needed.

Uses: Use as an accent or specimen tree. Several planted together in a group is very ornamental.

PAPER BIRCH *Betula papyrifera*

EUROPEAN WHITE BIRCH *Betula pendula*

Zones: 6 & 7

Betula pendula is an open-headed, deciduous tree with graceful, pendulous branches. It will reach 20′ (6m) in 10 years, with a mature height of 30-60′ (9-18m). It may have single or multiple stems. Characteristic white bark has black ridges after 4-5 years.

The diamond-shaped, light green leaves have lighter undersides. Fall color is golden yellow.

Soil: This tree does best in a moist, medium-coarse to medium textured, moderately- or well-drained soil.

Light: Position in full sun.

Pruning: Prune in summer and fall if needed.

Uses: Use as an accent or specimen tree. Several planted in a group is very ornamental.

245

BLACK OLIVE *Bucida buceras*

Bucida buceras is a medium size evergreen tree that reaches 50′ (15m) or more at maturity. Branches often have 1″ (2.5cm) long spines.

Greenish yellow flowers appear in 4″ (10cm) long spikes. Fruit are a ½″ (1.3cm) long, brownish black.

Medium green, leathery, 4″ (10cm) long leaves grow in "rosettes" and singularly, at branch ends and all along the stems.

Soil: *Bucida* grows well in a rich, well-drained alkaline soil with a 7.0 pH or greater.

Light: Position in full sun or partial shade.

Pruning: Prune as needed for desired shape.

Uses: Use as a tropical-appearing accent, specimen or shade tree.

This large, graceful, shapely deciduous tree reaches 100′ (30m) or more in height and about 70′ (21m) in width. The foliage has a beautiful, fine-textured appearance.

Large compound leaves have 9-17 slightly curved leaflets. Reddish brown nuts are encased in a 4-winged, dark brown husk that splits when the nut is ripe.

Soil: *Carya* needs a deep, well-drained soil. Give occasional, thorough watering in hot climates.

Light: Plant in full sun.

Pruning: Prune to shape and remove dead wood.

Uses: Use as a stately specimen or shade tree.

COMMON CATALPA   *Catalpa bignonioides*

Catalpa bignonioides is a hardy, deciduous tree with highly ornamental flowers, leaves and seed pods. With a symmetrical crown, it reaches about 60′ (18m) in height. The cultivar *C.b.* 'Nana' (shown in the inset) is grafted on to *C. bignonoiodes* boles, and forms a dense, umbrella-like head.

Large clusters of trumpet-shaped, white flowers are striped and marked with yellow and brown. Long bean-shaped pods follow the flowers.

The distinctive heart-shaped leaves are 10-12″ (25-30cm) long and 7-8″ (18-20cm) wide.

Soil: Plant in any well-drained soil. Protect from strong wind.

Light: Position in full sun or partial shade.

Pruning: Remove lower branches for a straight, smooth trunk. 'Nana' requires careful and regular shaping.

Uses: Use as a striking lawn, shade or street tree. Use 'Nana' as a small ornamental tree.

HACKBERRY or NETTLE TREE *Celtis occidentalis*

Celtis occidentalis is a wide-spreading deciduous tree with a moderate growth rate. Height may be 10′ (3m) in 15-20 years, with mature height at 40-50′ (12-15m). The bark often has a wartlike appearance.

Oval, pointed, medium to dark green leaves turn yellow in the fall.

Soil: Plant *Celtis* in any moderately- to well-drained soil as long as there is no restrictive soil layer for at least 10′ (3m). The tree will tolerate acid, alkaline or dry conditions.

Light: Position in full sun.

Pruning: Pruning is rarely needed.

Uses: Use as an accent, street or shade tree. It is tolerant of urban pollution and strong wind.

KATSURA TREE *Cercidiphyllum japonicum*

This conical, upright or spreading deciduous tree may have single or multiple stems. Height may be 20-25' (6-7.5m) in 10-15 years, with mature height of 40-60' (12-18m). A single trunk specimen forms an upright cone and spreads 30-50' (9-15m); multiple trunk tree spread is 40-60' (12-18m).

The characteristic dark brown bark is shreddy and shaggy looking on mature trees.

Heart-shaped leaves have a reddish tint in the spring, then turn deep blue-green. Fall color is orange and yellow.

Soil: *Cercidiphyllum* likes a moist, rich, well-drained soil. The tree is tolerant of a high lime content.

Light: Plant in full sun in Zone 6, and in full sun or light shade in Zones 7 & 8.

Pruning: Pruning is rarely needed.

Uses: Use as an accent, specimen or shade tree.

This small, thorny, tightly branched tree grows to about 16′ (5m) in height.

Waxy white fragrant flowers are followed by 2″ (5cm) fruit with light green skin and juicy flesh.

This small, 2-3″ (5-8cm), glossy green leaves are distinctly aromatic.

Soil: Plant *Citrus* in a deep, loose, sandy to loam soil. Good drainage is essential.

Light: Position in full sun.

Pruning: *Citrus* usually forms a shapely, symmetrical head, so little pruning is necessary. Dead or frost injured branches should be removed.

Uses: Use as a showy ornamental accent or specimen tree. Plant several together to form a small grove.

This small, globose, spiny tree with slender branches makes a stunning ornamental.

Fragrant white flowers are followed by deep orange-yellow, 3½″ (9cm) fruit with a loose skin and sweet pulp.

The small, lance-shaped, shiny green leaves are tightly set.

Soil: Plant *Citrus* in a deep, loose, sandy to loam soil. Good drainage is essential.

Light: Position in full sun.

Pruning: Remove dead or frost-injured branches if needed. Little pruning is necessary.

Uses: Use as a showy ornamental, accent or specimen.

YELLOWWOOD or VIRGILIA   *Cladrastis lutea (C. tinctoria)*

This spreading, deep-rooted deciduous tree with smooth gray bark has a height and spread of 15-20′ (4.5-6m) in about 10 years. Mature height will be 30-50′ (9-15m).

Clusters of fragrant white flowers bloom in late spring or early summer. A major flower crop is produced every 2-3 years. Flat brown seed pods ripen and drop in the fall.

Pinnate leaves with 4″ (10cm) long leaflets are bright green. Fall color is orange to yellow.

Soil: Plant in a deep, moist, well-drained soil with no restrictive soil layer for at least 10′ (3m).

Light: Position in full sun.

Pruning: Pruning is rarely needed. Cut in summer or fall to avoid excessive bleeding.

Uses: Use as a specimen, accent or shade tree.

MONKEY APPLE or BALSAM APPLE *Clusia rosea*

This evergreen tree has strikingly beautiful foliage, flowers and fruit. Mature height is usually 20-30′ (6-9m) depending on the planting site. It is so adaptable it will grow on rocks or even on other trees.

The 2″ (5cm) pink and white flowers are followed by round, 3″ (8cm) wide, greenish white fruit.

Large, thick, glossy green leaves are 8″ (20cm) long.

Soil: Plant in any kind of soil. *Clusia* makes a fine seaside tree.

Light: Position in full sun.

Pruning: Prune to desired size and shape.

Uses: Use as a striking, tropical-appearing ornamental accent or specimen tree.

MONKEY APPLE or BALSAM APPLE *Clusia rosea*

AMERICAN or COMMON PERSIMMON *Diospyros virginiana* Zones: 6-9

Diospyros virginiana is a slender tree with a broad, oval crown that reaches to 20-30' (6-9m) at maturity. The trunk has deeply fissured bark that forms a checkered pattern.

Small inconspicious, bell-shaped yellow flowers bloom in late spring. Round, yellow to orange, 1½" (3.7cm) fruit are wrinkled until ripe, then full and very sweet.

Broad, oval, 6" (15cm) glossy green leaves are bronzy or reddish when new, then pinkish and red in the fall.

Soil: Plant in a well-drained soil with ample moisture-holding capacity. Feed and water regularly.

Light: Position in full sun.

Pruning: Prune only to remove dead wood, open the interior crown or lightly shape.

Uses: Use as a small accent, specimen or shade tree. It also makes a beautiful espalier.

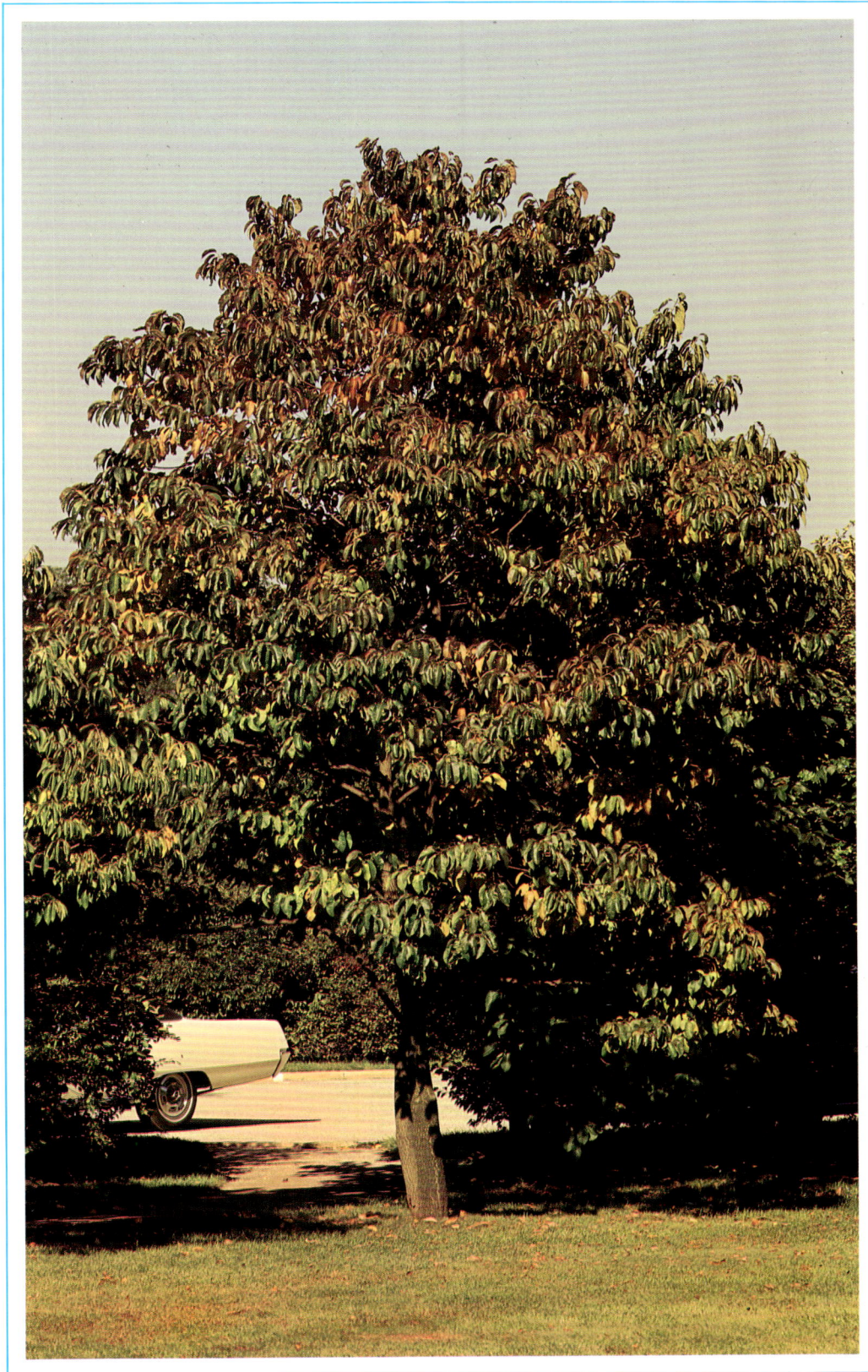

RUSSIAN OLIVE *Elaeagnus angustifolia*

This adaptable, fast-growing deciduous tree may have single or multiple stems. Height in 5-10 years may be 15-20′ (4.5-6m) and mature height is 25-30′ (7.5-9m). The spread equals the height.

Small, fragrant greenish yellow flowers bloom in early summer. Silvery green berrylike fruit resemble miniature olives.

The leaves are a 1½-3″ (3.7-8cm) long silver-gray.

Soil: Plant in any moderately- or well-drained soil. *Elaeagnus* tolerates air pollution, heat, wind, seaside conditions and low watering. It is highly effective for erosion control in problem areas. The tree tolerates city and industrial pollution.

Light: Position in full sun.

Pruning: Shear to desired shape and form.

Uses: Use as an accent or specimen tree wherever a light, silvery effect is desirable. Plant in a long row along an entranceway or barrier wall.

COPPER BEECH or PURPLE BEECH

Fagus sylvatica 'Atropunicea'

Zones: 6-8

This slow-growing, long-lived deciduous tree reaches a height of 15-20' (4.5-6m) in 10-15 years. It matures at 50-80' (15-24m) or more, with a spread of 50-60' (15-18m).

Inconspicious spring flowers are followed by small prickly nuts.

The 2-4" (5-10cm) stunning leaves are red when young, then turn copper-red or purple at maturity. This gorgeous foliage display lasts all season.

Soil: Plant *Fagus* in a moist, well-drained soil where there is no restrictive layer for at least 10' (3m).

Light: The tree does best in full sun. Give moderate watering during dry periods.

Pruning: Pruning is rarely needed. If live branches must be pruned, cut them in summer or fall to prevent excessive bleeding.

Uses: Use as a specimen, accent or shade tree. For a natural screen, plant 3' (90cm) apart.

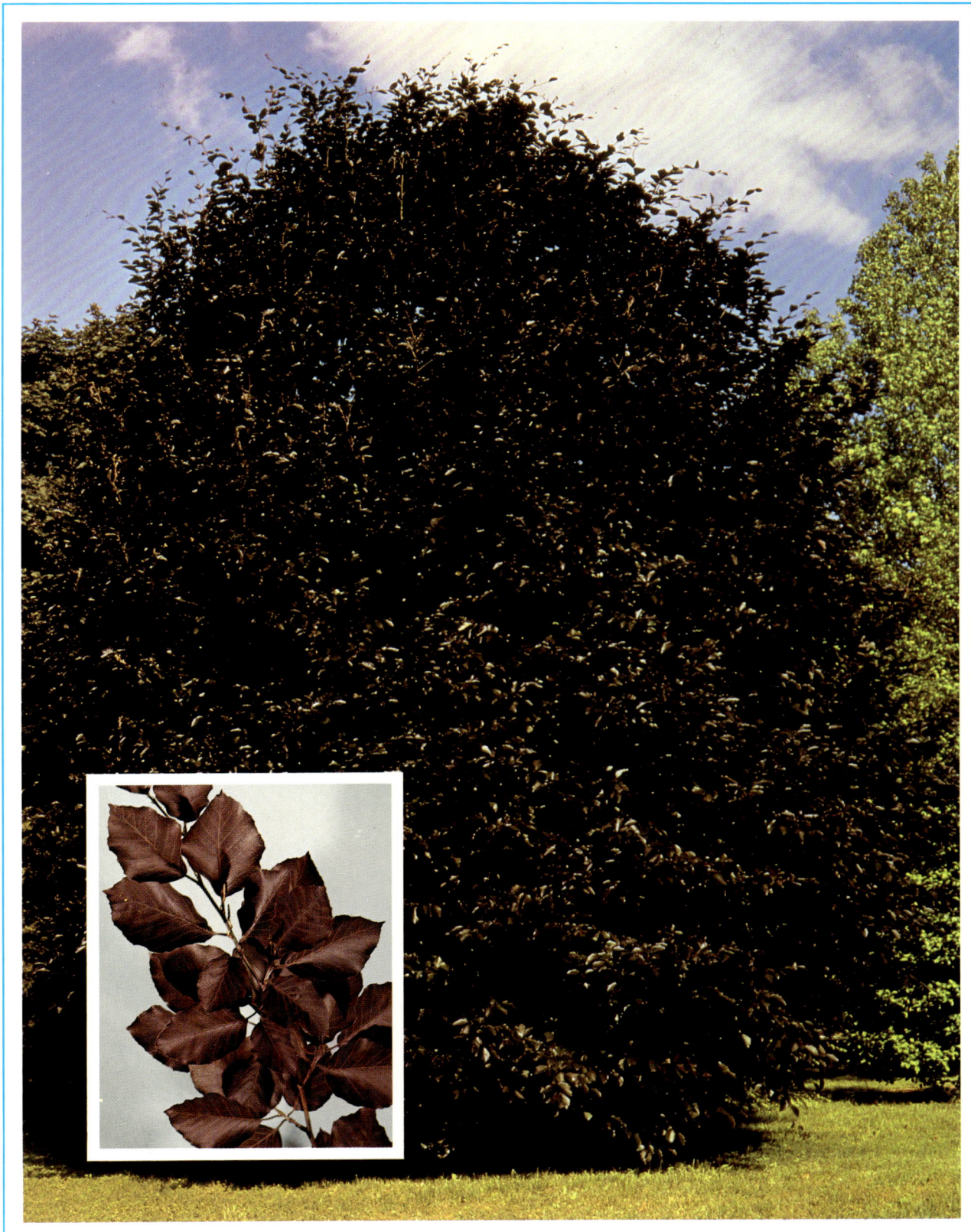

257

WHITE ASH *Fraxinus americana*

This fast-growing, oval or round-topped, deciduous tree has a mature height of 80-120′ (24-36m) and a spread of 30-50′ (9-15m).

Winged fruit occur on female trees only. They quickly germinate to produce unwanted seedlings close to the tree. Plant male trees if possible.

The leaves have seven, 6″ (15cm) leaflets that are medium green. The loose, airy composition of the foliage casts filtered shade that does not inhibit grass. Fall color is clear yellow. Fallen leaves quickly disintegrate, making raking hardly necessary.

Soil: Plant in any deep, well-drained soil that has no restrictive layer for at least 10′ (3m). The tree has a deep root system.

Light: Position in full sun.

Pruning: Pruning is rarely needed.

Uses: Use as an accent, shade or street tree.

MARSHALL SEEDLESS ASH

Fraxinus pennsylvanica 'Marshall Seedless'

Zones: 6-9

Fraxinus pennsylvanica 'Marshall Seedless' is a superior strain of *F. pennsylvanica* (Green Ash). It has rapid growth to 30-40′ (9-12m) and forms a compact, oval crown. This sterile variety leaves no unsightly seed drop.

The large leaves are a beautiful dark green, and are held longer than the species. Fall color is bright lemon yellow.

Soil: Plant in any deep, well-drained soil that has no restrictive layer for at least 10′ (3m). The tree has a deep root system.

Light: Position in full sun.

Pruning: Pruning is rarely needed.

Uses: Use as an accent, specimen or shade tree.

GINKGO or MAIDENHAIR TREE *Ginkgo biloba*

Ginkgo biloba is a slow-growing, deciduous tree that grows to 20′ (6m) in 12-18 years. It matures at 50-80′ (15-24m) in height, with a spread of 40′ (12m). Only male trees are desirable since female fruit have an unpleasant scent. Varieties 'Autumn Gold', 'Fairmont' and 'Saratoga' are good choices.

Fan-shaped, 2-3″ (5-8cm) green leaves have a leaf vein pattern that resembles the leaflets of Maidenhair fern.

Soil: Plant in a deep, loose, well-drained soil that has no restrictive layer for at least 10′ (3m).

Light: Ginkgo does best in full sun.

Pruning: Stake young trees to keep them straight.

Uses: Use as an unusual, showy accent, specimen, street or lawn tree.

THORNLESS HONEY LOCUST *Gleditsia triacanthos var. inermis*

This fast-growing, spreading, open-headed, deciduous tree will reach 25' (7.5m) in 10-12 years. It matures at 35-70' (10.5-21m) with an equal spread. The tree is easily established.

The 6-8" (15-20cm) long pinnate leaves are dark green with a fernlike appearance. Fall color is pale yellow. Fallen leaves quickly disintegrate, making raking hardly necessary.

Soil: Plant in a deep, loose, well-drained soil that has no restrictive soil layer for at least 10' (3m).

Light: Position in full sun.

Pruning: Prune in the fall if necessary.

Uses: Use as an accent, specimen, shade or street tree.

261

Guaiacum officinale is a beautiful, ornamental evergreen tree that grows to about 30′ (9m) in height. It is salt tolerant and makes a lovely seaside planting.

Large clusters of velvety blue flowers appear at branch tips, followed by angled, 1″ (2.5cm), orange-yellow fruit.

The glossy, oval, bright green leaves have four to six, 2″ (5cm) leaflets.

Soil: Plant in a moist, fertile, well-drained soil. Condition with peat moss or compost if necessary.

Light: Position in full sun.

Uses: Use as a showy, tropical-appearing accent or specimen tree.

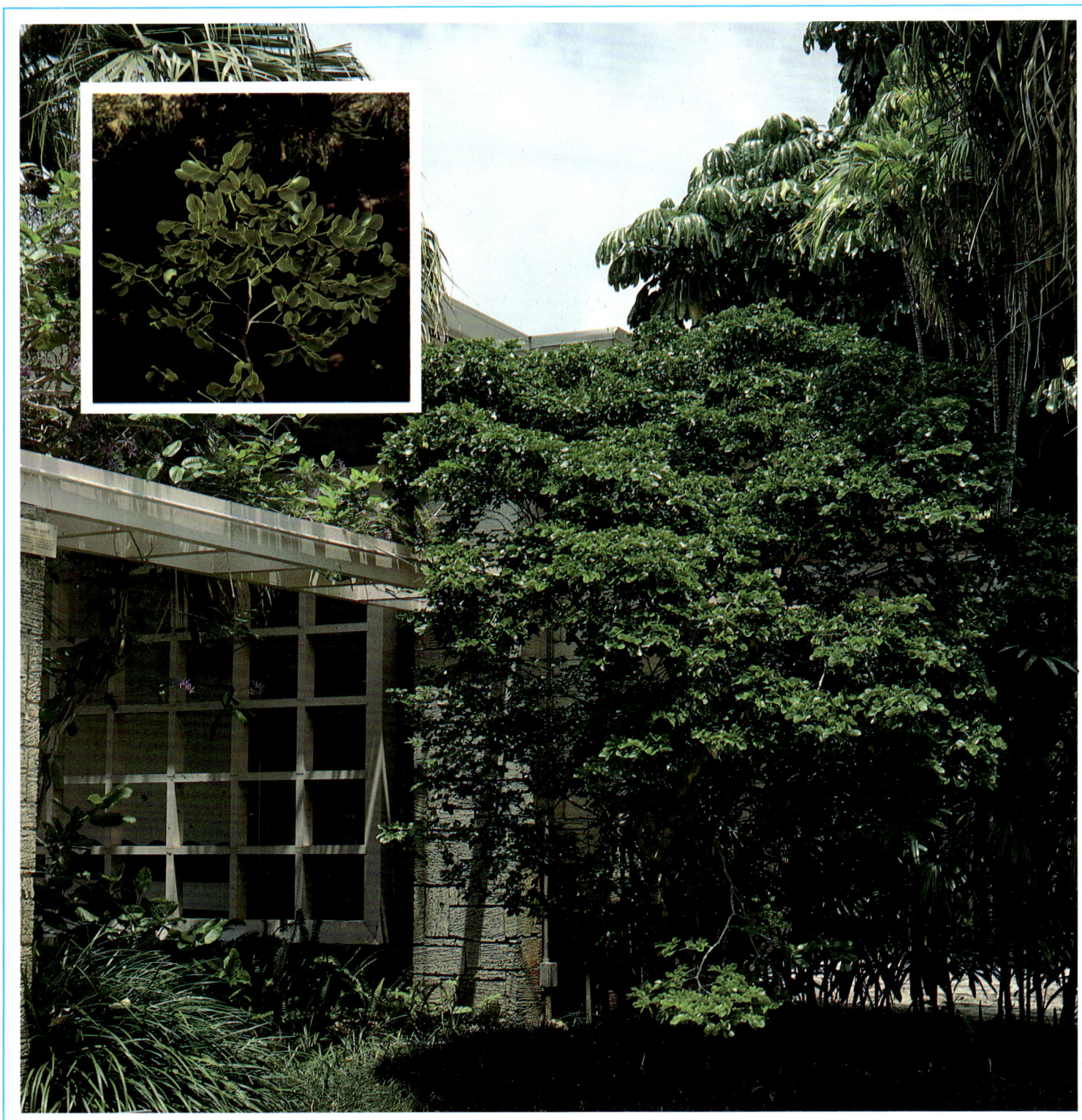

SWEET GUM *Liquidambar styraciflua*

This cone-shaped, upright, deciduous tree will reach 25-30′ (7.5-9m) high in 8-12 years in a moist soil, or in 10-15 years in dry conditions. It matures at 60-70′ (18-21m). Bark on the trunk is silvery brown and deeply furrowed, while branches and twigs have corky wings.

Distinctive star-shaped leaves are 3-7″ (8-18cm) wide, and turn purple, yellow or red in the fall in frost areas. The fruit is a burrlike capsule on a long stem.

The attractive branch pattern, furrowed bark, corky winged twigs and hanging fruit capsules add landscape interest all winter.

Soil: Plant in a neutral or slightly acid (pH 6-6.5), moist soil that has no restrictive layer for at least 10′ (3m). Add peat moss, compost or leaf mold to improve the moisture-holding capacity.

Light: Position in full sun.

Pruning: Stake young trees and prune only to shape. The tree branches from the ground up, and looks most natural that way.

Uses: Use as an accent, specimen or street tree.

TULIP TREE or TULIP POPLAR *Liriodendron tulipifera*

This large, very fast-growing deciduous tree reaches a height of 25-30′ (7.5-9m) in 10-12 years. It matures at 70-90′ (21-27m) with a spread of 35-40′ (10.5-12m).

Showy tulip-shaped flowers begin to appear after the leaves, at age 10-20 years. The unique blooms are greenish yellow with orange at the base.

Cone-shaped fruit follow the flowers and disintegrate when mature.

The bright green, 4-lobed, tulip-shaped leaves are lighter underneath. Fall color is clear golden yellow with brown flecks.

Soil: Plant in a deep, moist, well-drained soil that has no restrictive layer for at least 10′ (3m).

Light: Position in full sun.

Pruning: Stake when young and prune only in the winter.

Uses: Use as an accent, specimen or shade tree.

264

FRUITLESS WHITE MULBERRY *Morus alba 'Fruitless'*

This rapid-growing, deciduous tree may reach 20' (6m) high in 3-5 years in a hot climate. Mature height is usually 35' (10.5m) with a spread equally wide, or wider. This tree has a wide-spreading crown. The cultivar *M. alba* 'Pendula' is a small, weeping ornamental form (shown in the inset).

The light green leaves are variable in form, size and shape—often on the same tree. The large leaves provide excellent shade, and are easily raked in the fall.

Soil: *Morus alba* does best in a deep, moist, well-drained garden soil. It will tolerate considerable drought and dry soils, but growth rate will be reduced under these conditions.

Light: Position in full sun.

Pruning: Stake new plants to support the rapid height growth and crown expansion. Shorten young, long branches back to an upward-growing bud. Do not prune heavy branches back to stubs.

Uses: Use as a shade or ornamental lawn tree.

WAX MYRTLE or SOUTHERN BAYBERRY *Myrica cerifera*

Myrica cerifera is a small, beautiful, native evergreen tree or shrub which matures at about 35′ (10.5m). It is easily trained to a single stem and a round, dense crown.

Inconspicious flowers are followed by clusters of light green fruit coated with pale blue wax. The fragrant wax is used in making candles.

The 3″ (8cm) long, narrow leaves are serrated from middle to tip. Aromatic when crushed, they have small dark glands above and orange glands below.

Soil: *Myrica* thrives in moist, peaty soil.

Light: Position in full sun.

Pruning: Train to a single stem for a small, ornamental tree. Plant in groups for additional beauty.

Uses: Use as an accent, specimen, border, shade or seaside tree.

TUPELO or SOUR GUM *Nyssa sylvatica*

Nyssa sylvatica is a stunning, deciduous lawn or shade tree that has brilliant fall color even in areas with mild winters. It has a moderate growth rate, and reaches 30-50' (9-15m) in height. The crown is pyramidal when young, then spreads into a broad, irregular form with age. Red-tinged bark and crooked twigs add winter interest.

Bluish black, olivelike fruit follow inconspicious flowers.

The glossy, 2-5" (5-13cm) dark green leaves turn copper-red in the fall.

Soil: Plant this tree in most any soil. It thrives in soils with good to moderate drainage, but grows well even in poorly drained soils. It withstands short periods of drought when it has become well established.

Light: Position in full sun.

Pruning: Prune to shape only if needed.

Uses: Use as a beautiful lawn, shade or street tree.

This small, evergreen tree or shrub grows to about 20′ (6m) in height with a spread equally wide. It is easily trained to a single stem. *Ochrosia elliptica* has beautiful shiny foliage and very showy (but poisonous) fruit.

Small cream-white flowers are followed by 2″ (5cm) scarlet fruit.

The 3-6″ (8-15cm) leaves are set in whorls of 3 or 4, and are a bright, glossy dark green.

Soil: Plant in any good, well-drained soil. *Ochrosia* will tolerate a high soil pH (7.0 or greater).

Light: Position in full sun.

Pruning: Prune lightly for desired shape.

Uses: Use as a stunning accent, specimen or seaside planting.

CHINESE PISTACHIO *Pistacia chinensis*

Zones: 7-9

This medium size deciduous tree grows to about 60′ (18m), with a striking umbrellalike crown. Spread may be up to 50′ (15m) wide.

Fruit occur on female trees only, and are 1½″ (3.8cm), reddish brown drupes.

The green compound leaves have 10-16 paired leaflets. Stunning fall colors are scarlet, crimson, orange and yellow.

Soil: Plant in any good, well-drained soil. *Pistacia* is tolerant of alkaline conditions (pH 7.0 or greater).

Light: Position in full sun.

Pruning: Stake young trees and remove lower branches for a smooth trunk and high crown.

Uses: Use as a lawn, shade or street tree. It is also attractive as a corner planting.

This fast-growing, broad, open-headed deciduous tree reaches 20' (6m) in 5-8 years and matures at 40-100' (12-30m) with an equal spread. Characteristic gray-brown bark flakes off to expose greenish yellow patches that eventually become chalky white.

Inconspicuous flowers are followed by ball-shaped seed pods which persist after leaf fall. The pods are used in decorative winter arrangements.

Maple-shaped, 4-8" (10-20cm) wide leaves are dark green.

Soil: Plant in a deep, moderately- to well-drained soil with moderate moisture-holding capacity. There should be no restrictive soil layer for at least 10' (3m). Water deeply in dry periods when young and fertilize every one or two years.

Light: Position in full sun or light shade. The tree is tolerant of urban pollution.

Pruning: Prune in winter if needed.

Uses: Use as a shade, accent specimen or street tree.

CAROLINA POPLAR *Populus x canadensis cv. 'Eugenei'*

'Eugenei' is a very fast growing, deciduous tree which may reach 20′ (6m) in 3-5 years in a rich, moist, well-drained soil. Mature height may be 40-100′ (12-30m). This male cultivar is highly desirable for its "cottonless" characteristic. It has shown high disease resistance in many genetic field trials.

The triangle-shaped leaves are medium green with lighter undersides. Fall color is bright yellow.

Soil: Plant in a medium-coarse to medium textured soil that is well-drained, has a moderate moisture-holding capacity and has no restrictive soil layer for at least 6′ (1.8m). *Populus* has wide-spreading lateral roots, so plant well away from septic systems and drains.

Light: Position in full sun.

Uses: Use as a fast-growing shade or lawn tree. When positioned in a row, 10-12′ (3-3.6m) apart, the tree makes an outstanding windbreak or screen.

HOLLY OAK, HOLM OAK *Quercus ilex*

Quercus ilex is a beautiful evergreen tree that has a moderate growth rate to 40-60′ (12-18m) in height with an equal spread.

Flowers appear with the new leaves in June. Acorns, ¾″ (1.8cm), are light green, and two-thirds enclosed by their cups.

The leaves are variable in size and shape, 1½-3″ (3.8-8cm) long and either toothed or smooth edged. The upper surface is a rich dark green, while the lower is yellowish or silvery.

Soil: Plant in a moist, well-drained soil and water frequently until it is well established (2-3 years).

Light: Position in full sun.

Pruning: *Quercus ilex* withstands pruning and clipping well. Shape in winter or early spring.

Uses: Use as a good evergreen street or lawn tree. It will tolerate seacoast conditions, but will have a shrublike appearance.

PIN OAK *Quercus palustris*

This symmetrical, pyramidal, deciduous tree grows 20-25′ (6-7.5m) in 8-10 years. It matures at about 75′ (22.5m) with a spread of 25-40′ (7.5-12m). Slender branches are either spreading or pendulous, and lower ones are retained on the tree if it is planted in an open position. Acorns develop every 2 years.

The deeply cut leaves are glossy dark green, and fall color is crimson.

Soil: Plant in a moist, rich, acid (pH 5.5-6.5) soil. The tree will tolerate dry, rocky and sandy conditions. Use iron chelate or sequestrene in alkaline areas to improve growth and leaf color.

Light: Position in full sun.

Pruning: Prune young trees in winter or early spring. Remove lower branches for headroom as needed.

Uses: Use as a shade, accent or street tree.

This pyramidal to rounded, deciduous tree reaches a height of 20' (6m) in 5-10 years. It matures at 60-80' (18-24m) with a spread of 40-50' (12-15m).

Red flowers on female trees can be seen with the new leaves. The 3/4" (3.8cm) long acorns take 2 years to mature.

The 5-9" (13-23cm) long leaves have sharply pointed lobes. Fall color is burgundy.

Soil: Plant in a moist, rich, acid (pH 5.5-6.5) soil. The tree will tolerate dry, rocky and sandy conditions. Use iron chelate or sequestrene in alkaline areas to improve growth and leaf color.

Light: Position in full sun.

Pruning: Prune young trees in winter or early spring. Remove lower branches for headroom as needed.

Uses: Use as a shade, accent or street tree.

CORK OAK *Quercus suber*

Zones: 8-10

This evergreen oak has a moderate growth rate to 70-100′ (21-30m) high with an equal spread. The trunk and main branches are covered with a thick, corky bark (see inset).

The shiny, dark green, 3″ (8cm) leaves are toothed, and give a fine-textured appearance to the crown. Acorns form in one year.

Soil: *Quercus suber* must have good soil drainage. A loose, sandy loam would be best. Use iron chelate or sequestrene in alkaline areas to improve growth and leaf color. Mature trees can withstand considerable drought.

Light: Position in full sun or partial shade.

Uses: Use as a beautiful garden or lawn tree. Keep away from traffic areas, especially public parks, because the soft bark is easily carved and subsequently damaged.

SOUTHERN LIVE OAK *Quercus virginiana*

Zones: 7-10

Quercus virginiana is an evergreen or semideciduous tree, depending on cold winter regions. It has moderately fast growth to a mature 60′ (18m) in height, with a broad crown. The spread is twice as wide as the height. It is the most beautiful of all evergreen oaks.

The 5″ (13cm) long leaves are smooth edged, shiny dark green above and whitish beneath. Acorns are dark green and one-fourth enclosed by their cup.

Soil: *Quercus virginiana* thrives in a deep, rich soil with no restrictive layer at least 10′ (3m) deep.

Light: Position in full sun.

Uses: Use as a stately lawn tree. It makes an excellent seaside planting due to its salt tolerance.

WEEPING WILLOW *Salix babylonica*

This broad-headed deciduous tree has classic pendulous, flexible, weeping branches that often touch the ground. Growth is rapid, and the tree may reach 20′ (6m) in 3-6 years. It matures at 50-60′ (15-18m) with an equal spread.

Young branches and twigs are yellow to olive green, and mature bark is pale gray-green.

Inconspicuous 1″ (2.5cm) long catkins (flowers) appear before the leaves are fully expanded in the spring.

The long, narrow light green leaves are silvery underneath. Fall color is yellow.

Soil: Plant in a soil that is moist or wet all year. Water thoroughly if the soil dries in the summer. The shallow root system inhibits grass growth under the tree.

Light: Position in full sun.

Pruning: Prune lower branches in summer and fall to provide headroom, and to allow the tree to weep well.

Uses: Use as a specimen, accent or shade tree.

1320 SUNSET COURT

GLOBE NAVAJO WILLOW   *Salix matsudana 'Navajo'*

'Navajo' is a large, very hardy, wide-spreading round topped tree that grows to 70′ (21m) with an equal spread. It has a dense, tight branching habit.

The long, narrow, 3″ (8cm) leaves are light silvery green.

Soil: Plant 'Navajo' in a loose sandy soil. The tree thrives in a hot dry climate.

Light: Position in full sun.

Pruning: Prune lower branches in the summer and fall. Clip overlong branches to maintain a rounded crown.

Uses: Use as a specimen, accent, shade or street tree in a hot, dry climate.

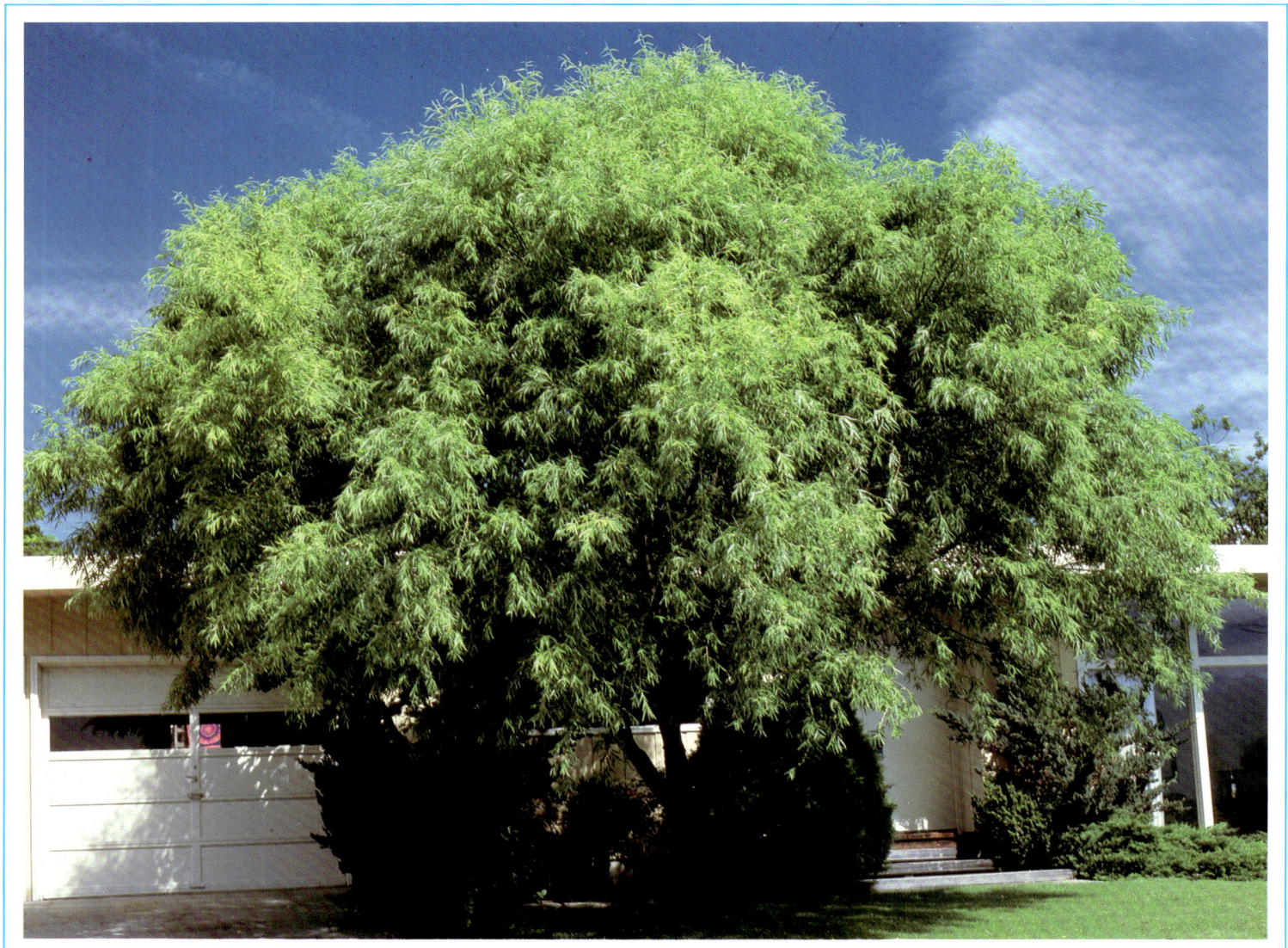

TWISTED HANKOW WILLOW *Salix matsudana 'Tortuosa'*

Zones: 6-8

This slow-growing, erect, deciduous tree may have single or multiple stems. Its unique, twisting branch habit adds winter interest. The tree matures at about 30′ (9m) high and spreads to 20-30′ (6-9m).

Young branches and twigs are yellow to olive green, and mature bark is yellow-gray.

The long, narrow, twisted leaves are light green above with silver beneath. Fall color is yellow.

Soil: Plant in moderately moist soil. It is well suited to hot, dry areas. 'Tortuosa' does not require as much moisture as *S. babylonica.*

Light: Position in full sun.

Pruning: Prune in summer and fall. Take out the lower branches for headroom.

Uses: Use as a specimen, accent or shade tree.

CHINESE TALLOW TREE *Sapium sebiferum*

Sapium sebiferum is an extremely round-topped deciduous tree that reaches 20-60′ (6-18m) in height with an equal spread. It may have multiple stems, but is easily trained to a single stem specimen.

Showy yellow-white flowers bloom in 15″ (38cm) clusters from July through August. Small, waxy grayish white fruit follow the flowers.

The roundish, poplarlike leaves are light green and flutter in the breeze. The dense foliage gives the tree an airy appearance. Fall color (in frost areas) is usually a brilliant red. Some trees may have leaves that are yellow and orange as well. The milky sap is poisonous.

Soil: Plant in a well-drained, slightly acid (pH 6.0-6.5) soil. Water regularly for fast growth.

Light: Position in full sun.

Pruning: Stake young trees and prune only to maintain the desired shape.

Uses: Use as an accent, specimen, shade or lawn tree.

LITTLE LEAF LINDEN *Tilia cordata*

This symmetrical, pryamid-shaped, deciduous tree grows to 20′ (6m) in height with a spread of 25-30′ (7.5-9m).

Fragrant yellow-white flowers bloom in midsummer. Tiny, inedible fruit follow the flowers, and persist into winter.

The 3″ (8cm) long leaves are equally wide, and are dark green above with silvery undersides. Fall color is yellow in frost areas.

Soil: Plant in a deep, moist, well-drained soil that has no restrictive layer for at least 10′ (3m).

Light: Position in full sun or light shade.

Pruning: Pruning is rarely needed. Remove suckers at the ground level.

Uses: Use as a lawn, street or shade tree.

LITTLE LEAF LINDEN *Tilia cordata*

Ulmus parvifolia 'Drake' is a medium size, vigorous, round-headed evergreen or semi-deciduous tree with a more upright habit in youth than the species. It develops pendulous outer branches with age.

The 2″ (5cm) long shining green leaves remain on the tree through the winter in frost free areas. Bark is mottled, often exposing the lighter inner bark when mature.

Soil: Plant in any moderately- to well-drained soil.

Light: Position in full sun.

Pruning: Stake young trees and clip off young branches along the trunk for the first five years.

Uses: Use as an accent, specimen or lawn tree.

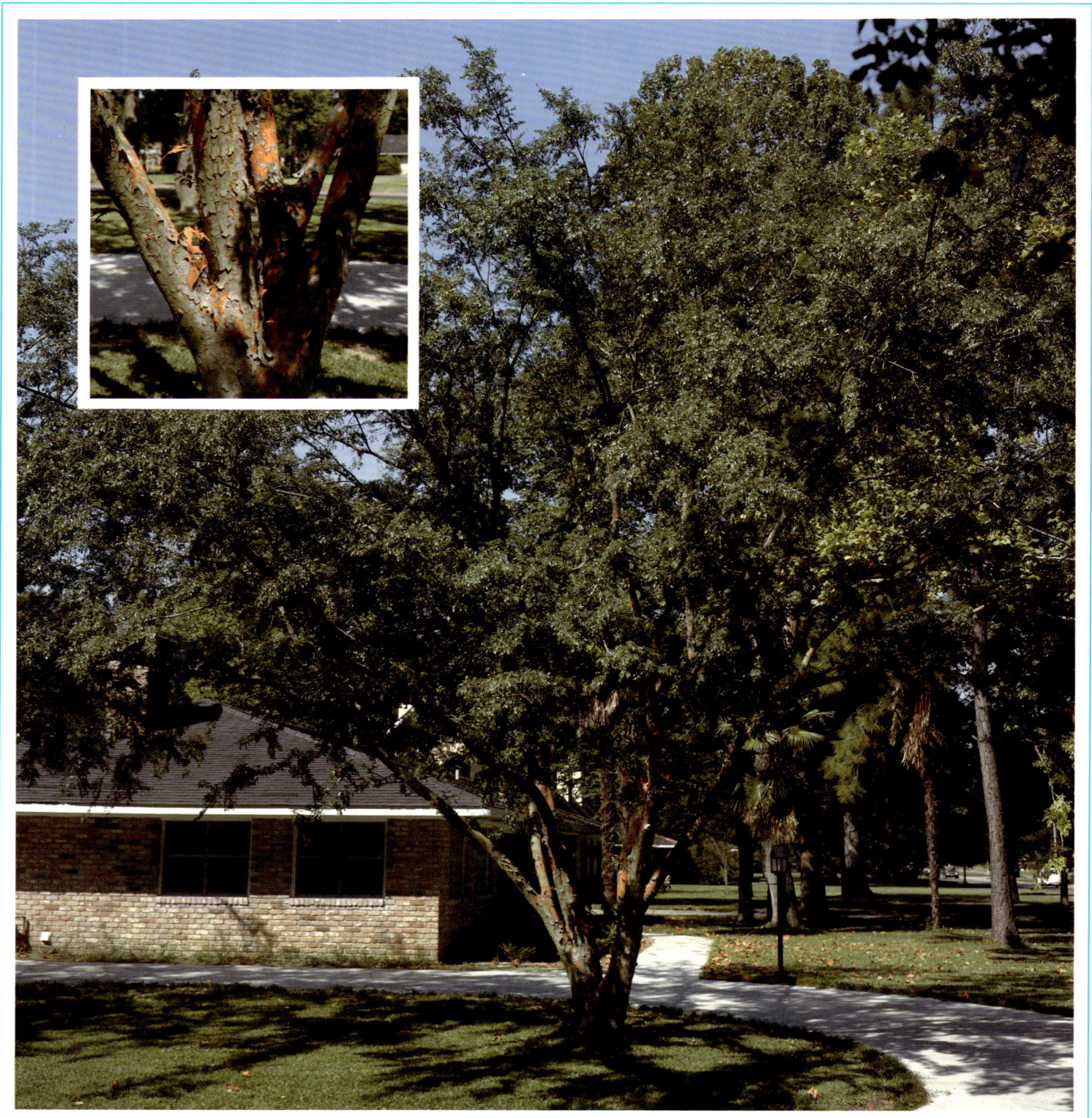

DRAKE ELM *Ulmus parvifolia 'Drake'*

Tropicals

CENTURY PLANT *Agave americana*

This large, fleshy succulent requires many years to mature, flowers only once, then dies; suckers may then result.

When the plant is 10+ years old, a 20′+ (6m+) branched flower stalk produces yellowish green flowers.

Leaves grow from a basal rosette to 5′ (1.5m) long and nearly 10″ (25.5cm) wide. Curved, grayish in color, the leaves have dangerous spines. Some cultivars may have yellow edges and a yellow central band or stripes. *Agave attenuata,* an alternate choice, is smaller, globose and without spines.

Soil: The plant does best in a sandy to sandy loam soil with good drainage.

Light: Prefers full sun or light shade and does not tolerate salt spray.

Uses: Century plant makes a unique specimen or may be used for pot culture. Keep away from traffic or play areas.

QUEEN PALM *Arecastrum romanzoffianum*

Arecastrum romanzoffianum is a rapid-growing palm with a bold, straight trunk that reaches 50′ (15m) at maturity.

The 10-15′ (3-4.5m) long, arching leaves are a feathery, glossy bright green. Because of their size, they are subject to breakage in high winds.

Soil: Plant in a rich, well-drained soil that has a good moisture-holding capacity. If organic matter is low, mix one-half the top soil from the hole with equal amounts of peat moss, compost or muck.

Light: Plant in full sun.

Uses: This palm makes an excellent accent, specimen or street tree.

QUEEN PALM *Arecastrum romanzoffianum*

BAMBOO *Bambusa spp.*

Bambusa spp. are clumping, evergreen grass plants with woody stems. They send up closely spaced new shoots from underground rhizomes.

Bambusa glaucescens 'Fernleaf', FERNLEAF BAMBOO (main illustration), has ½″ (1.3cm) in diameter stems, reaches 6-10′ (1.8-3m) in height and forms a 10-20′ (3-6m) wide clump. The closely spaced, fine-textured leaves give the plant its fernlike appearance. Leaf color is deep green on top with silver-blue underneath.

Bambusa oldhamii, OLDHAM BAMBOO (shown in the inset), has 3″ (8cm) in diameter stems, reaches 15-25′ (4.5-7.5m) in height and forms a 20-40′ (6-12m) wide clump.Dense green foliage graces the pendulous branches.

Soil: Plant in a rich, well-drained soil that is high in organic matter. Condition with peat moss or compost if necessary.

Light: Position in full sun.

Pruning: To limit lateral spread, insert a shovel 12″ (30cm) deep into the soil, and make a narrow trench around the circumference of a clump. Be sure to sever unwanted, expanding rhizomes. New shoots may be broken off as they appear aboveground, preventing resprouting.

Uses: Use 'Fernleaf' as a group planting, hedge/screen or ground cover. Use *B. oldhamii* as a large background, mass planting or large screen/windbreak.

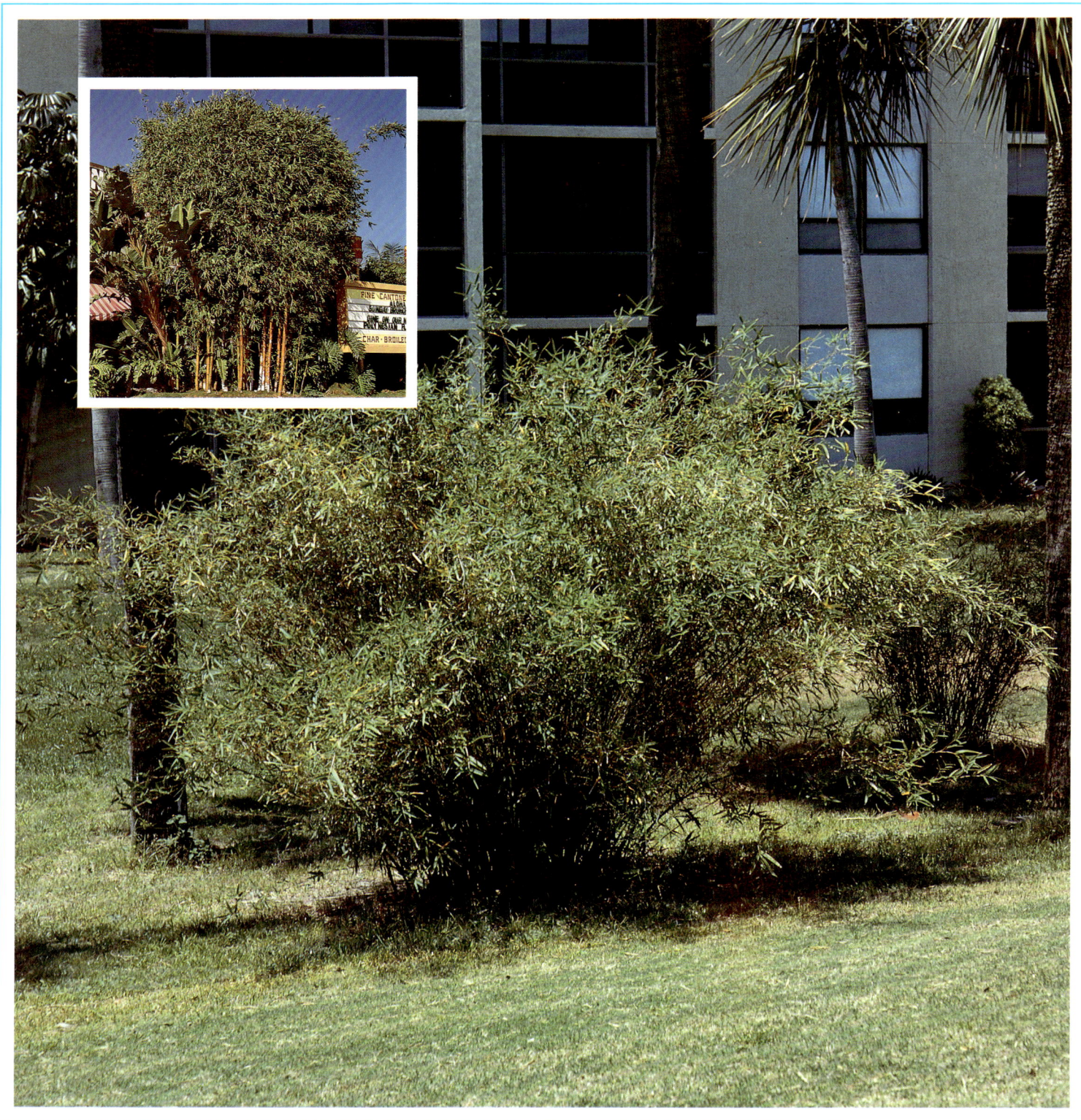

This large, tree-like plant has a tall trunk which grows to 30′ (9m) and a base which becomes a swollen, woody mass with age.

Panicles of small, inconspicuous whitish flowers may appear on very old trees.

Arching, pendulous 4-6′ (1.2-1.8m) green leaves form a rosette at branch ends.

Soil: Plant in good well-drained garden soil where half of the top soil from the hole has been given equal amounts of peat, compost or muck. Mulch around the plant with leaves, straw or compost. Water daily for several weeks, then water and fertilize regularly.

Light: It needs full sun. If transplanting from indoors for winter, gradually increase sun and cooler temperatures.

Uses: This palm makes an excellent accent, specimen or natural planting.

Butia capitata is a short, stocky, slow-growing palm which eventually reaches 10-20′ (3-6m) in height. The thick trunk is covered with persistent leafbases and the foliage extends in a graceful arch.

Very small inconspicuous flowers are yellow to red. The plant also produces a small orange fruit with edible pulp.

Bluish gray and silvery leaves are gracefully arched.

Soil: This palm is very hardy and will grow on a wide range of well-drained soils; feed and water it moderately.

Light: The plant needs full sun or light shade if not in inland areas.

Uses: Plant as an attractive accent or specimen.

EUROPEAN FAN PALM *Chamaerops humilis*

This slow-growing, extremely hardy palm grows in clusters of rough, fibrous stems to about 5′ (1.5m).

The bluish green 3′ (90cm) wide leaves extend from a compact crown at the end of each trunk. giving a fan-shaped appearance.

Soil: Plant this palm in any good garden soil that is well drained. It will tolerate mild drought once established.

Light: It will do well in sun or partial shade and is tolerant of wind.

Uses: The clumping nature of this palm makes it well suited for use as a screen. Accent or foundation planting would also be an attractive option. Good for informal hedge. Commonly used in tubs for patio.

289

CANE PALM *Chrysalidocarpus lutescens (Areca lutescens)* Zone: 10

This beautiful feather palm matures at only 20' (6m), and has multiple trunks that give a clumping effect. It is one of the most beautiful small palms.

The long, yellowish green leaves give a graceful, tropical effect.

Soil: Plant in a medium-coarse to medium textured, well-drained soil. Give moderate water during dry periods.

Light: Position in full sun near the coast or partial shade inland.

Uses: Use as a tropical accent, specimen or patio planting.

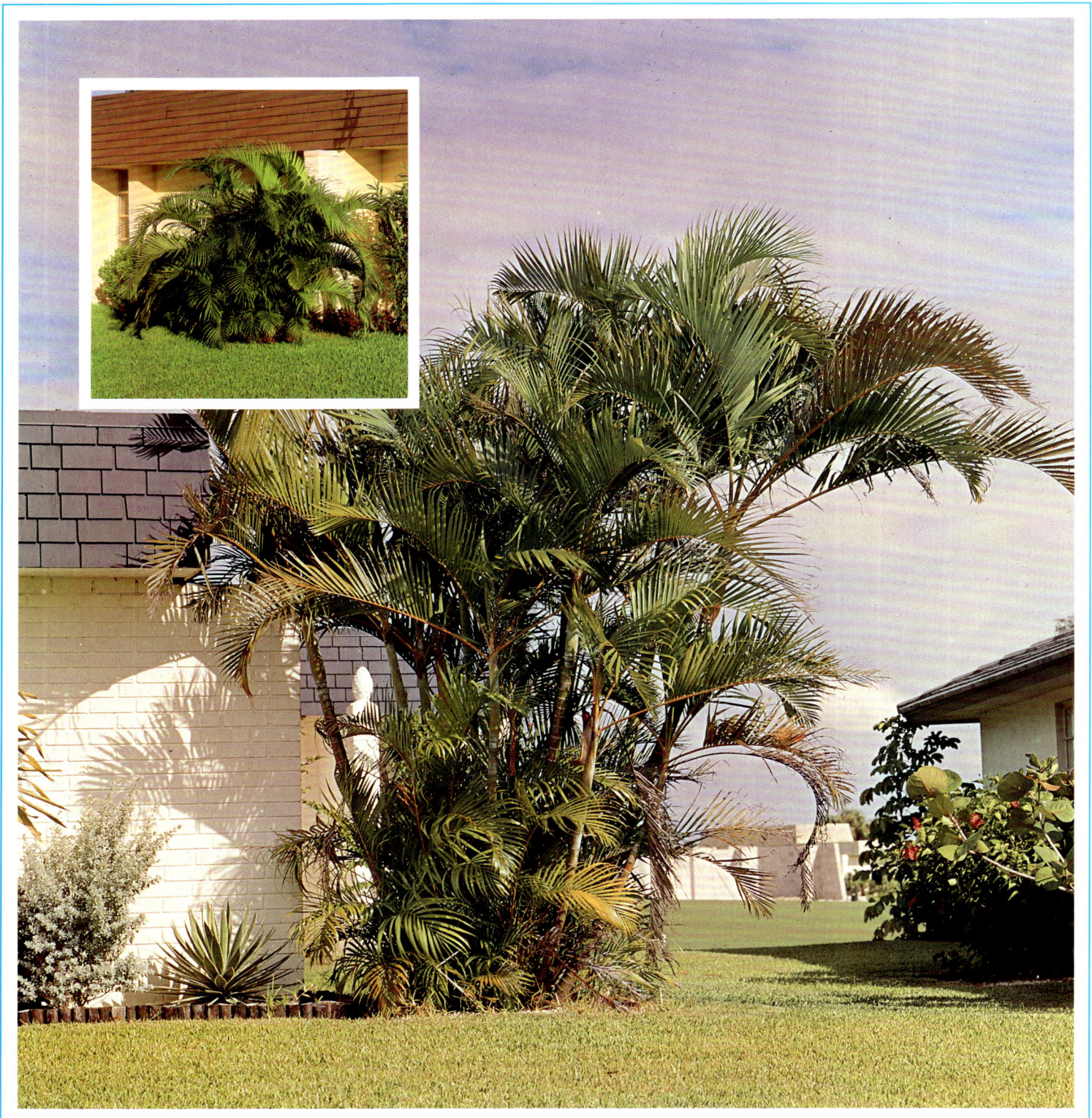

SILVER PALM *Coccothrinax alta*

Coccothrinax alta is a slow-growing, slender, solitary palm that grows to 30' (9m) in height. The silvery leaves are often used for making hats and baskets.

Large, deeply divided leaves have about 40 individual segments. The leafblades are light green on top with distinctive silver tones underneath.

Soil: Plant in a rich, well-drained soil with a moderate to high moisture-holding capacity. Condition the soil with compost or peat moss if necessary.

Light: Position in partial shade.

Uses: Use this stunning palm as a specimen for a tropical effect.

BLUE DRACAENA *Cordyline indivisa*

This slender, palmlike shrub or tree grows to 25' (7.5m) high with a single trunk which is often forked at the crown.

White flowers in 4' (1.2m) long clusters blossom in early spring.

Huge 6' (1.8m) long, flat green leaves extend from the crown; upper leaves are erect and lower ones are arching.

Soil: Plant in deep, medium-coarse to medium textured soil as cordylines extend a long "taproot". They like plenty of moisture but will tolerate some drought when established.

Light: It needs full sun and is suitable for seaside plantings.

Uses: This shrub or tree makes a fine accent, specimen, screen or border planting. It is suitable as a container planting as well.

DRACAENA CONGESTA *Cordyline stricta*

Zone: 10

Cordyline stricta has slender stems which either initiate from the base or branch upward from the lower part of a central stem. It will mature at about 15′ (4.5m) high.

Showy lavender flowers blossom in long clusters in the spring.

Narrow 2′ (60cm) long, sword-shaped, dark green leaves have a reddish tinge when young.

Soil: Plant in deep, medium-coarse to medium textured soil as *cordylines* extend a long "taproot". They like plenty of moisture but will tolerate some drought when established.

Light: It needs full sun and is suitable for seaside plantings.

Pruning: To keep lower and more compact cut long canes to the ground; new shoots will then replace them.

Uses: This would be particularly suited to narrow background areas or as an accent or specimen.

293

Cycas revoluta is a slow-growing, primitive plant related to conifers, which grows to about 10' (3m). The overall form resembles a pineapple plant.

Stiff, slightly arching, 2-3' (.6-.9m) green leaves with sharp pointed leaflets come out of a rosette at the top of a stout, palmlike trunk.

Soil: This is the hardiest cycad and it will thrive in most any soil with moderate moisture.

Light: It does best in partial shade.

Uses: It is excellent for a tropical effect as a container or patio planting, or it would be suitable as an accent, foundation, hedge or screen.

DRAGON TREE *Dracaena draco*

Zone: 10

This palmlike plant grows slowly to about 25' (7.5m) with an equal spread. Usually cultured as a houseplant, it makes an interesting and unusual specimen in an outdoor setting.

Greenish white flowers form in clusters at branch ends. Bright orange berries follow the blossoms.

Two foot long, sword-shaped leaves reach out and upward from a wide trunk.

Soil: Plant in deep, medium-coarse to medium textured soil. Dracaenas like plenty of moisture but will tolerate some drought when established.

Light: Plant in full sun and protect from wind.

Pruning: Trim off bare flower stems after blossoms drop.

Uses: Good for accent, specimen or as a traditional container planting.

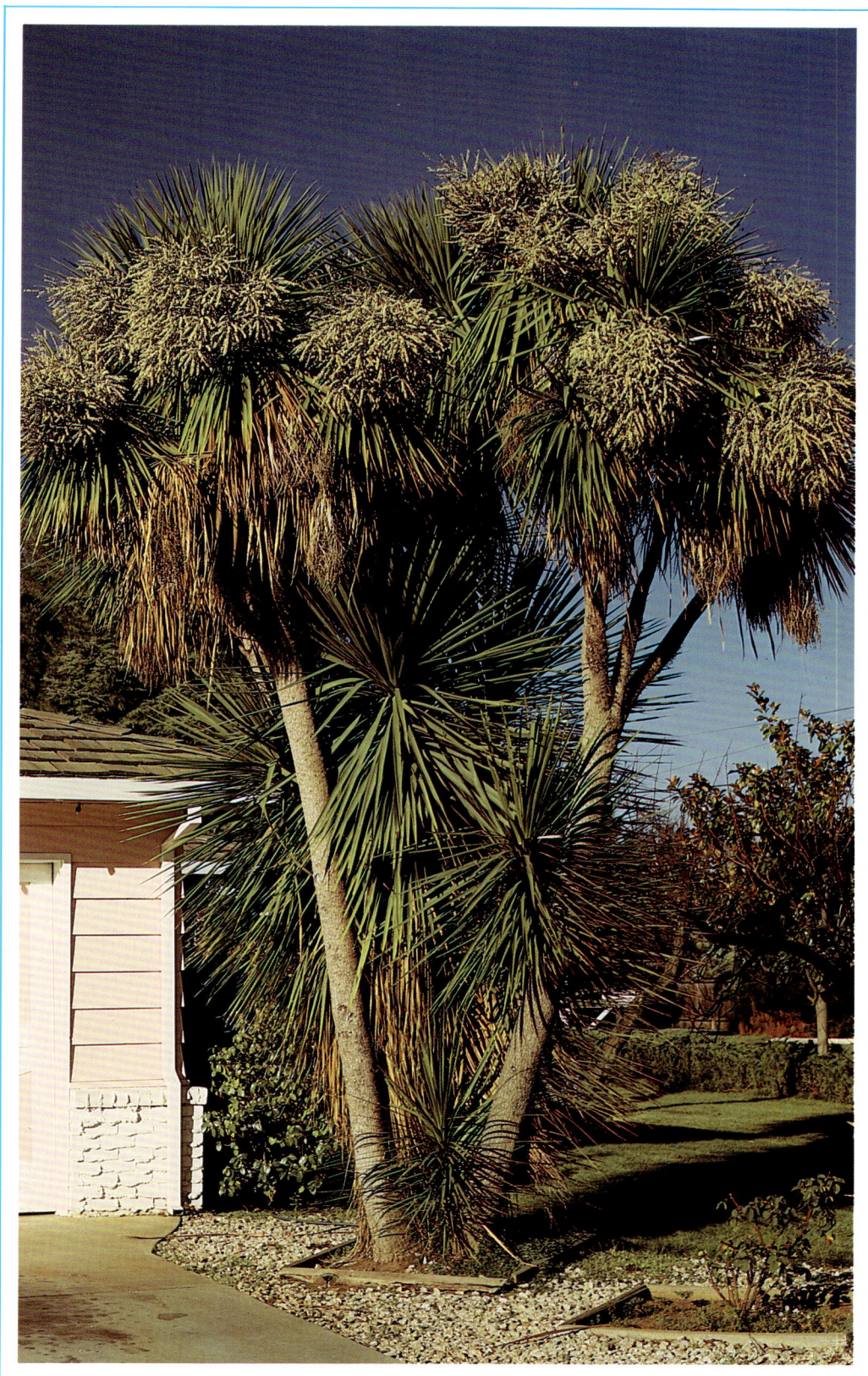

MADAGASCAR DRAGON TREE *Dracaena*

Dracaena is a slow-growing, palmlike plant with a slender, branching trunk that grows to 15′ (4.5m). Each cane (trunk) is topped by a dense terminal rosette of thick, fleshy leaves. The canes grow in a twisted fashion which adds interest.

The long, linear 16″ (40cm) leaves are a deep olive green.

Soil: Plant in deep, medium-coarse to medium textured soil. Dracaenas like plenty of moisture but will tolerate some drought when established.

Light: Plant in full sun and protect from wind.

Pruning: If this plant gets excessively tall, remove the crown and simply re-root it. New crowns initiate from the cut surface of the old stem.

Uses: Good for accent, specimen or as a traditional container planting.

BANANA *Musa spp.*

Musa x *paradisiaca* has many ornamental and edible forms. *Musa* x *paradisiaca 'Seminifera' (featured here) grows to 20'* (6m) or more with 9' (2.7m) bright green leaves. The stunning flower stalk has silvery purple bracts. Seedy, inedible fruit may be produced.

Musa acuminata 'Dwarf Cavendish' (shown in the inset) grows 6-8' (1.8-2.4m) tall and has leaves 5' (1.5m) long by 2' (60cm) wide. Yellow flowers appear in large clusters with reddish to dark purple bracts. Six-inch (15cm) bananas may be produced.

Soil: Plant in a rich, well-drained soil, high in organic matter. Feed and water regularly. Protect from wind as the huge leaves tear easily.

Light: Position in full sun.

Pruning: *Musa* produces offsets from the parent plant which may be replanted to form clumps. Simply break them off at their respective bases.

Uses: Use as a quick, tropical accent, specimen or shade plant.

DWARF DATE PALM *Phoenix roebelenii*

This small-scale palm has one stem with curved leaves extending gracefully to form a dense crown. Growth is very slow, to about 6′ (1.8m) at maturity.

The leaves (fronds) are a narrow, feathery dark green.

Soil: Plant in a deep, medium-coarse to medium textured soil. *Phoenix* likes plenty of moisture but will tolerate some drought when it is established.

Light: Full sun to partial shade.

Uses: Use as an accent, specimen or as a traditional container planting.

SOLITAIRE PALM *Ptychosperma elegans (Seaforthia elegans)*

Zone: 10

This handsome, solitary feather palm has a graceful, slender trunk with 6-8 pinnate, 3-6′ (.9-1.8m) long fronds rising from the center top. Mature height is 20′ (6m).

Fragrant white flowers are followed by small, bright red fruit.

The fronds have about 20 pairs of bright green pinnae (leaflets) which are jagged at the top.

Soil: Plant in a rich, well-drained soil that has a good moisture-holding capacity. If organic matter is low, mix one-half the top soil from the hole with an equal amount of peat moss, compost or muck. Give ample water.

Light: Position in partial shade.

Uses: Use this beautiful palm for tropical effect as an accent, street or lawn tree.

SOLITAIRE PALM

299

LADY PALM *Rhapis excelsa*

Zones: 9 & 10

Rhapis excelsa is an upright palm with long, slender, attractive "furry" canes that reach to 6-8′ (1.8-2.4m).

Clusters of delicate fronds at various levels, give a delicate, layered look to the plant.

Soil: Plant in a rich, well-drained soil that has a good moisture-holding capacity. If organic matter is low, mix one-half the topsoil from the hole with equal amounts of peat moss, compost or muck.

Light: Plant in sun or light shade. It tolerates temperature extremes from freezing to 100°F (38°C). Fertilize and water well if bright sun yellows the leaves. *Rhapis* is moderately salt tolerant.

Uses: This palm is excellent as a barrier, accent or foundation planting for large buildings. It is also well suited as a container planting for a patio.

Roystonea spp. are fast-growing, highly ornamental palms that are striking along streets, boulevards or when planted in groups.

Roystonea elata, FLORIDA ROYAL PALM (main illustration), is a stately feather palm that has a smooth gray trunk and rises over 100' (30m) high. Arching, plumelike 20' (6m) long, glossy green leaves rise out of a dense crown, and are arranged in several rows. Fragrant flowers bloom in a long inflorescense (upper right), and are followed by round, 1" (2.5cm) fruit.

Roystonea regia, CUBAN ROYAL PALM (lower right), has an erect, gray trunk and reaches over 60' (18m)

high. Gracefully arching, 6-10' (1.8-3m) long, feathery fronds are bright green, prominently ribbed and arranged in two planes on either side of the center axis.

Soil: Plant in a rich, well-drained soil high in organic matter. Condition the soil with leaf mold, compost or muck if necessary.

Light: Plant in full sun or partial shade. These palms are resistant to wind and salt spray.

Pruning: Support the trunks of these palms with braces to prevent swaying during heavy winds. Do not attach braces to the trunk with nails.

Uses: Use as a stunning street, park or lawn specimen.

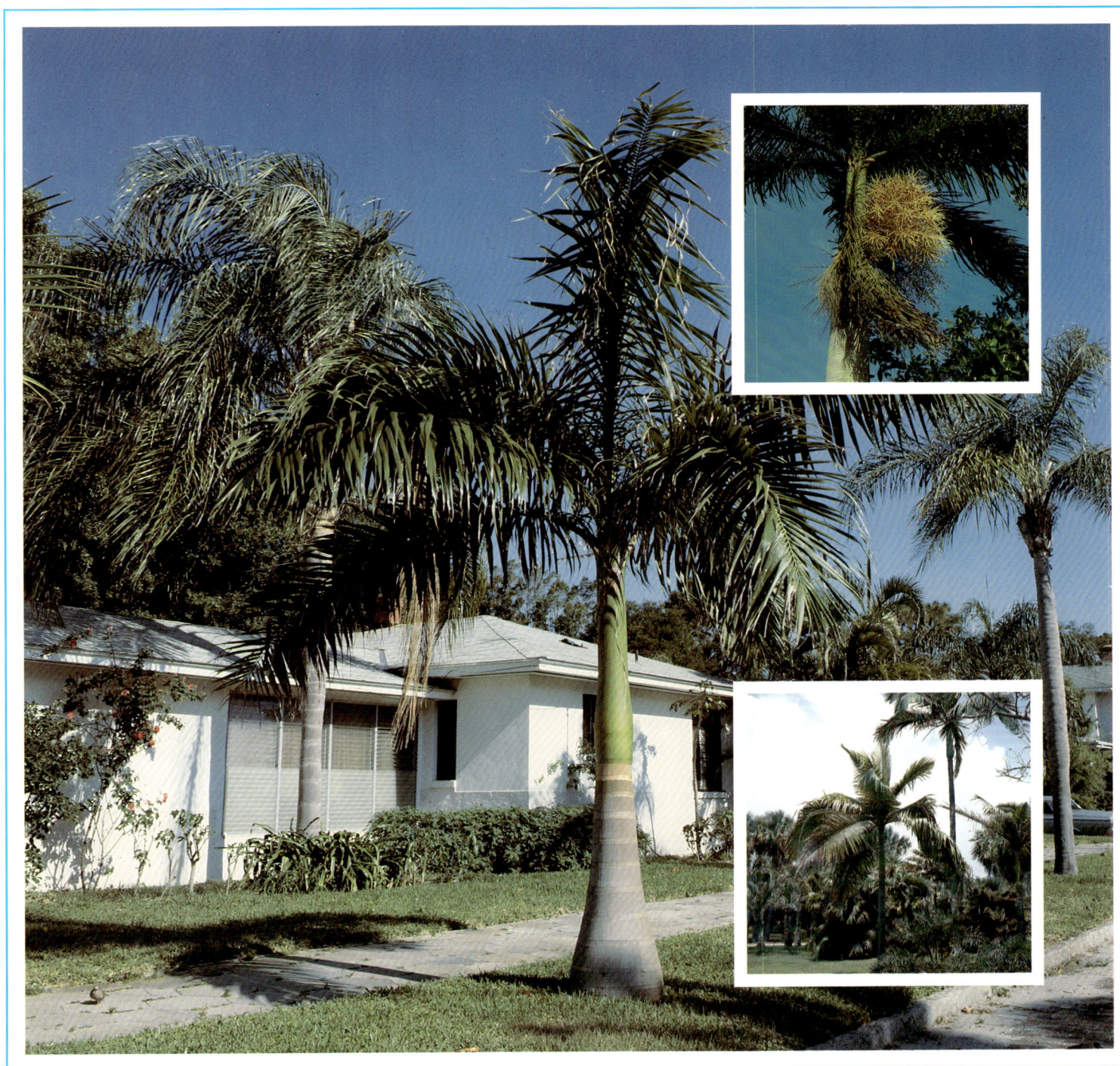

HAWAIIAN ELF SCHEFFLERA *Schefflera arboricola*

Schefflera arboricola is a large, fast-growing, tropical-looking evergreen tree or shrub. It will reach 20′ (6m) or more in height with an equal or greater spread. It is easily pruned to a smaller size.

Yellowish flowers in 1′ (30cm), flattened clusters turn bronze with age.

The dark green, leathery leaves have 3″ (8cm) long leaflets which become wider toward rounded tips. Plant the stems at an angle and the plant will have an attractive multitiered effect.

Soil: Plant in a rich, moist, well-drained soil with a high organic matter content. Condition with peat moss, compost or muck if necessary. Allow the soil to become moderately dry, then water thoroughly.

Light: Position in full sun or partial shade. *Schefflera* thrives in areas of high humidity.

Pruning: Cut out overlong stems. To improve form, cut back overgrown plants to the ground.

Uses: Use as a striking tropical accent or specimen.

BIRD OF PARADISE *Streletzia reginae*

This clumping, compact tropical plant grows to about 5' (1.5m) high and produces an incredible flower display.

The orange, blue and white flowers on long, stiff stems look like tropical birds.

Large, bluish gray leaves have an attractive red midrib.

Soil: Plant in a good, well-drained garden soil, high in organic matter with moderate moisture-holding capacity.

Add peat moss or leaf mold to improve the soil. It needs frequent and heavy feedings.

Light: Plant in full sun in coastal areas and in filtered light in hot inlands.

Pruning: Remove faded blooms.

Uses: *Streletzia* makes an outstanding specimen or accent planting. It is equally attractive hanging over a wall or bank.

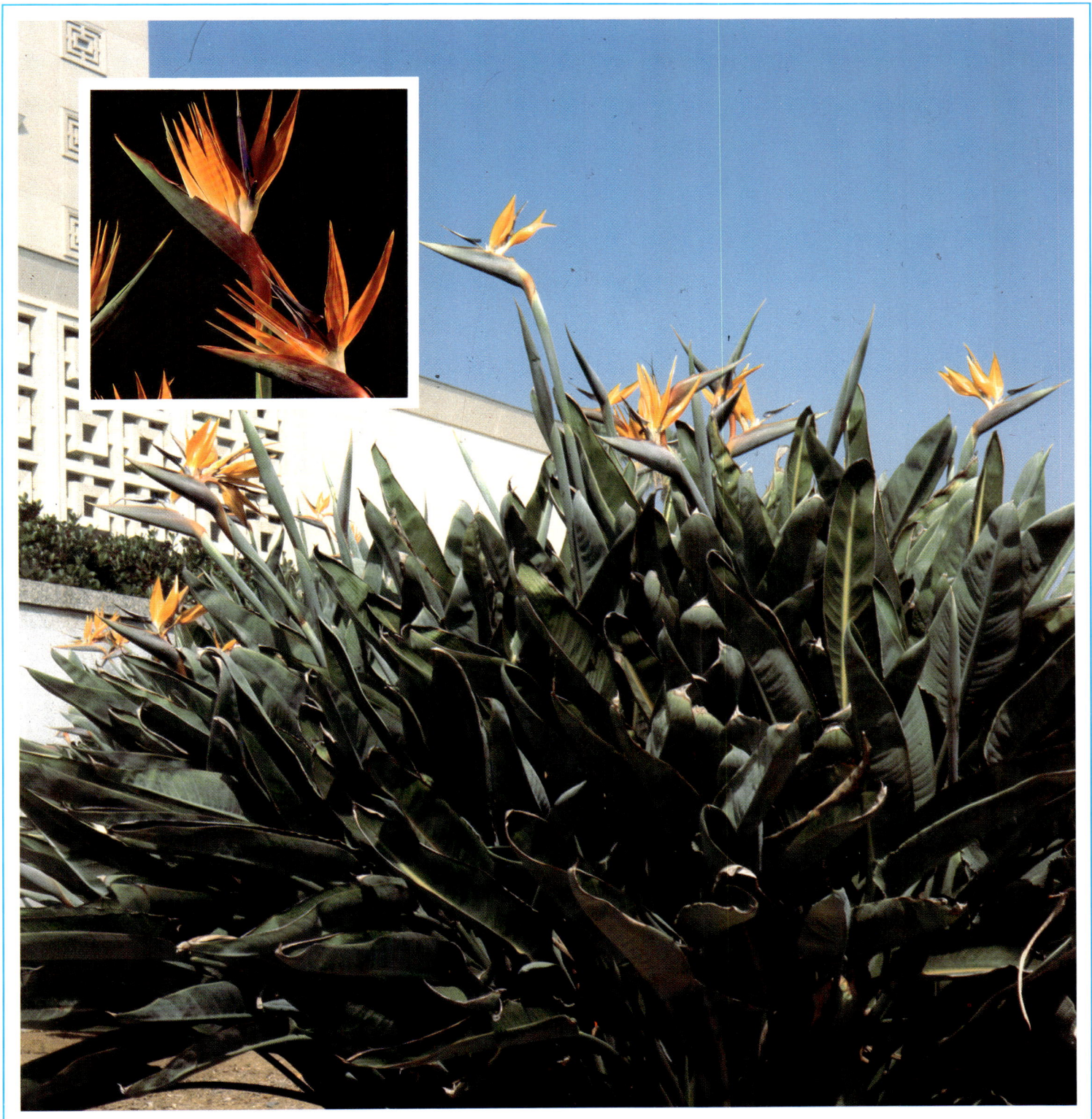

303

Microcoelum weddellianum is an excellent small palm with a straight, slender single stem. Mature height is only 7-8′ (2.1-2.4m).

The graceful, yellow-green leaves are feather-shaped. This palm is highly salt tolerant and is an excellent choice for along the coast.

Soil: Plant in a medium-coarse to medium textured, well-drained soil. Give moderate water during dry periods.

Light: Position in full sun along the coast or in partial shade inland.

Uses: Use as an attractive tropical accent, specimen or patio planting.

HARDY FAN LEAF PALM or
CALIFORNIA FAN PALM *Washingtonia filifera*

Zones: 9 & 10

This erect, single trunk, broad-crown palm grows to 60-80′ (18-24m). The leaf bases give the trunk a shaggy appearance.

Large, bright green, fan-shaped leaves on long stems hang down, tapering in toward the stout trunk.

Soil: *Washingtonia* does well in most well-drained soils. Mix topsoil with an equal part of peat moss or compost. Mulch by spreading leaves, straw or other organic material to reduce soil temperature, conserve moisture and add organic matter. Feed and water regularly.

Light: Plant in a sunny location.

Pruning: Support the trunk with braces to protect against strong winds. This palm is moderately salt tolerant.

Uses: Use as a street tree, park specimen, in a group or as a container planting when young.

Washingtonia robusta is a slender, tapering, single trunk palm that grows to 100′ (30m). The trunk of older plants has a natural curve.

Large, bright green, 4-6′ (1.2-1.8m) across leaves unfold on medium long, red-streaked leaf stalks which come out of a compact crown.

Soil: *Washingtonia* does well in most well-drained soils. Mix topsoil with equal parts of peat moss or compost. Mulch by spreading leaves, straw or other organic material to reduce soil temperature, conserve moisture and add organic matter. Feed and water regularly.

Light: Plant in a sunny location.

Pruning: Support the trunk with braces to protect against strong winds. This palm is moderately salt tolerant.

Uses: Use as a street tree, park specimen, in a group or as a container planting when young.

SPANISH BAYONET   *Yucca aloifolia*

Yucca aloifolia is a perennial plant with slow growth to about 10' (3m). The trunk may be single or branched, giving a layered effect.

White flowers up to 4" (10cm) across, bloom on 2' (60cm) spikes. Some flowers have petals tinged with purple.

The sharp-pointed, 2½' (75cm) long leaves are an intense dark green. The spiny tips are a hazard in areas of heavy traffic.

Soil: Plant in a well-drained soil. It will accept drought once established. Regular garden watering is suitable.

Light: This yucca does best in full sun.

Pruning: Remove faded flower stalks.

Uses: Use as a striking specimen among softer-leaved, tropical plants.

GIANT YUCCA   *Yucca elephantipes (Y. gigantea)*

Zones: 9 & 10

Yucca elephantipes is a big-scale perennial plant usually with several trunks, and reaches 15-30' (4.5-9m) at maturity.

Large spikes of creamy white flowers appear in the spring.

The 4' (1.2m) long, rich, dark green leaves are not spine tipped.

Soil: Position in a rich, well-drained soil, and give it plenty of water.

Light: Plant in full sun except in hot, inland areas with long dry spells. Give some mid-day sun protection in this case.

Pruning: Remove faded flower spikes.

Uses: Use this yucca as a large specimen or accent with or without other large-scale foliage plants.

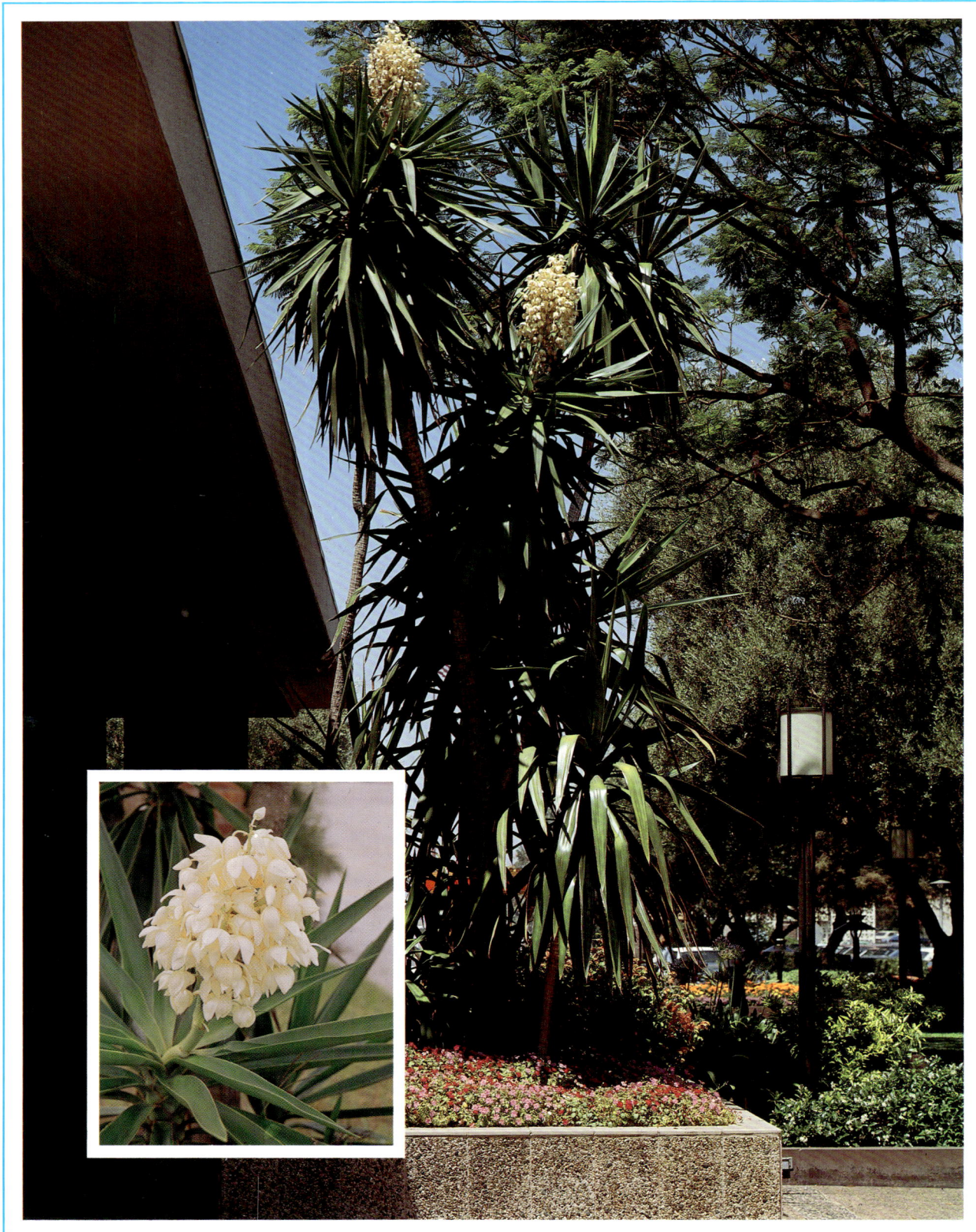

ADAM'S NEEDLE *Yucca filamentosa*

Zones: 6-10

This perennial plant is native to the southeastern United States. It is extremely hardy in the colder areas.

Lightly fragrant, white flowers bloom in tall, narrow, branching clusters.

The stiff, 2' (60cm) narrow leaves have long, loose fibers at the edges.

Soil: Plant in a well-drained soil. It will accept drought once established. Regular garden watering is suitable.

Light: Plant in full sun.

Pruning: Remove faded flower stalks.

Uses: Use as a striking specimen among softer-leaved, tropical plants.

Zamia pumila is a low-growing, spreading, cycadlike plant (primitive conebearing coniferlike plant) with a short trunk. Mature height is 4-6′ (1.2-1.8m), and spread is equal or greater than the height.

Twisting, twining, 3-4′ (1-1.2m) long leaves on prickly stalks have leathery, overlapping leaflets. Male and female woody cones are produced.

Soil: Plant in a fertile, well-drained soil. Feed and water regularly. *Zamia* tolerates a high soil pH (7.0 or greater).

Light: Plant in full sun or partial shade.

Pruning: Prune to desired size and shape.

Uses: Use as a unique, tropical-appearing accent or specimen.

Vines

CORAL VINE or QUEEN'S WREATH *Antigonon leptopus* Zones: 9 & 10

Antigonon leptopus is a climbing, deciduous or evergreen vine with tendrils that grow to 40′ (12m) and give an open, airy appearance.

Bright rose-pink, 1½″ (3.7cm) long flowers appear all along trailing stems from mid-summer through fall.

Dark green, 4″ (10cm), heart-shaped leaves persist in warm winter areas.

Soil: Plant in a medium-coarse to medium textured, well-drained soil. Mulch roots for winter protection below 25°F (-4°C).

Light: Position in full sun.

Pruning: Provide support as desired for specific location.

Uses: Use on a trellis, wall, eave or fence.

BOUGAINVILLEA   *Bougainvillea spp.*

Zone: 10

Bougainvillea is usually an evergreen, shrubby, climbing vine, but it may have a low-growing, bushy habit.

Spectacular blooms of showy bracts in large panicles may have single or double forms. Brilliant colors may be yellow, orange, red, pink or purple. Planting different varieties ensures a floral show for almost the entire year. The variety 'Barbara Karst' is featured here.

The narrow, oval leaves are usually medium green, but may be variegated.

Soil: Plant in a loose, fertile, well-drained soil, high in organic matter. The slightest disturbance to the roots will kill the plant so to plant it in the original container, cut out side slits and remove the bottom if possible.

Light: *Bougainvillea* thrives in full sun.

Pruning: Provide a sturdy support and anchor shoots all along their physical structure. Delicate leaves and blossoms are injured by strong wind.

Uses: Use as a stunning bank, wall or ground cover.

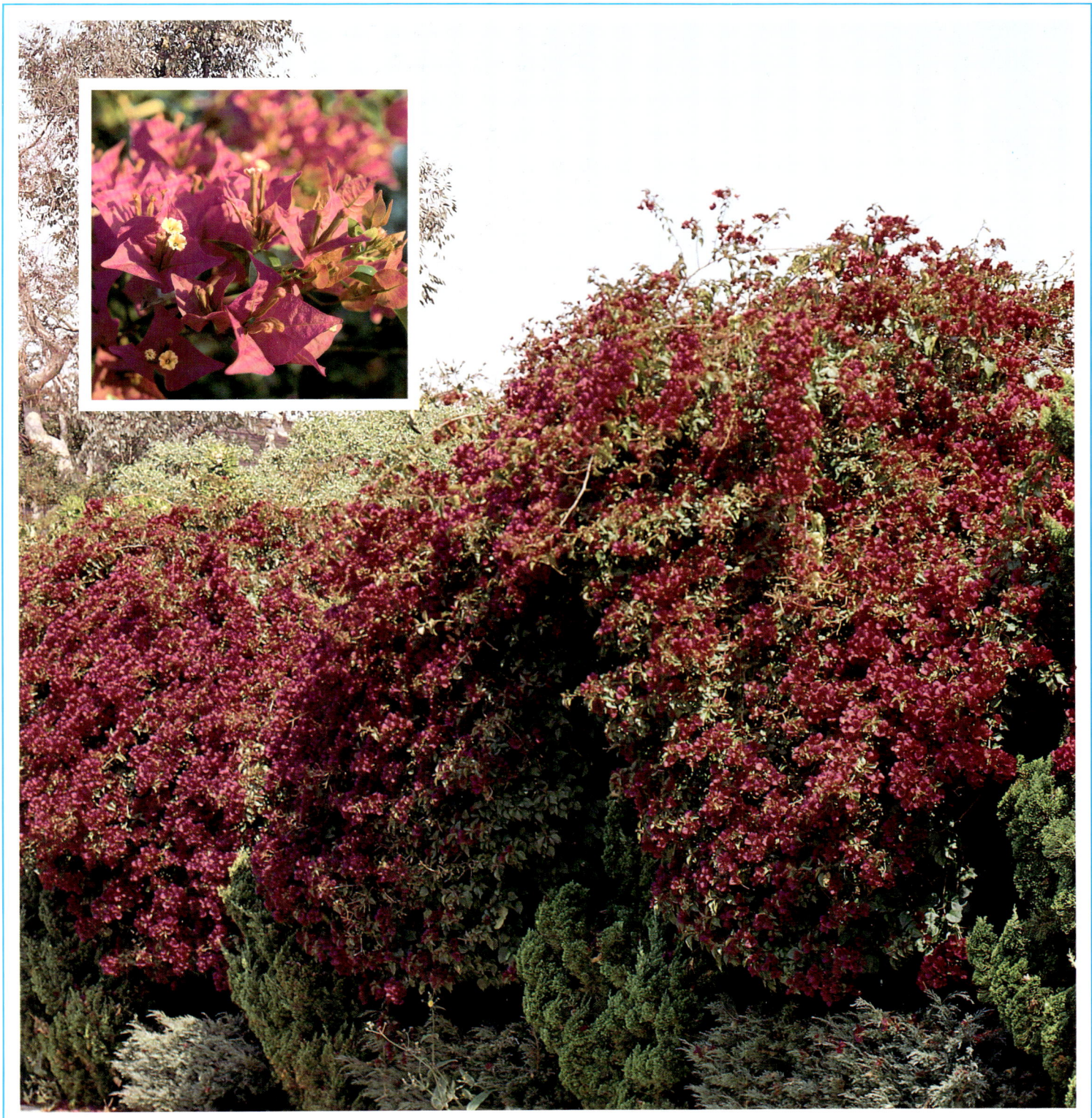

TRUMPET CREEPER or TRUMPET VINE   *Campsis radicans (Bignonia radicans)*   Zones: 6-10

Campsis radicans is a vigorous, deciduous vine that clings to wood, brick and masonry surfaces with aerial rootlets. Rapid growth takes it to 40′ (12m) or more.

Three-inch (8cm) long, tubular flowers are orange with scarlet lobes, and grow in showy clusters of six to twelve.

The medium green, strongly toothed leaves are divided into nine to eleven, 2½″ (6cm) leaflets.

Soil: Plant in any well-drained garden soil. Give moderate water.

Light: Position in full sun.

Pruning: Provide strong support. Thin old plants that are leggy and top heavy.

Uses: Use on a trellis, wall, bank or fence.

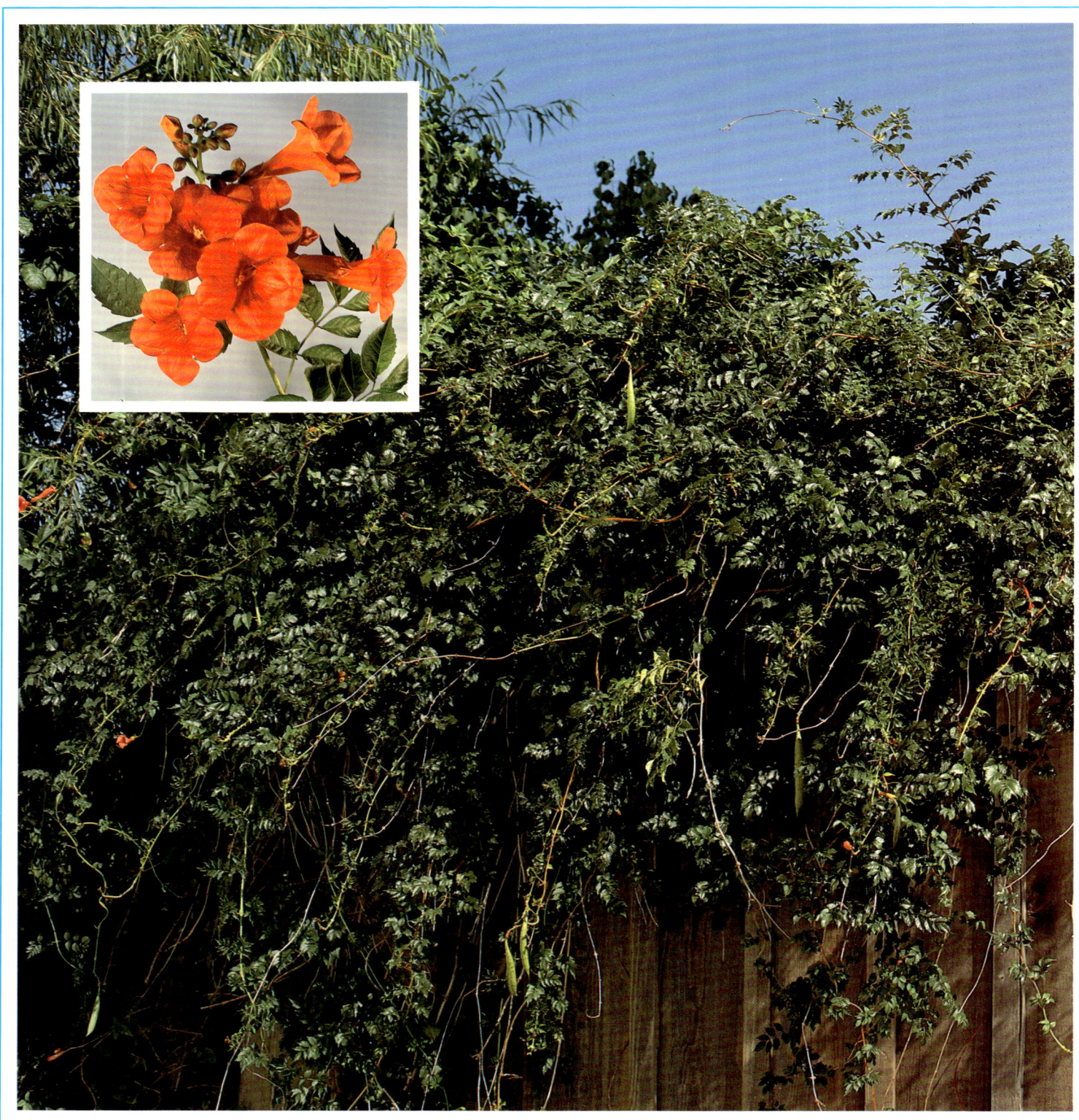

ORIENTAL BITTERSWEET *Celastrus orbiculatus*

Zones: 6-8

Celastrus orbiculatus is a hardy, twining vine with rope-like branches. It has a spectacular display of fruit clusters consisting of orange capsules that split to show red-coated seeds. Total length may be 40′ (12m).

The showy, yellow and orange fruit are prized for indoor arrangements. The fruit is not eaten by birds so it persists into winter.

The 4″ (10cm) leaves are round and toothed.

Soil: *Celastrus* thrives in most any moderately- or well-drained soil. Give moderate watering and feeding.

Light: Position in full sun.

Pruning: Support the stem and branches. Prune out tangled shoots. Cut out old fruiting branches in the winter.

Uses: Use this vine to cover walls, trellises, fences or as a ground cover.

JACKMAN CLEMATIS *Clematis x jackmanii hybrids*

These fast-growing, deciduous vines are natural climbers with twining leaf stalks. Rapid growth will produce 10′ (3m) or more in one season.

Showy flowers are produced in summer and fall on the current season's growth. The large, flat blossoms may be up to 10″ (25cm) across, and rich purple, rose-pink or burgundy-red in color.

The dark green leaves are divided into leaflets that twist and curve to provide support for the plant.

Soil: Plant in a moderately-coarse, moist, slightly alkaline (pH 7.0) soil. The species is shallow rooted and should be left undisturbed by cultivation. Protect roots and lower stems from heat and mechanical damage.

Light: Position in light shade. Roots must be in a cool position. Blossoms need protection from midday sun.

Pruning: Prune newly planted plants to 6-9″ (15-23cm) above the ground. Prune established vines to the ground when dormant.

Uses: Use on a wall, trellis or porch. *Clematis* makes a lovely container plant for patio or balcony. It would be very showy back of a shrub border and roots would remain shaded and cool.

CANDIDA CLEMATIS   *Clematis lanuginosa 'Candida'*

Clematis lanuginosa 'Candida' is a showy, deciduous, vine with twining branches and clinging leaf stalks. 'Candida' grows to less than 10′ (3m), but produces an incredible floral display.

Large, 6-9″ (15-23cm), white flowers bloom on old and new wood in June in cool climates, or in March or April in warm climates.

The leaves are an oval, pointed, smooth edged dark green.

Soil: Plant in a moderately-coarse, moist, slightly alkaline (above pH 7.0) soil. The species is shallow rooted and should be left undisturbed by cultivation. Protect roots and lower stems from heat and mechanical damage.

Light: Position in light shade. Roots must be in a cool position. Blossoms need protection from midday sun.

Pruning: Prune in early spring to remove dead or non-productive shoots. Cut back spent flowered portions for another crop the same season.

Uses: Use as a stunning accent or specimen vine in a small area.

Ficus pumila is an evergreen vine that climbs and attaches itself to wood, masonry or metal. Though growth is slow in youth, the plant has almost unlimited size potential, and may cover a very large area by a mature age.

Tiny, delicate, heart-shaped leathery green leaves bear no resemblance to other *Ficus* species.

Soil: *Ficus* thrives in a rich, moist, but well-drained soil. Beautiful foliage results with frequent, light feeding. Allow the soil to become moderately dry, then water thoroughly.

Light: Plant in sun or partial shade. Do not plant on a hot south or west wall, or it will turn yellow and fail to climb.

Pruning: Control vigorous expansion by removing fruiting stems occasionally.

Uses: This vine is excellent for covering masonry walls.

CAROLINA JESSAMINE *Gelsemium sempervirens*

Gelsemium sempervirens is a twining, shrubby evergreen vine that grows to about 20′ (6m).

A profusion of fragrant yellow, trumpet-shaped flowers bloom early spring and summer.

Light green, 1-4″ (2.5-10cm) long leaves grace long, slender branches. ALL PLANT PARTS ARE POISONOUS!!.

Soil: Plant in any well-drained garden soil. Water regularly and feed during bloom season.

Light: Position in full sun.

Pruning: Support and secure on a firm structure. Slender branch ends will sway beautifully in the wind when left free.

Uses: Use this vine on a trellis, wall, fence, porch, bank or on the side of a house.

STAR JASMINE *Jasminum multiflorum (J. pubescens)* Zone: 10

Jasminum multiflorum is a shrubby, evergreen vine which can reach a height of 20' (6m) when climbing a support. Young leaves and twining shoots are densely pubescent.

Pure white, star shaped flowers are about 1" wide and are borne in clusters on the tips of side branches. Flowers may be fragrant or odorless. Blossoms appear throughout the year, though the most profuse blooming occurs in summer and fall.

Leaves are dark green and 1-3" (2.5-8cm) long.

Soil: Plant in a well drained garden soil which has been enriched with compost, leaf mold, or peat moss.

Light: Position in full sun or partial shade.

Pruning: Prune in late fall to promote fullness or to shape.

Uses: Use as a vine trained to a fence or trellis, as a groundcover, or prune into a shrub (as shown here).

CHRISTINE LANTANA

Lantana camara 'Christine'

Zones: 9 & 10

Lantana camara 'Christine' is an evergreen vining shrub with coarse, upright growth to 3-4′ (.9-1.2m). Masses of colorful blooms are produced all year long.

Stunning cerise-pink flowers bloom in 1-2″ (2.5-5cm) clusters.

The leaves are a coarse textured, finely toothed, rich green.

Soil: Plant in any moderately- or well-drained garden soil.

Allow soil to become moderately dry, then water thoroughly. Feed lightly.

Light: Lantana does best in full sun. It is subject to mildew when shaded.

Pruning: Prune dead wood in early spring.

Uses: Use as a bank or wall cover. Lantana is an excellent soil binder where erosion could be a problem. It also makes an effective ground cover.

RADIATION LANTANA *Lantana camara 'Radiation'*

Lantana camara 'Radiation' is an evergreen vining shrub with coarse, upright growth to 3-4' (.9-1.2m). Masses of colorful blooms are produced all year long.

Rich orange-red flowers bloom in 1-2" (2.5-5cm) clusters.

The leaves are a coarse-textured, finely toothed rich green.

Soil: Plant in any moderately- or well-drained garden soil. Allow soil to become moderately dry, then water thoroughly. Feed lightly.

Light: Lantana does best in full sun. It is subject to mildew when shaded.

Pruning: Prune dead wood in early spring.

Uses: Use as a bank or wall cover. Lantana is an excellent soil binder where erosion could be a problem. It also makes an effective ground cover.

GOLD FLAME HONEYSUCKLE *Lonicera heckrottii*

This deciduous or semi-deciduous vine or small shrub has vigorous, sprawling growth to 12-15′ (3.6-4.5m). It is one of the most beautiful climbing honeysuckles.

Flowers are 1½″ (3.8cm) long, and open from coral-pink buds. They develop coral-pink outside and bright yellow inside. Profuse clusters of these flowers are stunning from early spring to late fall.

The 2″ (5cm) oval leaves are blue-green.

Soil: Plant in a loose, well-drained garden soil. Give moderate feeding and watering during bloom period.

Light: Position in full sun along the coast or partial shade in hot, dry inland areas.

Pruning: Prune or train to desired size and form.

Uses: This *Lonicera* would be striking on an arbor, wall or along eaves. It can also be used as a shrubby hedge/screen with support.

DROPMORE SCARLET HONEYSUCKLE
Lonicera heckrottii 'Dropmore Scarlet'   Zones: 6-10

'Dropmore Scarlet' is a deciduous or semi-deciduous vine or small shrub with vigorous, sprawling growth to 12-15′ (3.6-4.5m). Like the species, *L. heckrottii* (GOLD FLAME HONEYSUCKLE, p. 322), it is also one of the most beautiful climbing honeysuckles.

Brilliant scarlet tubular flowers bloom in clusters from early spring until late fall.

The oval leaves are medium to dark green.

Soil: Plant in a loose, well-drained garden soil. Give moderate feeding and watering during bloom period.

Light: Position in full sun along the coast or partial shade in hot, dry inland areas.

Pruning: Prune or train to desired size and form.

Uses: This *Lonicera* would be striking on an arbor, wall or along eaves. It can also be used as a shrubby hedge/screen with support.

HALL'S JAPANESE HONEYSUCKLE

Lonicera japonica 'Halliana'

Zones: 6-10

Lonicera japonica 'Halliana' is a vigorous, twining, deciduous or semi-deciduous vine. It will climb to 15' (4.5m) or more and cover about 150 sq. ft. (14 sq. m).

Fragrant pure white to pale yellow flowers bloom all summer.

The oval leaves are deep green.

Soil: Plant in a loose, well-drained garden soil. Give moderate feeding and watering during bloom period.

Light: Position in full sun along the coast or partial shade in hot, dry inland areas.

Pruning: Prune to desired size and shape. Remove old branches.

Uses: Use on a trellis, fence, wall or as a bank/ground cover.

HALL'S JAPANESE HONEYSUCKLE

LATE RED HONEYSUCKLE
or WOODBINE _Lonicera periclymenum var. serotina_

Lonicera periclymenum var. _serotina_ is a shrubby, sprawling climber.

Fragrant dark purple flowers with yellow insides bloom profusely in terminal whorls all summer.

The oval, green leaves are blue-green on the underside.

Soil: Plant in a loose, well-drained garden soil. Give moderate feeding and watering during bloom period.

Light: Position in full sun along the coast or partial shade in hot, dry inland areas.

Pruning: Prune to desired size and shape.

Uses: Use as a bank or wall cover, hedge/screen, or with support, as a shrubby accent/specimen.

BOSTON IVY or JAPANESE CREEPER *Parthenocissus*

This fast-growing, deciduous creeping vine is a natural climber with clinging, rootlike tendrils. The tendrils penetrate the support, and side branches fill out growth to add depth and density. Maximum height can be up to 80′ (25cm).

Fruit are blue-black berries that ripen in fall and are eaten by birds.

The shiny leaves, 8″ (20cm) across, display deep burgundy fall color.

Soil: Plant in a moist, fertile well-drained soil.

Light: Position in full sun or light shade. *Parthenocissus* tolerates urban pollution and seashore conditions.

Uses: Use on walls or trellises. It makes a stunning background for flowering specimens. It is also well suited as a bank or ground cover.

CHINA FLEECE VINE or SILVER LACE VINE   *Polygonum aubertii*   Zones: 6-8

This fast-growing deciduous vine has twining stems and dense growth. It may grow as much as 20-30′ (6-9m) in a single year. If the top is killed by severe frosts, the plant will grow back from roots and flower in one season.

Dense clusters of fluffy, greenish white fragrant flowers bloom in late summer.

The light yellow-green, 2″ (5cm) long leaves are arrowhead shaped.

Soil: Plant in almost any well-drained soil. The plant tolerates poor soil conditions.

Light: *Polygonum* likes full sun. It is drought tolerant and resists insect and disease infestation.

Pruning: Little pruning is needed. Clip overlong shoots if desired.

Uses: Use as an informal vine for thick growth along a fence or on a strong trellis.

JAPANESE WISTERIA *Wisteria floribunda*

Wisteria floribunda is a vigorous growing, woody, twining vine that needs an arbor or fence to provide the best view of incredible, pendulous clusters of showy blooms.

White, lavender, violet, violet-blue or pink flowers (depending on variety) bloom in stunning, 18″ (45cm) clusters in April and May.

The compound, 12-16″ (30-40cm) long bright green leaves are divided into 15-19 leaflets.

Soil: Plant *Wisteria* in any well-drained soil that is not alkaline (pH 7.0 or greater). If necessary add iron chelates. Water and feed generously during bloom season.

Pruning: Rub off buds on trunk for a single stem specimen. Pinch branch tips for a broad, multiple stem form. Provide firm support for developing stems.

Uses: Use on a trellis, wall or fence. *Wisteria* may be trained into a beautiful single-trunk tree.

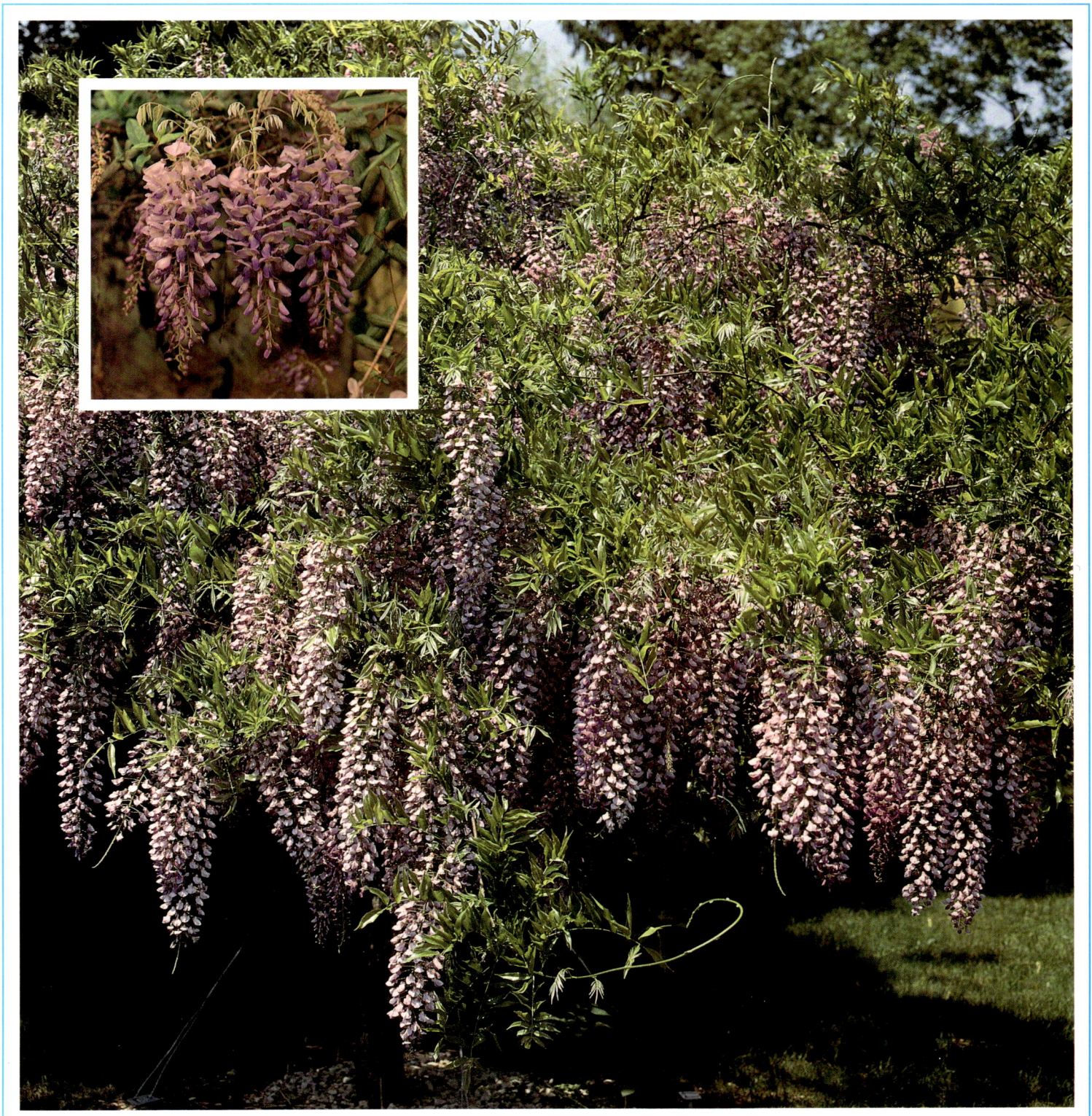

Bibliography

Bailey, Liberty Hyde and Ethel Zoe Bailey. 1976. *Hortus Third: A Concise Dictionary of Plants Cultivated in the United States and Canada.* Macmillan Pub. Co., Inc., New York and Collier Macmillan Pub. Co., London. 1290 p.

Black, Robert J. and David F. Hamilton. Native Florida plants for home landscapes. Fla. Coop. Ext. Serv., OH-25. Inst. of Food and Agr. Sci., Univ. of Fla., Gainsville, FL 32611. 6 p.

Burch, D.G. and D.L. Ingram. 1984. Shrubs for South Florida. Fla. Coop. Ext. Serv., Cir.-498. Inst. of Food and Agr. Sci., Univ. of Fla., Gainsville, FL 32611. 19 p.

Clark, David E., Ed. 1979. *Sunset New Western Garden Book.* Lane Pub. Co., Menlo Park, CA 94025. 512 p.

Crockett, James Underwood & Editors of TIME-LIFE BOOKS. 1971. *Roses.* Time-Life Books, New York, N.Y. 160 p.

Donselman, Henry. Palms resistant to lethal yellowing for South Florida. Fla. Coop. Ext. Serv., OH-48. Inst. of Food and Agr. Sci., Univ. of Fla., Gainsville, FL 32611. 4 p.

Galle, Fred C. 1974. Southern Living Azaleas. Oxmoor House, Inc., Book Division of the Progressive Farmer Co., P.O. Box 2463, Birmingham, AL 35202. 96 p.

Graf, Alfred Byrd. 1978. *TROPICA: Color Cyclopedia of Exotic Plants and Trees From the Tropics and Sub-tropics.* Roehrs Company, East Rutherford, N.J. 07073. 1120 p.

Halfacre, R. Gordon and Anne R. Shawcroft. 1979. *Landscape Plants of The Southeast.* Sparks Press. P.O. Box 26747, Raleigh, N.C. 27611. 325 p.

Helmer, M. Jane Coleman. 1985. *Pictorial Library of Landscape Plants. Volume 1, Northern Hardiness Zones 1-5.* Merchants Publishing Co., 20 Mills St., Kalamazoo, MI 49001. 343 p.

Logsdon, Gene. 1975. *The Gardeners Guide To Better Soil.* Rodale Press, Inc., Emmaus, PA 18904. 247 p.

Matthes, John and Robert J. Black. Ground covers for Florida homes. Fla. Coop. Ext. Serv., OH-30. Inst. of Food and Agr. Sci., Univ. of Fla., Gainsville, FL 32611. 6 p.

Midcap, James T., Robert J. Black and Shannon Smith. Ornamental trees for South Florida. Fla. Coop. Ext. Serv., OH-22, Inst. of Food and Agr. Sci., Univ. of Fla., Gainsville, FL 32611. 4 p.

Midcap, Jim, Shannon Smith & Robert Black. Ornamental palms for South Florida. Fla. Coop. Ext. Serv., FS-21. Inst. of Food and Agr. Sci., Univ. of Fla., Gainsville, FL 32611. 4 p.

Phillips, Roger. 1978 *Trees of North America and Europe.* Random House, Inc., New York. 224 p.

Appendix A

SITE SELECTION AND SOIL CONDITIONING

There are several soil/site factors crucial to the establishment and future well-being of the plants recommended in this book. A moderate soil texture (sandy loam or loam) is best for most species. A loose, friable (crushable) structure is necessary for maximum root expansion and efficient movement of air and moisture through the soil. A generous quantity of organic matter is needed to: 1) hold soil moisture, 2) provide necessary nutrients, 3) support and nourish soil organisms which aid in the release of soil nutrients and 4) moderate harsh soil texture.

Good internal soil drainage is essential for efficient air movement within the rooting zone. The majority of the plants, require a soil that is well drained, yet holds sufficient moisture during dry periods. A soil with poor internal soil drainage will have poor air circulation, less soil biological activity, slow release of nutrients and possible root disease. A few of the trees and shrubs are well adapted to wet sites, a greater number to very dry sites and some very flexible species will do well over a wide range of soil/site conditions.

When nature has varied from moderate, and the desired plant is not flexible, soil conditioning is needed. The structure, aeration and drainage of heavy clay soils may be improved by the addition of shredded bark, chopped corn or sugar cane stalks, wood chips, peanut hulls, straw or sand. Structure, moisture-holding capacity and fertility of coarse, sandy soils may be improved by adding peat moss, leaf mold, compost, peanut hulls, tobacco stems and/or seaweed (for coastal sands).

If drainage is still a problem in heavy soils that have been conditioned as suggested, shallow ditches placed out of sight and graded off the landscape may be needed. For small, wet areas, extract a cylinder(s) of soil with an auger to 6' (1.8m) deep, fill with gravel to within one foot from the surface and add conditioned soil in the remaining foot.

Appendix B

LANDSCAPE PLANTS LISTED BY HEIGHT

BROADLEAF EVERGREENS

Low Growing
under 3' (90cm)

Buxus microphylla var. koreana 'Wintergreen'
Carissa grandiflora 'Boxwood Beauty'
Cotoneaster glaucophyllus
Cotoneaster microphyllus
Hebe x 'Patty's Purple'
Hebe x 'Veronica Lake'
Ilex cornuta 'Burfordii Nana'
Ilex cornuta 'Compacta'
Ilex crenata 'Globosa'
Ilex crenata 'Helleri'
Ilex vomitoria 'Stokes'
Rhododendron Kurume Hybrids
Santolina chamaecyparissus
Teucrium chamaedrys

Medium
3-6' (.9-1.8m)

Abelia x grandiflora
Abelia x grandiflora 'Edward Goucher'
Berberis julianae
Buxus microphylla var. japonica
Buxus sempervirens 'Welleri'
Camellia japonica 'Finlandia'
Carissa grandiflora 'Fancy'
Eriobotrya deflexa
Euonymus fortunei var. vegeta
Euonymus japonica 'Aureo-marginata'
Euonymus kiautschovicus
Gardenia jasminoides
Hibiscus rosa-sinensis, Compact Bush Form
Ilex crenata 'Convexa'
Ilex vomitoria 'Nana'
Mahonia aquifolium
Raphiolepis indica
Rhododendron, Southern Indica Hybrids
Ternstroemia gymnanthera
Viburnum suspensum

Tall
over 6' (1.8m)

Aucuba japonica
Aucuba japonica 'Crotonifolia'
Camellia japonica cvs.
Cocculus laurifolius
Dizygotheca elegantissima
Dodonaea viscosa
Elaeagnus macrophylla 'Ebbingii'
Elaeagnus pungens
Eucalyptus camaldulensis
Fatsia japonica
Ficus benjamina
Ficus lyrata
Grevillea robusta
Hibiscus rosa-sinensis, Open Upright Form
Hibiscus rosa-sinensis, Tall Compact Form
Hibiscus rosa-sinensis, Upright Bush Form
Hibiscus syriacus
Ilex aquifolium
Ilex cornuta 'Burfordii'
Ilex opaca
Ilex vomitoria
Kalmia latifolia
Ligustrum lucidum
Magnolia grandiflora
Nerium oleander
Osmanthus fragrans
Osmanthus heterophyllus 'Aureus'
Photinia x fraseri
Photinia glabra
Pittosporum tobira
Plumbago auriculata
Portulacaria afra
Prunus caroliniana
Pyracantha coccinea 'Lalandei'
Pyracantha fortuneana 'Graberi'
Pyracantha koidzumii
Raphiolepis ovata
Schefflera arboricola
Thevetia thevetioides
Tibouchina urvilleana
Viburnum japonicum

CONIFEROUS EVERGREEN SHRUBS

Low
under 3' (90cm)
Chamaecyparis obtusa 'Nana'
Juniperus conferta 'Blue Pacific'
Juniperus sabina 'Tamariscifolia'
Thuja occidentalis 'Hetz Midget'

Medium
3-6' (.9-1.8m)
Juniperus chinensis 'Armstrongii'
Juniperus chinensis 'Pfitzerana'
Juniperus scopulorum cvs.
Pinus mugo var. mugo

Tall
over 6' (1.8m)
Chamaecyparis pisifera 'Cyanoviridis'
x Cupressocyparis leylandii
Cupressus glabra
Cupressus sempervirens 'Glauca'
Juniperus chinensis 'Torulosa'
Juniperus scopulorum cvs.
Juniperus scopulorum 'Welchii'
Juniperus virginiana 'Skyrocket'
Podocarpus gracilior
Podocarpus macrophyllus
Thuja occidentalis 'Nigra'

CONIFEROUS EVERGREEN TREES

Medium
20-35' (6-10.5m)
Pinus nigra
Sciadopitys verticillata

Tall
over 35' (10.5m)
Araucaria bidwillii
Araucaria heterophylla
Cedrus atlantica

Cedrus deodara
Pinus elliottii
Pinus glabra
Pinus halepensis
Pinus pinea
Pinus radiata
Pinus strobus
Pinus thunbergiana
Taxodium distichum

DECIDUOUS SHRUBS

Low
under 3' (90cm)
Berberis thunbergii 'Kobold'
Berberis thunbergii 'Rose Glow'
Cotoneaster apiculatus
Lagerstroemia indica 'Dixie Series'
Spiraea japonica 'Coccinea'
Stephanandra incisa 'Crispa'
Syringa patula

Medium
3-6' (.9-1.8m)
Cytisus x praecox
Deutzia gracilis
Euonymus alata 'Compacta'
Exochorda x macrantha 'The Bride'
Hydrangea paniculata 'Grandiflora'
Hydrangea quercifolia
Kerria japonica 'Pleniflora'
Plumeria rubra cvs.
Spiraea cantoniensis
Syringa palibiniana

Tall
over 6' (1.8m)
Aesculus parviflora
Berberis thunbergii 'Aurea'
Chaenomeles japonica
Cornus alba 'Argenteo-marginata'
Cornus sericea Baileyi

Cotinus coggygria
Enkianthus campanulatus
Enkianthus campanulatus 'Palibinii'
Forsythia x intermedia
Hamamelis mollis
Hydrangea arborescens 'Grandiflora'
Hydrangea macrophylla hybrids
Kolkwitzia amabilis
Lagerstroemia indica
Ligustrum sinense 'Variegatum'
Magnolia stellata
Plumeria rubra 'Acutifolia'
Potentilla fruticosa
Rhododendron, Ghent Hybrids
Rhododendron, Mollis Hybrids
Rhododendron roseum
Rhus typhina 'Laciniata'
Sambucus canadensis
Sambucus canadensis 'Aurea'
Spiraea prunifolia
Spiraea x vanhouttei
Syringa x prestoniae hybrids
Syringa vulgaris cvs.
Tamarix aphylla
Viburnum x carlcephalum
Viburnum carlesii
Viburnum x juddii
Viburnum lantana
Viburnum opulus 'Sterile'
Vitex agnus-castus
Weigela florida

FLOWERING TREES

**Small
under 20' (6m)**

Aesculus x carnea 'Briotii'
Caesalpinia pulcherrima
Chionanthus virginicus
Cornus florida
Cornus florida 'Rubra'
Malus 'Almey'
Malus floribunda
Malus 'Red Jade'
Prunus persica cvs.
Pyrus calleryana 'Bradford'

**Medium
20-35' (6-10.5m)**

Callistemon citrinus
Callistemon viminalis
Cercis canadensis

Cornus kousa
Crataegus crus galli
Crataegus laevigata 'Paulii'
Koelreuteria paniculata
Laburnum x watereri
Magnolia x soulangiana
Malus hybrid 'Radiant'
Prunus serrulata 'Kwanzan'
Tabebuia chrysotricha

**Tall
over 35' (10.5m)**

Albizia julibrissin
Chorisia speciosa
Delonix regia
Halesia carolina
Prunus padus

SHADE AND ORNAMENTAL TREES

**Small
under 20' (6m)**

Acer ginnala
Citrus aurantiifolia
Citrus reticulata 'Cleopatra'
Elaeagnus angustifolia
Morus alba 'Pendula'
Ochrosia elliptica

**Medium
20-35' (6-10.5m)**

Acacia baileyana
Clusia rosea
Diospyros virginiana
Guaiacum officinale
Morus alba 'Fruitless'
Myrica cerifera
Salix matsudana 'Tortuosa'
Sapium sebiferum
Tilia cordata
Ulmus parvifolia 'Drake'

**Tall
over 35' (10.5m)**

Acer rubrum
Acer rubrum 'Drummondii'
Acer saccharinum
Acer saccharum
Asimina triloba

Betula nigra
Betula papyrifera
Betula pendula
Bucida buceras
Carya illinoinensis
Catalpa bignonioides
Catalpa bignonioides 'Nana'
Celtis occidentalis
Cercidiphyllum japonicum
Cladrastis lutea
Fagus sylvatica 'Atropunicea'
Fraxinus americana
Fraxinus pennsylvanica 'Marshall Seedless'
Ginkgo biloba
Gleditsia triacanthos var. inermis
Liquidambar styraciflua
Liriodendron tulipifera
Nyssa sylvatica
Pistacia chinensis
Platanus occidentalis
Populus x canadensis cv. 'Eugenei'
Quercus ilex
Quercus palustris
Quercus rubra
Quercus suber
Quercus virginiana
Salix babylonica
Salix matsudana 'Navajo'

TROPICALS

Low
under 6′ (1.8m)

Agave americana
Cordyline indivisa
Strelitzia reginae
Yucca filamentosa
Zamia pumila

Medium
6-10′ (1.8-3m)

Bambusa glaucescens 'Fernleaf'
Musa acuminata 'Dwarf Cavendish'
Yucca aloifolia

Tall
over 10′ (3m)

Bambusa oldhamii
Cordyline stricta
Dracaena draco
Dracaena marginata
Musa x paradisiaca 'Seminifera'
Schefflera arboricola
Yucca elephantipes

PALMS

Small
under 20′ (6m)

Butia capitata
Chamaerops humilis
Cycas revoluta
Microcoelum weddellianum
Phoenix roebelenii

Medium
20-35′ (6-10.5m)

Beaucarnea recurvata
Chrysalidocarpus lutescens
Coccothrinax alta
Ptychosperma elegans
Rhapis excelsa

Tall
over 35′ (10.5m)

Arecastrum romanzoffianum
Roystonea elata
Roystonea regia
Washingtonia filifera
Washingtonia robusta

GROUND COVERS

Low
under 3″ (15cm)

Ajuga reptans cvs.
Hedera canariensis
Hedera helix cvs.
Pachysandra terminalis
Trachelospermum asiaticum
Vinca minor

Medium
6-18″ (15-45cm)

Carissa grandiflora 'Green Carpet'
Cotoneaster adpressus var. praecox
Cotoneaster dammeri cvs.

Tall
over 18″ (45cm)

Abelia x grandiflora 'Prostrata'
Calluna vulgaris, cvs.
Cotoneaster horizontalis
Euphorbia milii
Nephrolepis exalta
Scaevola frutescens

Appendix C

LANDSCAPE PLANTS LISTED BY USE

HEDGES AND SCREENS

Low
Under 30″ (90cm)

Berberis thunbergii 'Crimson Pygmy'
Carissa grandiflora 'Tuttlei'
Lantana camara 'Dwarf Yellow'
Myrtus communis 'Compacta'

Medium
3-6′ (.9-1.8m)

Codiaeum variegatum
Galphimia gracilis
Lonicera 'Clavey's Dwarf'
Myrsine africana
Physocarpus opulifolius 'Luteus'

Tall
over 6′ (1.8m)

Acacia verticillata
Coccoloba uvifera
Cortaderia selloana
Cotoneaster salicifolius
Cytisus scoparius 'Burkwoodii'
Elaeagnus angustifolia
Eugenia uniflora
Ixora spp.

Ixora duffii 'Superking'
Ligustrum japonicum
Ligustrum japonicum 'Aureum'
Ligustrum japonicum 'Howardii'
Murraya paniculata
Osmanthus fragrans
Osmanthus heterophyllus 'Purpureus'
Podocarpus macrophyllus
Prunus laurocerasus
Rhamnus frangula 'Columnaris'

SALT TOLERANT SPECIES

Low
under 6′ (1.8m)

Carissa grandiflora 'Boxwood Beauty'
Carissa grandiflora 'Green Carpet'
Cordyline indivisa
Cytisus x praecox
Euonymus fortunei var. vegeta
Euonymus kiautschovicus
Euphorbia milii
Hebe x 'Patty's Purple'
Hebe x 'Veronica Lake'
Ilex vomitoria cvs.
Juniperus spp.
Lonicera spp.
Raphiolepis indica
Zamia pumila

Medium
6-15′ (1.8-4.5m)

Acacia verticillata
Bougainvillea spp.
Butia capitata
Carissa grandiflora 'Fancy'
Cordyline stricta
Dodonaea viscosa
Elaeagnus angustifolia
Elaeagnus macrophylla 'Ebbingii'
Elaeagnus pungens
Euonymus japonica 'Aureo-marginata'

Juniperus spp.
Nerium oleander
Ochrosia elliptica
Pittosporum tobira
Raphiolepis ovata
Scaevola frutescens
Yucca aloifolia

Tall
over 15′ (4.5m)

Acacia baileyana
Acer saccharinum
Bucida buceras
Chionanthus virginicus
Clusia rosea
Coccoloba uvifera
Coccothrinax alta
Cortaderia selloana
Elaeagnus angustifolia
Eucalyptus camaldulensis
Guaiacum officinale
Ilex vomitoria
Myrica cerifera
Pinus pinea
Quercus ilex
Quercus virginiana
Roystonea spp.
Tamarix aphylla

VINES

Antigonon leptopus
Bougainvillea spp.
Bignonia radicans
Celastrus orbiculatus
Clematis x jackmanii hybrids
Clematis lanuginosa 'Candida'
Ficus pumila
Gelsemium sempervirens
Hedera helix
Hedera canariensis

Jasminum multiflorum
Lantana camara 'Christine'
Lantana camara 'Radiation'
Lonicera heckrottii
Lonicera heckrottii 'Dropmore Scarlet'
Lonicera japonica 'Halliana'
Lonicera periclymenum var. serotina
Parthenocissus
Polygonum aubertii
Wisteria floribunda

WINDBREAK TREES

Cortaderia selloana
Cupressocyparis leylandii
Cupressus glabra
Pinus halepensis
Pinus nigra

Pinus radiata
Pinus strobus
Populus x canadensis cv. 'Eugenei'
Prunus caroliniana

SOIL EROSION CONTROL PLANTS

Low
under 3' (90cm)

Abelia x grandiflora 'Prostrata'
Calluna vulgaris
Cotoneaster apiculatus
Cotoneaster dammeri cvs.
Cotoneaster glaucophyllus
Cotoneaster horizontalis
Cotoneaster microphyllus
Hedera spp.
Lantana spp.
Nephrolepis exaltata
Santolina chamaecyparissus
Vinca spp.

Medium
3-6' (.9-1.8m)

Cytisus x praecox
Cytisus scoparius 'Burkwoodii'
Euonymus alata 'Compacta'
Juniperus spp.

Tall
over 6' (1.8m)

Bougainvillea spp.
Celtis occidentalis
Cercis canadensis
Coccoloba uvifera
Cotoneaster salicifolius
Cotoneaster adpressus var. praecox
Dodonaea viscosa
Elaeagnus angustifolia
Elaeagnus macrophylla 'Ebbingii'
Elaeagnus pungens
Nyssa sylvatica
Plumbago auriculata
Rhus typhina 'Laciniata'
Salix matsudana 'Navajo'
Salix matsudana 'Tortuosa'

Appendix D

SOIL PREPARATION FOR ACID-LOVING PLANTS

The ideal acidity range for acid-loving plants is pH4.5-5.5. Additions of peat moss, leaf mold or compost, plus aluminum sulfate, may bring about the correct adjustment if your soil is already neutral (pH7) or slightly acid (pH6.5 or below). Where soil is alkaline (pH higher than 7), plan to make a special acid (or peat) bed, as follows:

Excavate an area 36"x36" (90x90cm) *for each plant* to a depth of 18" (45.2cm). Replace the soil with a mixture containing equal volumes of acid peat moss, leaf mold and coarse sand. Then add one cup of aluminum sulfate and mix in well. For a longer lasting acid soil mix, raise your bed above ground level by using railroad ties or non-limestone rocks for the edges.

Acid-loving plants that are close to buildings will be affected by lime that washes into the soil from mortar and cement blocks. Regular additions of aluminum sulfate, sulfur, iron sulfate or proprietary mixtures for soil acidification will help adjust the soil acidity for these plants. Consult your supplier for the correct compound to use, then apply at the manufacturer's recommended rates.

Index

Map Labels

Provinces/States:
BRITISH COLUMBIA, ALBERTA, SASKATCHEWAN, MANITOBA, WASHINGTON, OREGON, CALIFORNIA, NEVADA, IDAHO, MONTANA, WYOMING, UTAH, ARIZONA, NEW MEXICO, COLORADO, NORTH DAKOTA, SOUTH DAKOTA, NEBRASKA, KANSAS, OKLAHOMA, TEXAS, MINNESO[TA], IOWA, MINNEAPOL[IS]

Cities:
Vancouver, Calgary, Saskatoon, Regina, Winnipeg, Seattle, Spokane, Yakima, Portland, Pendleton, Eugene, Medford, Great Falls, Butte, Billings, Bismarck, Fargo, Redding, Boise, Pocatello, Sheridan, Rapid City, Sioux Falls, Sacramento, Elko, Reno, Salt Lake City, Cheyenne, Denver, Pueblo, North Platte, Omaha, San Francisco, Fresno, Las Vegas, Flagstaff, Albuquerque, Kansas City, Wichita, Los Angeles, Amarillo, Tulsa, Oklahoma City, San Diego, Phoenix, El Paso, Fort Worth, Dallas, San Antonio, Houston

Zone markers: ① ② ③ ④ ⑤ ⑥ ⑦ ⑧ ⑨ ⑩

The zone numbers listed with each subject in the **Pictorial Library** refer to the zones of hardiness as shown on this map. Usually the plant material will do well in the lowest zone number it is rated for or any higher number. In some instances the varieties which are rated for a particular zone may be used in the next lower zone. This is true under special circumstances such as a well protected area, a plant given exceptional protection or care, or within an unusual localized weather pattern such as is found along the Gulf Coast or other large bodies of water.